P9-CEJ-451

STAND-OFF
IN
TEXAS

"Just Call Me a Spokesman
for the DPS"

Mike Cox

EAKIN PRESS ★ Austin, Texas

FIRST EDITION

Copyright © 1998
By Mike Cox

Published in the United States of America
By Eakin Press
A Division of Sunbelt Media, Inc.
P.O. Box 90159
Austin, Texas 78709
email: eakinpub@sig.net

ALL RIGHTS RESERVED.

2 3 4 5 6 7 8 9

ISBN 1-57168-246-5

First, for the usual suspects, my wife Linda and our daughter Hallie. But also for the men and women of the Texas Department of Public Safety and particularly for my colleagues and former colleagues in the DPS Public Information Office—information officers Laureen Chernow, Sherri Deatherage Green, and Tela Goodwin Mange, along with administrative technicians Alicia Neville Cox (no relation), Lisa Hunter, Laura Luckie, Beth Warren, and Laverne Purcell.

When Mike Cox visited Fort Davis in 1955, he was not there in an official capacity as a spokesman for the DPS. That would happen about forty years later.

Contents

Preface vi
Taking RoweVista 1
Normally, Jay Leno's pretty funny 6
Just call me a spokesman for the DPS 9
A pistol in the mashed potatoes 23
Wackos in Waco 38
"Welcome to Koresh World" 48
A brief history of the first Republic of Texas 71
Old Fort Davis didn't have log walls 83
A brief history of the second Republic of Texas 94
The siege begins 111
The plane leaves at 7:00 in the morning 122
Saving America from New World Order tyranny 139
"This is not the Alamo" .152
The Terry and Mike show 167
The line in the sand 175
The Republic's flag comes down 186
Burros and booby traps .194
Shots fired! 199
Preventing a second disaster 207
Silver bullets 220
Remembering the Alamo, Killeen,
      Waco, and Fort Davis 237
Follow-up: ROT 247
Epilogue 256
Appendices 257
Bibliography 281
Index 285

Preface

This book almost didn't get written.

The story behind that statement is the best way I can think of to bring up one of the major themes of this book: We learn from experience—our own and those of others.

Every fall, the Texas Rangers of Company D get together on a ranch in South Texas for a dove hunt and barbecue. Years ago the captain invited me, and since then someone keeps forgetting to scratch my name off the list. The birds are more plentiful some years than others, but the food and fellowship are worth the trip even if I don't see a single dove.

The trip in 1996, however, came close to being my last.

One of the ranch hands dropped me off at a stock tank. "Be back to pick you up at sundown," he promised. A drooping mesquite tree offered shade and concealment, so I unfolded my camouflage stool, dropped two shells of No. 7 shot into my 12-gauge shotgun, and settled down to wait for the birds to start flying in for water.

Before long a lone mourning dove whistled in right over my head and I fired instinctively. The bird exploded in feathers, plummeting into the high brush behind the earthen dam.

I realized that the dove, which hadn't seen me, had flown in way too close. After my near point-blank shot, there couldn't be enough meat left to flavor even a thin broth. I decided to let it lay where it fell and dropped in another shell. But as shadows grew longer I knew I didn't have much hunting time left. A big flight never materialized, and I began feeling guilty about leaving that bird out in the brush. There could have been a few shreds of meat on it. Besides, Texas law says you must make an effort to find the game you've shot.

Looking down from the top of the dam, I saw it was a steep descent.

I'd better break open my shotgun, I told myself, *just in case I slip.*

That was important because I hunt with an over/under shotgun. Like a side-by-side double-barrel, the gun cannot fire when it is open. I find it's easier to keep it open than to fumble with the safety every time I want to shoot. Open, the gun is safer than with a safety on. Safeties can fail or be forgotten, but the gun absolutely cannot be fired when it is open.

So I broke open the gun and carefully worked my way down the earthen dam. Soon I was standing in brush nearly chest high. As I started searching for the downed bird, I got to thinking about something else: rattlesnakes. I hate snakes. To be on the safe side—just in case I saw a snake that needed shooting—I snapped the shotgun closed.

A few moments later, I found the bird. My first impression had been correct. There was no game to drop into my bag. I swiveled a half-turn to my left to pitch the useless carcass back into the brush for the coyotes when my gun went off.

Few things sound louder than a gunshot when you're not expecting it. I did not feel anything, but I'd been told that with a gunshot wound there is a moment or two of shock before the brain catches up with the pain.

I looked down at my leg, expecting to see blood.

The lead pellets had missed me by inches, leaving a small crater of disturbed earth right next to my boot. An old-fashioned pocket-sized snakebite kit, with its rubber tube, razor blade and suction cup, would have been useless if I'd blown my foot off with my own gun. I'd have bled to death before someone came to my rescue. The ranch hands and Rangers would have had to search the brush for my body, just as I had searched for the dove.

When I calmed down enough to try to figure out what had happened, I decided a tough mesquite twig had become caught in the trigger guard. As I had moved forward, there was just enough pressure to pull the trigger.

Breaking the gun open again—there was still a shell in one barrel—I climbed back up on top of the dam. I sat down on my stool, took a deep breath, and savored a glorious sunset—one that could have been my last.

As you might imagine, I did a little soul searching.

How could I have done something so stupid? I wasn't a novice. I'd started hunting when I was a young boy, and I knew the rules. I should have put the safety on or left the gun open—snakes or no snakes. A shotgun is deadlier than the biggest, meanest rattler that ever slithered out of its den.

But I survived, and we learn from those experiences we survive. Needless to say, I'm a lot more careful with shotguns these days. Looking back, I can say I've survived a number of experiences, not all of them caused by my own carelessness.

This is my seventh full-length book but the first based almost entirely on personal experience. I hope that by sharing some of my experiences in this book, I can offer you an interesting read and maybe at the same time save you from shooting yourself in the foot—in the figurative sense—when dealing with the media during a crisis.

Texas Stand-off is actually three books—or at least, three different genres in one. It is part true crime, part memoir, part textbook. Call it true.mem.text. No matter its category, what went into the writing of this book was experience, memory, and research.

I've written true crime before, and my weekly book columns, "Texana," are occasionally reminiscent or reflective. But this is the first time I've attempted to write true crime based on my own on-the-scene experiences. Frankly, it was hard for me to include myself as a character in this book.

Like many writers I've kept a personal journal from time to time, but my early newspaper training makes it difficult for me to write in the first person for publication. As a young reporter, I was taught never to use "I" in a news story or even a by-lined column. If for some reason a writer was forced to refer to himself, it had to be done as "this reporter" or "this writer," or through the use of the royal "we"—as in "We woke up this morning and had a cup of coffee."

The "we" was newspaper code for "I." Mercifully, the royal "we" has abdicated and is practically archaic.

Using "I" or "me" was not the only tricky thing about writing this book. Since I am writing about events that occurred in the course of my job, I had to be careful to make a distinction between what I personally observed, heard, and felt on the one hand and the public record on the other. Although I am a spokesman for the Texas Department of Public Safety, it is not Mike Cox the DPS public information officer who is speaking here, but Mike Cox the free-lance writer.

The distinction is critical.

As a writer and as a fervent supporter of the First Amendment, in relaying my experiences following the 1991 mass murder at the Luby's Cafeteria in Killeen, the 1993 Branch Davidian siege outside Waco, and the 1997 Republic of Texas stand-off in Jeff Davis County, I have not hesitated to admit my own personal mistakes and to call things as I saw them—something I would not rush to do as an official spokesman for a state agency.

I have been as candid in my reflections as possible. Everything I have written about involved me, was related to me by other participants, or comes from the public record.

Perception being reality, different people had different experiences and different reactions to them at Killeen, at Mount Carmel during the Branch Davidian siege, and at Fort Davis in Jeff Davis County. Each of us on the scene at the Republic of Texas stand-off saw things differently. While the press slept in the vans at the media encampment or enjoyed rooms at nearby motels, some law enforcement officers slept on the ground next to their rifles in the chilly mountain air. While those of us on the outside clustered around the Salvation Army trucks for coffee, the people inside the Republic of Texas "embassy" watched their supplies of food and water dwindle. While many of us reveled in the sense of wide-open spaciousness, others knew they faced possible prison terms.

All I can say is that the pages which follow tell the stories of Killeen, Mount Carmel, and Fort Davis as I perceive those events.

In addition to my reporting and reflections, I've included quite a bit of primary material—including documents concerning both the original Republic of Texas and its late twentieth-century counterpart. I've also provided various media relations check lists, codes of ethics, and a newly developed methodology for assessing militia groups.

I hope I have been able to offer an insider's look at three of the bigger news stories in recent Texas history, although this book is not intended as a definitive account of the Republic of Texas stand-off, nor of the massacre in Killeen, nor of the siege in McLennan County (a tragedy commonly dubbed "Waco," even though it happened ten miles from that city).

The textbook part of this book is based on my thirty-plus years of experience in the communications field, first as a reporter, columnist, and occasional city editor and now as a government spokesman and president-elect of the National Association of Government Communicators. The list of books by government spokesmen is not a long one, nor is the media relations bibliography. I hope my experiences and suggestions will be helpful to others in the field who have yet to face a major media crisis, as well as anyone—law enforcement officer, legal counsel, corporate communications staffer, aspiring public servant—who may one day face off against the business end of a TV camera.

That lens can look as scary as the barrel of a shotgun.

—MIKE COX
Austin, Texas

Taking RoweVista

The three figures in camouflage fatigues believed war had broken out—the second Texas Revolution.

They'd been en route to their primary target, the silver-domed Jeff Davis County Courthouse in the small West Texas town of Fort Davis, when their two-way radio crackled out a change in orders. They were instructed to take this target instead.

Clutching assault rifles, they jumped from their convoy of vehicles—an old green Volkswagen and a white American Motors Eagle station wagon. Keeping low profiles, they scuttled quickly across the rocky front yard toward their second objective. Speed and stealth could make all the difference between failure and success. But without better cover, catching the occupants of the home off guard would be almost impossible.

Joe Rowe and his wife, Margaret Ann, had just finished a late Sunday breakfast. It was nearly noon. The couple, both fifty-one years old, were sitting in RoweVista, their dream-come-true adobe house in the Davis Mountains Resort. The Rowes were enjoying their coffee while gazing out at the nearby mountaintops, still lightly snow-dusted on that crisp spring morning.

Rowe, a retired Shell Oil Company pipeline technician, noticed the strange vehicles in his driveway. But these were not neighbors dropping by unannounced for a friendly visit. These people looked more like commandos.

Even so, the sudden approach of three people with guns

1

did not startle the Rowes as much as it might have most cou-
ples sitting peacefully at their kitchen table. They were well
aware of the existence of the so-called Republic of Texas and
of its nearby "embassy." Joe and Margaret Ann had known
there was bound to be trouble sooner or later. It looked like
that day—April 27, 1997—was the day.

Alert now to danger, Joe watched as one of the gunmen
ducked behind the station wagon while another cut around to
the side of the house. The third person secured a position
behind a short adobe wall not far from the porch, his weapon
pointed menacingly in the Rowes' direction.

"Go dial 911," Rowe instructed his wife.

Grabbing his Ruger 9mm semi-automatic pistol, Rowe
strode quickly from the kitchen to the laundry room, where an
opaque glass door led to their porch. He raised the handgun.

For an instant, Rowe had one of the figures clearly in his
sights. At that distance, he could have blown the man's head
off. He almost squeezed the trigger. But there were two more
people in his yard with rifles. He thought of his wife in the
other room. It wasn't worth the risk.

He opened the door partway and took cover behind it.
"What do you want?" he called out. "Get outta my yard."

"We're from the Republic of Texas," one of the men shouted
back, "and you're our prisoners of war."

Rowe pondered for a moment the startling concept of
being a POW in his own home in his own country—a century
and a half since the last time there actually had been a
Republic of Texas. He watched their dog Niskin Luca patter
across the front porch. The thought occurred to Rowe that the
man with the rifle might shoot his dog, just to underscore his
point.

Rowe decided not to take any chances. "If you won't kill
my dog," he offered, "I'll lay my gun down."

In the sheriff's office in Marfa, a dispatcher answered the
telephone.

"This is M.A. Rowe," Mrs. Rowe said frantically. "The
R.O.T. is in our yard with guns, with rifles. Send somebody
out here."

As his wife reported the attack on their home, Rowe

moved to put his pistol on a nearby stool. He was not fast enough. The man in camouflage suddenly stood and fired a three-shot burst through the glass door. The jacketed 7.62mm projectiles blew out the glass door, splintered wood around the door frame, and shattered the glass in the door to the shower in a nearby bathroom. Shards of flying glass dug into Rowe's arm. The pain was so intense he thought he'd taken a bullet.

"You son of a bitch!" he yelled. "You shot me anyway!"

Mrs. Rowe screamed into the phone. "They're shooting into the house! You're hit! My husband's hit! Hurry up . . . Oh dear Lord . . . They shot my husband."

As Rowe clutched his bloody arm, another of the gunmen, Richard Franklin Keyes III, charged through the front door.

"Drop the phone!" he ordered, aiming his weapon at Mrs. Rowe.

She did as she was told, but the 911 operator in neighboring Presidio County had heard the shots over the open telephone line. Moments before, the operator had written down the time, 11:43 A.M., and the pertinent information: Three armed subjects were forcing their way inside a home in the Davis Mountains Resort.

The gunman who had fired the burst through the door was the ranking member of the assault team, U.S. Army veteran Gregg Paulson. He entered the Rowe home through the laundry room door. Behind him came the third member of the team. Rowe saw that the military-style camouflage had fooled him. The third "gunman" was a woman. She was Paulson's wife, Karen.

All three now stood inside RoweVista.

Their first tactical operation had been a success. Taking control of the courthouse in Fort Davis would have been more dramatic, but less significant strategically. They now held a position with a commanding view of the only road leading to the "embassy" of the Republic of Texas and two prisoners of war.

Paulson ordered the couple to sit down in their living room and be quiet.

But Rowe's arm wound was bleeding heavily. In recent

weeks he'd had two heart attacks and was taking prescription anticoagulants.

"Could I please have a dish towel?" Mrs. Rowe asked, fearful that her husband was losing too much blood. He was pale, and his off-white beard added no color to his face.

None of the soldiers replied.

"Hand me a dish towel," she said, more firmly than before. "There's one right next to you on the sink. Look, we don't have guns, and we can't harm you. Now, hand me the dish towel."

One of the intruders finally gave her the towel, which she folded and wrapped tightly around her husband's arm.

The objective had been taken, but the assault team had more work to do. Keyes started running water into the Rowes' bathtub, just in case forces of the de facto Texas government were to surround them and cut off the water. Then Keyes stormed outside and roughly hauled down the red, white, and blue Lone Star Texas state flag that Rowe flew above his property. Property—Rowe reminded himself as he watched the gunman's harsh actions—he'd owned for a decade and had lived on now for three years.

Next Keyes hopped into the station wagon, drove it out to the road, and parked it crossways downhill from RoweVista at a cattle guard. Climbing out, he fired twice into each of the vehicle's tires, turning the 1980 model Eagle into an improvised barricade.

As far as Keyes and his team were concerned, every acre of land—and every structure—in the Davis Mountains Resort lying behind his roadblock was now under the control of the Republic of Texas.

Using a pair of binoculars and a telescope belonging to the Rowes, the members of the assault team established two lookout points with a commanding view of the only road leading to RoweVista and, beyond there, the Republic of Texas embassy.

The shots fired at RoweVista echoed off the surrounding Davis Mountains, and would continue to do so, figuratively, all across Texas and the nation.

Late April is not hunting season. Eleven shots fired close

together could only mean trouble. A neighbor phoned the Rowes to see if something was wrong.

"Yes," Mrs. Rowe replied quickly.

"Do you want us to come up?" the concerned neighbor asked.

"Absolutely not," came the emphatic answer.

Her strained voice confirmed her neighbor's fears.

Soon phones were ringing in Fort Davis, Midland, Austin—and all across the country. In Dallas, nearly 500 miles away from Fort Davis, my wife Linda and I and our just-turned-three-year-old daughter Hallie were at a book and paper show. My pager went off.

Early the next morning, I'd be on my way to West Texas.

Normally, Jay Leno's pretty funny

Two days after the attack on the Rowes' home, the revolution was still under way, though it had settled into a war of words.

I was lying in bed in my motel room in Alpine—a cool, clean haven from the heat and dust—trying to wind down from the day's tension at the site of what the media has already dubbed the Republic of Texas stand-off. Television was certainly no help. I switched on the TV just in time for the 10:00 news and watched scenes of Highway Patrol Troopers, with .223-caliber Ruger Mini-14 rifles slung on their shoulders, standing in front of a phalanx of black-and-white patrol cars against the backdrop of the rugged Davis Mountains. Interspersed were closeups of me, surrounded by microphones and cameras, showing distinct signs of sunburn and fatigue. The story was on all the network channels and CNN.

Finally, "The Tonight Show" came on. *Maybe now I can relax*, I thought. *Take my mind off the events of the last three days and get some sleep to be ready for tomorrow*. But host Jay Leno, in his opening monologue, was cracking jokes about the stand-off.

"The Tonight Show," he began, affecting a serious, informative tone, "is now seen in many foreign counties, including Spain, Taiwan, and the Republic of Texas.

"The Texas law enforcement officers have surrounded the Republic's embassy and have been yelling, 'Come out! Come out!'" Leno continued. "Finally, they said, 'We can't, we're not gay!'"

That joke played on the other big news of the week: The highly hyped upcoming Wednesday night episode of "Ellen" in which actor Ellen DeGeneres comes out, admitting to her family, friends, and co-workers that she is a lesbian. It would be a first for network television. And, in a delicious case of art imitating life, at least for the media and the show's producers, DeGeneres also had revealed that she was not just playing the part for this ABC sitcom. She was really gay.

Of course, Leno said, the people he really felt sorry for in all this fuss down in Texas were the citizens of our sister republic to the south, Mexico.

"If Texas is an independent republic," he deadpanned, "those poor Mexicans are going to have to go all the way to Oklahoma to get to the United States!"

I laughed. Someone from Texas must have written that joke.

One of Leno's jokes sounded familiar: "Why don't they just put a fence around the place and call it a prison?" I'd heard a variation of that one four years earlier during another so-called stand-off, the long siege at David Koresh's Branch Davidian compound near Waco. As if someone had clicked on the "backward" button on a computer screen Web page image, that gag pulled up a familiar scene from my own personal forty-eight-year-old "hard drive."

> *"See those round gray things on top of the bunker?" the uniformed lieutenant asked me, pointing toward the debris. "They're skulls." I raised my binoculars and looked toward the concrete box we called the bunker. Little wisps of smoke and steam still rose from the charred remains of the compound. The lieutenant was right. I counted nine of them. Nine human skulls on top of the rectangular concrete structure, virtually the only thing left standing. Nine people died on top of that bunker, or at least that's where their bodies ended up as the building collapsed in flames. All that was left of them were those bones, turned gray by the intense fire.*

*Like millions of others, I saw those people die on
live television as a wind-swept fire destroyed Koresh's
religious commune on the fifty-first day of a stand-off
with federal officers. For the next several days, I
watched a progression of body bags carried past my
vantage point in one of the DPS command post vans.
My job was to count the bags and try to explain to the
world what had happened.*

That bad memory brought another: A few months after
Waco, I still hadn't snapped back the way I should have. Sure,
the deaths at the compound had been tragic. And the pressure
from the news media relentless. But as we say in Texas, this
hadn't been my first rodeo. Still, I was having trouble sleeping,
and terrible, chronic indigestion. Something just didn't feel
right, so I finally made an appointment with my doctor . . .

*"You have an abnormally low red blood count,"
he said after the first tests.
"You've got some funny cells in your esophagus,"
a second doctor said after another test. "I need to take
another sample for biopsy."
And, after that next test, the words that hit like a
.45 slug in the gut: "It's cancer."
The third doctor, my oncologist, said the tumor in
my esophagus was not very old. For all he and I knew,
the pressure I'd been under because of Waco had put
just enough strain on my immune system to give a
bunch of wannabe cancer cells their big chance.*

But all that was then—unpleasant memories to be sure—
but no longer breaking news. With television satellite trucks
and the Internet, realities change quickly. Now I had another
problem, an ongoing crisis near a little town hardly anyone
had ever heard of.

I'd be doing another live press conference the next day to
update the world on the latest developments. I needed to stay
calm and rational and try to keep things in perspective. We
were all determined that Fort Davis would not be another
Waco. At least, I hoped not.

Just call me a spokesman for the DPS

"Okay, I'm recording for broadcast," the reporter said over the phone. "How do you want to be identified?"

"Just call me a spokesman for the Texas Department of Public Safety," is my standard reply.

My official title is chief of media relations for the DPS, Texas' state law enforcement agency, but that's a description I use only in memos and on my business cards. Ask the DPS' Human Resources Bureau what I am and they will check the computer and tell you I am a director of programs. Ask a reporter what I am, and more than likely he or she will say, "Oh, he's the flack for the DPS." That description contains the f-word of the public-relations field, media slang usually applied with some disdain.

No matter what I'm called, after thirteen years with the DPS it's sometimes still hard for me to believe that I'm paid not to ask questions, but to answer them. Especially when I think back to mid-summer of 1974, when Fred Gomez Carrasco—a San Antonio drug kingpin serving time at the state prison in Huntsville—took eleven hostages in the library of the Walls Unit. I was a reporter for the *Austin American-Statesman*, one of dozens of journalists camped out in front of the prison administration building. We attended periodic briefings from prison officials and desperately tried to get more information any other way we could. After nearly two weeks, the stand-off ended in a wild shootout with Texas Rangers and FBI agents. The inmates killed two hostages before they went down. Carrasco died from a self-inflicted pistol shot. The other inmate crumpled in a flurry of law enforcement gunfire.

Back then, if someone had asked me what I expected to be doing by the time I was in my mid-forties, I would have guessed I'd still be working for newspapers—not as a reporter, but as a managing editor or maybe even the editor. Never did I expect to someday find myself on the other side of the police barricades, passing on official information to today's voracious and sometimes openly hostile print and television reporters.

For one thing, not until near the end of my twenty-year career in newspapers did governmental entities in Texas generally begin embracing the idea of having public information officers.

The DPS Public Information Office dates from the late 1940s, and so far as I know, it is the oldest public information operation of any law enforcement agency in Texas. By way of comparison, the Austin Police Department, which I covered off and on for fifteen years, did not appoint an officer to deal full-time with the news media until the late 1970s.

The first spokesman I ever met was Bill Carter, a veteran of the old International News Service, which later was merged with United Press to create United Press International. Carter was a friend of my granddad's and belonged to a group known in the early to mid-1960s as "Connally men." He had been on Governor John B. Connally's staff, but left the governor to go to work for the DPS as head of the Public Information Office— the job I now hold. In 1965, when I was sixteen and writing a high school news column for the afternoon *Austin Statesman*, Carter issued me my first DPS press card. I was enormously proud to have tangible proof that I was a real reporter, and had high hopes that the very official looking identification card Carter had his secretary, Laverne Purcell, type out for me would impress the girls and, if I could find a good eraser and a matching typewriter font to alter my date of birth, allow me to buy beer. Unfortunately, the press card did neither. Twenty years later, Laverne would still be the secretary in the Public Information Office when I went to work there.

Carter wrote excellent speeches, crisp news releases, and great letters in response to citizen inquiries (I later read some of his old carbons), but he never had too much to say to the press. By the time my press card came up for renewal two years after he approved my first one, I really was a reporter, working for the *San Angelo Standard-Times*. But as a young reporter in San Angelo, Lubbock and Austin, I seldom ever called the DPS Austin Headquarters for information. Most of the time I got what I needed from Troopers or Texas Rangers in the field.

The first non-law enforcement spokesman I ever worked with on a regular basis was a former newspaper city editor, Glenn Cootes. In 1970 he was hired by the City of Austin to set up its first-ever Public Information Office, which also included the city's print shop and telephone switchboard.

Though theoretically a spokesman, "the old man," as we affectionately called him, did not like to be quoted. This may explain why he held the job for as long as he did—more than fifteen years. I'll never forget one of his favorite lines: "I can't tell you that! This is the information office."

At least half the time, he was right. For the real information, I had to go to the city manager, one of the department heads, the council members, or the mayor.

From Cootes, I learned that a good spokesman knows when not to speak.

To me and to my friend Larry BeSaw, the other reporter I covered city hall with, Cootes became "a city editor without portfolio," as he used to say. "When I was a city editor," he told us, "my reporters had to turn in six stories a day." If BeSaw and I didn't generate the same number from city hall, Cootes said we weren't doing our jobs. Of course we'd have to get our facts elsewhere, since Cootes' shop was only the Public Information Office.

Hanging on his office wall was one of his favorite old-time Texas expressions, a few short words which say a lot about the public information field and life in general: "Root hog or die."

But the coffee pot was always on in his office, which was right down the hall from the mayor's. BeSaw and I, and occasionally one of the more inquisitive TV types, spent many hours in Cootes' office with a Styrofoam cup—colorfully embossed with the city seal—in our hands. What we did glean from Cootes was perspective, the subtle little things a reporter needs to know to do the job right. The perspective he shared was the city council's and the city manager's perspective, of course, but it was a start.

BeSaw and I could tell by Cootes' reaction to either our published stories or our hints about what we were working on, how close or how far off target we were.

At my going-away party in May 1985, when I left the Austin newspaper to go to work for the Department of Public Safety, Cootes said, "I have to give you a test before you can take the new job." He pulled a page of copy from his coat pocket and read it with dramatic flourish. He had written an exaggeratedly puffy press release, extremely laudatory of the DPS and its highly trained personnel. I knew any editor would immediately throw it in the trash.

"Now," he said, waving the "release" for effect, "tell me what you're going to say when your boss gives you this or something like it and tells you he wants it in the newspaper the next day—word for word, just like it's written. Think about it. Are you sure you want to leave the paper?"

One spokesman who was good at getting releases into the newspaper was Joe Riordan, an old-style public relations man. Before the Texas Legislature created the Public Utility Commission, Southwestern Bell (this also was several years before the breakup of AT&T) and other utilities franchised by the city had to come to the city council with their rate increase requests. BeSaw and I covered those periodic hat-in-corporate-hand efforts, which is how I met Riordan. He was the local spokesman for the telephone company.

Riordan was from St. Louis, then Southwestern Bell's headquarters. As a youth, he had been a radio actor. As an adult, he still could perform wondrous tricks with his voice— from his natural enough Irish to his veddy British upper-class accent imitating a pompous English officer in World War II.

As a corporate spokesman, and before the concept of ethics in journalism had fully flowered, Riordan could do things that public spokespersons never can, such as picking up the check for lunch and drinks. Plenty of drinks. Or finding good tickets to the annual Texas versus Oklahoma football game in Dallas, even when it had been sold out for months. Or always seeming to suffer a terrible losing streak whenever he played poker with us.

In our defense, when we got a tip that the mayor pro tem had been doing some advertising work for Southwestern Bell through his public relations firm—a clear violation of the city charter—BeSaw and I proved up the story and the newspaper ran it on page one. The mayor pro tem resigned from office because of it. Later, when a lawsuit brought to light more distasteful matters involving the telephone company, BeSaw and I started digging. We wrote a series of articles which won a Headliner's Club Award, Texas' top journalism award.

To Riordan's credit, despite his lavish corporate spending, he never asked us to do anything we shouldn't have. Riordan, like Cootes, contributed greatly to my concept of what being a spokesman is about, including:

  • The more you know about your agency or company, the better. Riordan could explain the concept of long distance tariffs—which I still can't—in the time it took to stir a gin and tonic. Well, maybe a couple of gin and tonics.

  • It never hurts for a spokesman to be a nice guy, even if you can't pick up the check and buy the drinks on the government's nickel.

  • A good sense of humor will carry you a long way.

Looking back, my transition from paid question-asker to paid question-answerer seems logical enough now. Someone who has been in the news business understands the news-gathering techniques of reporters and the needs of the media better than someone who lacks that background.

After assessing what I do for a living, a colorful old retired police officer once told me: "Well, I guess it takes a thief to catch a thief."

I believe the best spokespersons are former newspaper reporters, but that's just my personal prejudice. I have several colleagues who came from the broadcast side, and they're topnotch. Still, on the wall of my office is a framed excerpt from the first page of what surely was one of the earliest books about what we spokespersons do—Charles Washburn's 1927

Press Agentry. The copy I have once belonged to Stanley Walker, the legendary city editor of the *New York Herald-Tribune.*

The author, probably one of Walker's many protégés, inscribed the book to Walker, saying: "Thanks for more than you know . . . ."

Walker moved from Texas newspapers to the Big Apple but came home to Texas in his late forties and stayed the rest of his life. He must have shared my belief about newspaper reporters. In the same blue pencil he used for the sharp editing that helped to make him famous, Walker marked this passage at the beginning of Chapter One:

> Even a short term on a newspaper is better than a long term in school. There is something about a newspaper that puts a man on his mettle, something that gives him the drive, the perseverance, the self-assurance and the stamina that is to be found nowhere else. The newspaper teaches a man to think and to observe.

Even if you buy the notion that all newspaper people have the admirable traits that Walker described, the transformation from reporter to spokesman is not immediate, except in the sense of where your paycheck comes from. And it is not easy. After joining the DPS, the first time a big story involving the agency broke on my watch I felt like the proverbial old fire horse watching a newfangled motorized fire engine pull out of the station on the third alarm. Even now that I'm used to not being the one to write the big stories I am involved in, I still experience the same adrenaline rush.

Another transition problem: It's tough for a former reporter to know something important has happened or is about to happen and not be able to tell anyone about it.

Also, there's an inclination on the part of a beginning spokesman to want to be too helpful to those in the media. Naturally, you want to impress your former colleagues and take care of your old friends. When your agency and the media are at odds over some issue, you hope there's a middle ground agreeable to all. But in the spokesperson business, these are quick ways to get into trouble.

I've learned that sometimes you're going to make the media mad, even though your position is clearly the correct one for you to take. You run an equal risk of making management mad.

At least my first day on the job in the DPS Public Information Office was not as scary as the one a fellow spokesman experienced when he went to work for one of the federal agencies in Washington. I was in the nation's capital for a board meeting of the National Association of Government Communicators, the largest professional organization for government spokespersons, and one evening Lew Brodsky told me his story.

He was sitting behind his big new desk for the first time, still sifting through the drawers to see what his predecessor might have left behind, when his secretary came in. "Someone with CBS is here to see you," she announced.

The new public affairs officer hastily checked his calendar and his memory. "I don't have an appointment with anybody from CBS," he said. "What does he want?"

"All I know is there's a man out there with CBS," his secretary said, "and he's insisting he has to talk to you right now."

Brodsky panicked. *My God*, he thought. *CBS! What have we done? Are Mike Wallace and a "60 Minutes" camera crew here on an ambush interview for something I don't have any idea about?*

Wisely, he told the secretary to stall the man while he frantically phoned everyone in the building he could think of who might have some idea what was going on. But no one had any clue why CBS would be showing up at the agency unannounced.

Soon, his secretary stuck her head back in.

"This man says he absolutely has to see you right now," she said.

The new spokesman took a deep breath. "Okay," he said, "Show him in."

When the door opened a man with his name stitched in a white oval on his greasy blue overalls strode purposely into the office.

"City Building Service," he announced. "I'm here to check your air conditioner."

If you are an air conditioning specialist, that's a job which is relatively easy to describe. Many job titles are more or less self-explanatory: "I'm a policeman . . . a doctor . . . a lawyer . . . a car salesman," and so on.

But what exactly is a "spokesman"?

My four-year-old daughter Hallie doesn't quite understand yet that her daddy gets paid primarily to answer questions, with a few other duties thrown in. Nor does she know yet that her parents probably would never even have met except for the fact that her mother, Linda Aronovsky, was the spokesperson for Austin's Emergency Medical Service when I was still covering the police beat for the Austin newspaper. Hallie also doesn't care that I have had dealings with people from the real CBS. (So far my only serious confrontation with "60 Minutes" has been a polite argument with a correspondent, the late Harry Reasoner, who mistakenly maintained that North Carolina barbeque is better than Texas barbeque. Otherwise, he was a fine journalist.) All Hallie knows is that Daddy sometimes drives a white car with black letters on the doors and occasionally shows up on TV, provided she doesn't have *101 Dalmatians* playing on the VCR.

Briefly, my job is to see to it that the news media get the facts on issues involving the DPS and that the public stays informed while at the same time allowing law enforcement officers to go about their business without me causing too many interruptions. One thing I am not is a public relations practitioner. Former Senior Ranger Captain Bill Wilson, a college football star before he came to the DPS, once offered the best distinction I've ever heard between someone in public relations and in public information: "A PR person tries to get something *in* the newspaper," Captain Wilson told Larry Todd, one of my predecessors in the DPS Public Information Office. "A PIO tries to keep something *out* of the newspaper."

That may be a little too black and white. As a spokesman, I have done some of both, but the appropriations act specifically bars Texas state agencies from engaging in public relations. We inform—when we can—but we don't use tax dollars to do hard sells on the public. I can't give away football tickets or fix the kind of tickets you get from Troopers.

Sometimes, it's not so much a matter of getting something into a newspaper or keeping something out of it, but figuring out exactly the right way to articulate that something. This has become known as "spin control." A person who is highly skilled at this is called a "spin doctor."

Long before these terms were coined, an old-time Texas newspaperman, Boyce House, offered a good example of the skilled application of the spokesman's art:

> The candidate for State office was getting ready to open his campaign.
>
> "Only thing I'm afraid of is they'll find out that my father was hanged," he confided to friends.
>
> "The press agent will fix that up all right," they reassured him, and the publicity man wrote:
>
> "During a public spectacle, the candidate's father fell from a scaffolding and death was instantaneous."

Like many jobs, mine is usually day-after-day routine. A college student assigned to write a paper on driving while intoxicated calls to ask basic questions. Someone whose great-granddaddy was a Texas Ranger wants to know if we have any information on his ancestor. A textbook publisher needs generic photographs of a crime laboratory. An outraged citizen complains because one of our driver license clerks asked for her Social Security number. A reporter needs information on a fatal accident near Sonora. The page proofs of the annual report must be read and newspapers clipped. A legislative staffer needs statistics for a speech her boss will make. A visiting constable from Aberdeen, Scotland, wants a Texas Highway Patrol patch for his collection.

That's a typical day. But unlike many jobs, when I walk into the office on any given day, I never know for sure where I'll be or what I'll be doing by 5:00 P.M., although I am seldom able to leave the office at quitting time. The excitement of the unexpected was one of the aspects I liked about working for newspapers and is certainly one I enjoy most about working for a large law enforcement agency.

Police officers, especially during the occasional crisis, have enough problems dealing with the situation without having to take time out to talk with the press. That's not their area of expertise. I don't arrest drunk drivers or write search warrants and then go kick in doors with a pistol in my hands. And most police officers I know don't want to write a news release or stand in front of a video camera. Some officers I know would just as soon be involved in a gunfight as to be interviewed by a reporter.

Thanks to modern communications technology, someone from my office is on call twenty-four hours a day and theoretically immediately available—provided we're within pager or cellular phone range.

Cops sometimes think of us as reporters. Reporters tend to see us as cops in our black DPS jackets, even though the big white letters on our backs say "PIO" (public information officer.)

My staff and I often are caught in the middle—sometimes uncomfortably so. We need the balancing skills of the Flying Wallendas to walk the highwire between the two groups and our dual responsibilities of being forthright while not saying something that would adversely affect the outcome of a high-risk situation, endanger the progress of an ongoing investigation, or interfere with a person's right to a fair trial.

Spokespersons—since we don't use the f-word, "government communicators" is the accepted generic term for those of us paid with tax dollars—are neither reporters nor snake oil salesmen. The position has evolved over the years into a role of high visibility and considerable power. The visibility is obvious when something big happens. Not only are spokespersons frequently quoted but when the flow of breaking news slows down, the media start doing profiles on the spokespersons.

When the United Nations hired a new spokesperson in the summer of 1996, the *New York Times* did a story on her: "Official Voice of the U.N. Is a Blunt Ex-Journalist."

When the State Department named James Rubin as its new assistant secretary of state for public affairs (their title for spokesman), *USA Today* ran a long (for them) story: "Briefings 101: Crash course on the podium/James Rubin's access will help when he takes over State Department briefings. So will his practice."

The power is bestowed both by the news media—and therefore the public in general—and by the people to whom we report. This is a circle, though not an unbroken one.

The most visible spokesperson in the world, and probably the most powerful, at least by association, is the presidential press secretary. As an example of how far spokespersons have come, it was press secretary Marlin Fitzwater—not then-President George Bush—who announced the beginning of the 1991 Gulf War with these words: "The liberation of Kuwait has begun."

Spokespersons get power from the media when journalists are willing to settle for our being in front of the camera instead of the president or for whomever else we work. We get power from the president, or for whomever else we work, when he or she gives us broad authority to speak in his or her behalf. The more trust your boss has in you—and you in your boss—the more power you have, and the more responsibility. If your boss doesn't have to sign off on every sentence you utter or write before you can release it, you are, in effect, making policy when you issue statements in the name of your agency or company.

In the 1996 hit summer movie *Independence Day*, the president's spokesperson—by getting her ex-husband-absent-minded scientist through to the president so he could clue the Chief in on the deadly plans of the aliens—played a role in saving not only the nation but the whole world.

A government communicator also had a hand in the genesis of one of America's hottest myths, the so-called Roswell Incident.

On July 8, 1947—a day that will live in UFO conspiracy infamy—First Lieutenant Walter Haut, press officer with the 509th Bomber Group at Roswell Army Air Field in New Mexico, issued a press release announcing that the military had in its possession the wreckage of a "flying disk" found on a nearby ranch.

When a newspaper gets a press release like that, especially when it comes from the government of the United States, it doesn't take a slow news day to get it published. Haut's press release, which he later maintained his colonel ordered him to write, prompted this banner headline in the *Roswell Daily Record*: "RAAF Captures Flying Saucer On Ranch in Roswell Region."

The next day at Carswell Air Base in Fort Worth, Brigadier General Roger Ramey, commander of the Eighth Air Force, said the report was all a mistake. The object in question was only a weather balloon, he said.

More than a half century later, Air Force spokespersons were still answering questions about this bizarre incident. In July 1997, more than 100,000 people trekked to Roswell for the fiftieth anniversary celebration, visiting the site of the supposed crash, buying souvenirs, wearing alien costumes, and wondering what really happened.

It all started with a press release from a public information officer.

I have never issued a news release on a UFO, but I have fielded telephone calls to the DPS about UFOs from the media and general public. If it is not immediately clear which section of the DPS' 1,800-employee state headquarters should receive a telephone inquiry from the public, our PIO gets it on the assumption we will know how to handle it.

Especially the weird calls.

My strangest UFO call came from Hollywood. A researcher for a production company working on a movie about a UFO landing at the South Texas community of Poteet during the annual Strawberry Festival wanted to know what the DPS would do about it if such an event actually happened.

"Does the DPS have jurisdiction to investigate alien spacecraft?" the researcher asked quite seriously. "Would the Texas Rangers get involved?"

"Well," I replied in an equally serious vein, "if an alien spacecraft exceeded the speed limit on a state highway, I'm sure the Highway Patrol would issue the operator a ticket. We don't play favorites in Texas, although we try to be courteous to out-of-state tourists. And if an alien commits a felony crime while in Texas, the local sheriff can certainly ask for help from the Rangers."

Then, practicing a finely honed public information officer

job skill, I referred the caller to someone else—the Air Force.

Most of the time, I am asked more serious questions.

"Do you have a policy covering how long a Trooper can be placed on suspension with pay during an internal investigation?" or "What's the DPS' stance on gun control?" (The answer to that one is easy: We leave those sorts of discussions up to the lawmakers and advocacy groups.)

If you stay in the spokesperson field long enough, eventually you will become fairly well known in your city and maybe your state—at least to the folks in the media. During a crisis, you may be on television every day. People will wrongly start to assume you're a celebrity. Before long, you will be invited to judge contests and give speeches to Rotary Clubs. You may even be asked to join. When you walk into a room, some co-worker inevitably will say, "Well, here's the TV star."

Speaking of TV stars, in the fall of 1996 ABC began airing a sitcom called "Spin City." The show starred Michael J. Fox in the role of deputy mayor of New York City. One of the supporting characters, Richard Kind, played the mayor's hapless press secretary. A running gag in the show was that no one ever clued the spokesman in on what was really going on at city hall. Of course, he was pretty clueless in his own right. Though touted as a show about "personal relationships," the two-word title described it best—a spoof of how politicians attempt spin control by what they say or don't say. The show was funny, but after watching a few episodes, I knew how law enforcement officers must feel when they see caricatures of their profession on TV.

Even though I've been kidded about being a "TV star," I've gone on vacation following day after day of continuous exposure on the news and still enjoyed perfect anonymity. This probably only proves that most people don't watch the news or read newspapers. Or don't remember what they've seen or read if they do.

But fame and power, as Caesar was pointedly reminded, are fleeting.

One major gaff, well-covered by the media, can be a career-changing experience for a spokesperson. Soon thereafter it is announced that you are returning to the private sector to pursue other career opportunities, or you go on camera to declare tearfully that you feel you need to start spending more time with your family—even if your children are all grown and have left home. Any way it plays out, a spokesperson who goes too far or says the wrong thing has to fall on his own sword or face a figurative firing squad.

Aside from mishaps for which you can be held personally accountable, politicians lose elections. Job layoffs occur. Colleagues move on. The person who hired you retires. The agency is reorganized and you don't fit into any of the boxes on the new organizational chart.

As a spokesman for one of the larger state police forces in the nation, I don't carry a gun or wear a uniform, but if I did I'd want the symbol on my shoulder patch to be a lightning rod. As it is, as far as the press is concerned, I'm a flack without a flak jacket.

A pistol in the mashed potatoes

October 16, 1991, was Bosses' Day, another one of those holidays like Secretary's Day that I suspect was created by one of the large greeting card companies in cahoots with the florist industry. The accepted way to honor the boss is to take him or her to lunch, so maybe the restaurant industry kicked in some funding for research and development. On that particular Wednesday, bosses all across the nation were receiving funny cards and being invited to lunch by their staffs.

The DPS secretaries on the director's staff had decided to honor their bosses by spreading a potluck luncheon in the conference room used for the monthly Public Safety Commission meetings. The food was good and, as usual, I ate too much of it. Then, full, contented, sleepy and cognizant of the conventional wisdom that there is no such thing as a free lunch, I headed down the hall to another conference room for a meeting with my own boss, Lieutenant Colonel Dudley Thomas, who was then the assistant director of the department, and a group of other bosses. We planned to wade through another draft of a DPS report to the Sunset Commission, an agency charged by the Legislature with periodically reviewing state agencies.

"Feel free to page me or come get me if something comes up," I had jokingly told my then-secretary Alicia Cox, who had replaced Laverne Purcell when she retired. We both got a lot of kidding about Alicia's last name, but no, we weren't married or otherwise related.

When I first met Colonel Thomas he was a Highway Patrol

captain stationed in Austin and I was still a police reporter. He runs a meeting well. I like his stories and he usually laughs at my jokes. As a manager, he succeeds in striking a balance between being affable and businesslike. If I seem to be having trouble figuring out if he's kidding when he tells me something, he'll add, "I'm serious as a train wreck."

But I just don't like meetings. On a nice fall afternoon like that, I would rather have been out fishing on the small private lake I lease than sitting in on this editing session. Knowing that Colonel Thomas probably felt the same way made me feel a little better, but only slightly.

We had not worked our way through very many report pages when Alicia walked in. I felt momentarily cheered at the prospect of interruption. At first I thought she was kidding around, taking my flippant comment about rescuing me from the meeting way too literally. But then I saw the expression on her face. She handed me a yellow telephone message slip.

The message, taken at 1:17 that afternoon, was from Gary Patterson, supervisor of the Headquarters communications center: "Had hostage situation in Killeen / perp. is dead as are 12 others—will call w/details as they receive them."

I read the note to the lieutenant colonel and excused myself so I could find out what had happened and whether the DPS was involved in any way.

Back in my office, the telephones had already begun to ring. I made a quick call to our district office and learned a few more details.

The shooting had occurred at a Luby's Cafeteria. Someone crashed a pickup truck into the front window of the crowded eating place, stepped out, and started shooting people. Some DPS officers, not yet identified, had returned fire. I assumed some of our Troopers may have been eating lunch in the cafeteria when the shooting began. For years, the Luby's in Austin had offered its food at half-price to officers in uniform. I didn't know about the cafeteria in Killeen, but that was my guess.

I called Laureen Chernow, the public information officer for the Department's Division of Emergency Management, and asked for her help. Though her job description was fairly similar to mine, the Division of Emergency Management is partially federally funded, and though managed by the DPS and in the same building, also is part of the Governor's Office. The DPS' other public information officer was out on extended sick leave. In his absence I was the acting chief of media relations, but I was it. Laureen was my only generally available backup, though she still had her own shop to run. In addition to Laureen, I recruited Chief Frankie Waller, then head of Personnel and Staff Services for the Department, to help answer media calls. Since joining the DPS in 1970, he'd risen quickly through the ranks and was supervising hundreds of support personnel at Headquarters.

A short time later I was sitting in the front seat of a black-and-white Highway Patrol car as Trooper Kenneth Duderstadt rushed me to Killeen. I would have been on our Austin-based helicopter, but it was down for maintenance.

As we sped north on Interstate 35, I glanced over at the speedometer and watched the red needle quivering at 107 miles an hour. I didn't look a second time.

Duderstadt, a veteran Trooper nearing retirement, had the car's emergency lights on but not the siren. I mentioned it, thinking maybe he had forgotten to flip the switch.

"A siren doesn't do any good when you're running this fast," he explained. "Nobody can hear it."

I was beginning to believe no one could see us, either. The traffic code says a driver who observes an approaching emergency vehicle should pull over to the right, either off the road or at least into the far right lane of traffic. Very few motorists were extending us the courtesy of obeying the law as we rushed toward Killeen. I half-seriously began to compose an obituary that it would be up to someone else to write:

> Cox, 42, a DPS spokesman, had been on his way to Killeen to provide the media information on the DPS' role in the Luby's shooting when an 18-wheeler changed lanes in front of the patrol car.

Trooper Duderstadt hit the brakes and jerked me back to reality. He'd had to slow down to 65 miles an hour because the car in front of us in the left lane wasn't moving over. I could see that the driver was an older woman seemingly lost in her own thoughts. She never even looked into her rearview mirror. A law-abiding if inattentive driver, she was sticking exactly to the speed limit. Finally, the Trooper cut over into the right lane and passed her. If she even noticed us flashing by, I couldn't tell.

Maybe she was doing the same thing we were: Listening on the car's AM/FM radio to the unfolding news from Killeen—a city of some 65,000 that at the beginning of World War II had been only a small ranching community when the Army announced it was opening a huge tank training camp nearby. When we had left Austin, the first reports told only that several people had been shot and killed. As we raced toward the scene, the number of people reported as killed or wounded continued to rise.

Apparently, Texas was the venue of the latest mass murder. Someone had "gone postal," the irreverent slang term I'd heard used to describe such incidents, which with amazing frequency seem to involve postal employees in facilities operated by the U.S. Postal Service. This time someone had picked a cafeteria as a place to act out his rage.

Seven years before, it had been California's turn. On July 18, 1984, James Oliver Huberty gunned down twenty-one people at a McDonald's in San Isidro, California, before police killed him.

The shooting at Luby's was beginning to sound worse.

By the time we covered the seventy-five miles from Austin to Killeen, the radio reported that the shooter was dead by his own hand. As we pulled up outside the cafeteria we saw that all the ambulances had left. A MAST helicopter from nearby Fort Hood, which during the Cold War was billed as the largest Army post in the free world, was still on the ground on the right-of-way across State Highway 190 from the shopping center that included the cafeteria. A large crowd had gathered, held back by yellow plastic crime-scene tape. The only people left inside were police officers and the dead.

A huge media contingent had built up on the east side of the building. More reporters and camera crews were arriving.

Already, satellite dishes were trained toward the southwest, beaming the news to the rest of the world.

I walked to the front of the cafeteria with Trooper Duderstadt and started talking to one of the ranking Highway Patrol officers. On the first page of my legal pad, I wrote: "9mm semi-automatic—18-19 rounds/'I hate Killeen'/reloaded & shot himself/MVT conference/530 12W> <Geo. Hennard>."

Those jottings represented the story as far as anyone knew it at the time: The gunman had used a 9mm pistol, fired several clips, yelled things like "I hate Killeen," and finally had turned his weapon on himself.

The number-letter combination I'd written down was the license plate on the truck inside the cafeteria. The shooter was believed to have been George Hennard. I put the <> marks around his name because that was for my information only. The identification was not yet positive. The initials "MVT" referred to the DPS' Motor Vehicle Theft Service. The officers involved in the shooting had not been Troopers getting a discount on their lunch, as I had first thought. They were plain-clothes DPS auto theft investigators who had been teaching a training class nearby. They had rushed to the Luby's when the shooting started.

"You want to see what it's like inside?" one of the officers asked me. Well, not particularly. As a young reporter, I never minded looking at dead bodies. I thought it was exciting, just like in the movies or TV. I saw my first in San Angelo, in the summer of 1967, when someone committed suicide by shooting himself behind an ear with a .22.

Back then, when nurses still wore starched white uniforms and distinctive caps perched on their hair, Shannon Hospital did not mind having reporters in its emergency room. The helpful charge nurse, a tough but likable redhead who'd spent some of her younger days working at a hospital in Chicago, would call the *Standard-Times* to tip us when she knew an ambulance carrying a shooting or accident victim was coming in. If I was covering police, I'd race over to be there in time for the unloading. When the victim was rolled in (this was when funeral homes also provided ambulance service, which I always thought was the ultimate conflict of interest), I noticed the dead man had a black eye. *Aha!* I thought, *somebody beat him up, then shot him.* I could see a page-one story developing: "Angelo man beaten, shot."

But the murder story I envisioned soon evaporated. I stood nearby as the attending physician, who had not been able to do anything but pronounce the young man dead, assured one of his stunned relatives that "he didn't feel a thing" when he died. When I got a chance to ask the doctor about the black eye, he explained the bruise was caused by the impact of the bullet, which entered the back side of his head and stopped behind one of the eyes. It was a suicide, not a murder, he said.

In the intervening years, I'd seen a lot more dead bodies— suicides, murders, drownings, assorted accidental deaths (I remember a man who broke his neck when he fell out of a tree in a river bottom while threshing pecans), fires, and plane crash victims. But any thrill from the process had long since vanished, wandering off hand-in-hand with my youthful idealism.

Now, on this warm October afternoon, going inside Luby's was something I felt I had to do to get a better understanding of what had taken place there a few hours earlier. But I would not have done it out of curiosity.

Legal pad in hand, I walked through the broken door into the cafeteria. Two bodies lay in the foyer. Empty shell casings littered the carpet. Shattered glass crunched under my feet. I looked down and saw blood on the glass.

The pickup the gunman had crashed into the building was still inside. I wrote down "Ford p/u - 530 12W Ranger XLT bike in back 1987." The interior of the cafeteria looked more like a scene in a horror movie than the real world. Tables overturned. Curtains sucking like a chest wound in and out of a broken plate glass window. Trays loaded with cold food some people never got to eat. One of those people had chosen fried chicken, fried okra, mashed potatoes with gravy, and a roll. Lying on top of the entrée, its barrel thrust between the okra and the potatoes, was a Ruger P89, a 9mm semi-automatic. The killer had discarded the weapon after emptying it into some of the people who had been standing in the line. That Salvador Dali-like image is stamped into my mind as vividly as the impression the obscenely out of place pistol made in the food. Sometime later that evening, Missey Micheletti, DPS' head photographer, took a picture of that pistol on the plate. If there were a Pulitzer Prize for crime scene photography, she should have won it for that powerful picture. One 35mm color image told the whole horrible story.

I moved down the serving line, carefully stepping around three bodies, past the wrecked pickup truck, into the front portion of the eating area. The dining area floor was covered with bodies. I wrote "old woman at table—" and then noted "mostly females—."

After that, I quit trying to write down what I saw. I knew I couldn't go into that much detail when I described my walk-through to the media. Fortunately, not being an investigator, all I had to do was generalize, which would be gruesome enough. There was no need for specifics. I'd leave that to the Rangers and crime lab folks.

A police reporter who remains on the job long enough sees a lot of bodies, but they come one, two, or three at a time. Usually only one at a time. Few people in any field ever see a score or more dead human beings in one place at one time, not even doctors and usually not even morticians. Only combat veterans and those who have had to respond to a tragedy with mass casualties like this one know what it's like.

For one thing, the mind has trouble processing what the eyes are seeing. Healthy people newly dead look as though they could get up again. You keep staring, straining to catch some movement. They should be breathing, but they are not. The awful stillness simply does not compute.

The assault on my senses was not exclusively visual. There were smells. Of food. Of gun smoke. Of blood.

I had seen—and smelled—enough. I had to talk to somebody outside of this bloody still life, if for no other reason than to confirm there was still normalcy elsewhere. Walking back to the front of the cafeteria, I called Linda, my wife, on the primitive cellular telephone I had. The instrument was a hand-me-down, passed on by the sergeant who handled headquarters security. "It'll make an excellent trotline weight," he had assured me. The phone seemed to be able to hold a charge for only a few minutes, and I'm being only slightly sarcastic in saying that it worked best if the wind was blowing in the direction you were calling.

Linda remembers that I sounded agitated over the phone. She says I told her I was standing in blood looking at a room full of dead people. I can hardly remember the conversation. What I can recall is the almost overriding feeling that I had to connect with someone away from there.

My reaction surprised me. I had not expected the crime scene to bother me as much as it had. Maybe my reaction was cumulative, verging on system overload. A little more than a month earlier, on September 11, a Continental Express jet with eleven passengers and three crew members had crashed in flames about eight miles southwest of Eagle Lake, Texas, in Colorado County. I had flown to that scene from Austin in the DPS helicopter and had seen the charred bodies of those victims—clustered in the center of the plane by centrifugal force as it plummeted to earth—as I collected information to release to the media about the crash. Fourteen fire-blackened bodies.

But I did not have time to dwell on that still fresh memory now. While the interior of the cafeteria was deathly calm, outside was still chaos. Local police officers and DPS Troopers ringed the building. Stunned Luby's employees, uninjured customers who hadn't yet left, people who feared that a friend or someone in their family might be among the dead, and those who had no business there—the morbidly curious—stood on the other side of the crime scene tape and watched as police moved in and out of the cafeteria.

Rumor thrives in such chaos, which is the only word to describe the first few hours at the cafeteria and in the whole city of Killeen. The media had picked up on three rumors, all wrong, which had the potential of making things worse. The first rumor had it that two gunmen had entered the cafeteria, and one of them had escaped and was still at large. That report made the second rumor, that a sniper was still firing somewhere else in Killeen, more plausible. The third rumor was that someone was reporting a shooting at a school.

None of these rumors was true, and I called my office in Austin so they could get the word to the media. As soon as I could, I would brief the reporters on the scene and assure them of the same thing. Whatever had happened was over. A lot of people were dead, but the man who had killed them was dead too.

The first three rumors I had to contend with could have caused panic. The next three were merely erroneous pieces of information: No, five pounds of cocaine had not been found in Hennard's truck. No, a woman and her baby had not been crushed beneath that truck. No, Hennard had not eaten lunch at Luby's before coming back with his semi-automatic blazing.

Rumors flourish most readily when there is a lack of official information. The Killeen Police Department and municipal officials were overwhelmed by the situation and had had little time or inclination to talk with the media. As soon as I had a good idea of what had happened, particularly the basic details of the DPS response to the shooting, I went to the barricades separating the media from the crime scene, identified myself, and held a briefing.

A man armed with two pistols had crashed his pickup truck twenty feet inside the cafeteria, and had then strolled around shooting people until Killeen police and the two DPS investigators cornered him in the hallway leading to the restrooms. There, after an ejecting hull caught in his pistol in what police and others familiar with firearms call a "stovepipe jam," the man had shot himself. The whole bloody episode had lasted roughly twelve minutes.

"It's terrible," I told the reporters in describing what I'd seen inside. "You have to pinch yourself to make yourself believe this is real. There are bodies all over the place. I saw a large group of [bodies] in the southeast corner. I saw two bodies in the foyer. I saw a couple of bodies [actually three] in the serving line. It's an almost surrealistic, nightmarish scene."

Though I had the name of the gunman, I decided not to release it, since the Killeen Police Department would be the lead agency in investigating the shootings. I tried to focus on the DPS' role, what the scene looked like, and what the DPS would be doing to aid Killeen police: The Texas Rangers would be assisting in the investigation, and a DPS crime lab team was en route from Austin.

After the briefing I went back to the cafeteria to try to learn more about the part played by the DPS in the incident. Five DPS Motor Vehicle Theft Service investigators—Lieutenant Kenneth Henson and Sergeants Bill Cooper, Jody W. Fore, Marvin Guthrie and Roy Parrack—had been conducting a training class on stolen auto identification techniques for the Killeen Police Department at the nearby Sheraton Hotel, only 200 yards from Luby's. They had just finished lunch at the hotel when Hennard started shooting and the people who could began running from the cafeteria.

MVT Captain David M. Griffith had driven down from Dallas immediately after hearing about the shooting. Griffith told me that the two men with the most involvement—Sergeants Cooper and Fore—had gone with Ranger Sergeant Clayton Smith to the Killeen police headquarters to give a statement. Griffith gave me a general rundown and said that he would put me in touch with the two sergeants as soon as they were finished with that process.

Cooper had been standing outside the hotel, still on his lunch break, when he heard glass breaking and a muffled pop, followed seconds later by several more pops. Then Cooper saw people running from the Luby's. When he saw a woman who appeared to have blood on her shirt, he ran to his car to get his pistol. Once he was armed, he went to the woman and asked her what was happening.

"He's crazy, he's got a machine gun and he's killing people," she screamed.

Cooper asked where the man was.

"He's inside the restaurant."

Someone else yelled: "He's killing everybody!"

Sergeant Cooper ran toward the cafeteria. Killeen police officer Al Morris, who had been attending the training session, also ran to the cafeteria. Fore, Parrack, and Guthrie drove their cars to the scene.

When Cooper reached the cafeteria, he could see someone walking around inside with a pistol. From only forty feet away, he thought the man might be a plainclothes officer.

While Cooper was still trying to figure out if the man was a police officer or the bad guy, he saw the gunman walk up to an elderly couple. The woman was shielding her husband, who had already been shot. Then she realized she was about to die too.

"She just kind of bowed her head, and he shot her right in the top of the head," Cooper said.

Cooper realized he'd had a chance to shoot the killer, but then Hennard had moved out of his line of fire.

As I listened to Cooper's account of Hennard's execution of the woman, I suddenly noticed I couldn't read the notes I was writing on the legal pad. My eyes had filled with tears. As a reporter, I interviewed parents who'd just learned their sons had been killed in Vietnam, new widows and new widowers and witnesses to all sorts of terrible things, but I don't think any eyewitness account I had ever heard moved me as deeply as the story Cooper was telling.

Once Cooper and three Killeen police officers were inside the Luby's with Hennard, he began shooting at them. The Killeen officers returned the fire. From seventy-five yards, Sergeant Fore took four shots at Hennard. As Cooper crawled over the dead and wounded to get closer to the gunman, one shot from Hennard shattered glass right over the sergeant's head. Cooper now was only about twenty feet from Hennard, who had taken refuge in the hallway leading to the cafeteria's restrooms.

Using a serving cart for cover, Cooper aimed his pistol at Hennard. As he drew down on the gunman, Cooper could see that Hennard's pistol had jammed.

"Police!" Cooper yelled. "Drop the gun!"

Again, Cooper could have fired. But in his judgment, it would have been illegal to shoot the man. At that moment, Hennard was not threatening Cooper's life or anyone else's.

"It's not that I didn't want to," Cooper later recalled. "It would have been right by moral standards. But there was no way I could do it. State law says you can't."

Cooper had made a decision. Now Hennard made one. As the DPS investigator watched, his 9mm still trained on the gunman, Hennard (who was lying on his stomach) jerked the clip from his pistol, knocked out the empty shell casing that had jammed it, slapped another clip in, and jacked a round into the chamber.

The handgun was ready to fire again.

But he did not point the weapon at Cooper, which would have enabled the investigator to shoot. Instead, he turned over on his back and put the pistol against his right temple.

"He shot himself!" Cooper yelled.

Still training his gun on the now still form, Cooper rushed up, jerked loose the Glock still clenched in Hennard's hand, and checked for a pulse. There was none.

The massacre was over. The day after his thirty-fifth birthday, something had caused George Hennard to go berserk with two pistols. Payback, as we say in Texas, had been a son of a bitch.

When I had all the details I needed from the DPS officers involved, I thanked them and walked off toward an empty area in the parking lot, outside the circle of the lights. I stood there alone in the darkness, hoping no one would see me, until I felt I'd be able to talk to the media without tears rolling down my cheeks. People often tell me I have an exciting job, and I do. But this was not exciting. It was just hard. And what I was experiencing was only secondhand. I couldn't even begin to understand how Cooper and the other people more directly affected by the tragedy must have felt.

Following my briefing, several of the television stations, including WFAA out of Dallas, asked me to do "live shots" with them for the 10:00 news. Behind me was the cafeteria, illuminated by the tall street lamps in the parking lot and all the television lighting. During the daytime, no one had been able to see through the reflective glass windows, which had put officers at a distinct disadvantage during the shooting. Hennard could easily see where they were, but they could not see him. Now that it was dark, the reverse happened. From outside it was easy to see the crime scene work under way, as well as the covered bodies. Finally, someone realized this and the curtains were closed, blocking the view of the media and curious onlookers.

By midnight there wasn't much else I could do. The crime lab team had wrapped up its work at 11:30, though Ranger Sergeants Johnny Aycock and Fred Cummings would be there for some time yet, making measurements for a crime scene drawing, inventorying the contents of the truck, and gathering the possessions of the wounded and dead. Soon the bodies would be removed and taken to Dallas for autopsy, but I did not have to be around for that. I told Trooper Duderstadt, who had patiently waited around for me, that I was ready to go home. This time we took it easy on a lightly traveled back road. As soon as we got to the DPS, I thanked Duderstadt, transferred to my car, and went home.

I sat on our couch with Linda, who had stayed up to wait for me, and watched the coverage of the massacre for a while on CNN, then went to bed. I was tired—physically and mentally. But I couldn't get the interior scene out of my mind. Even worse, Sergeant Cooper's description of seeing the couple killed recycled in my head as regularly as CNN's "Headline News."

Back at the office the next morning, I told Colonel James Wilson and Lieutenant Colonel Thomas that I believed Sergeants Cooper and Fore deserved commendation for what they'd done in Killeen. I was disappointed that the morning newspapers had not snapped to the fact that their actions, along with those of the Killeen police, undoubtedly had saved lives. When the officers had cornered Hennard, he had begun shooting at them, not at the unarmed customers inside the cafeteria.

I called Jim Phillips, a friend of mine on the *Austin American-Statesman*, and went through the story of the DPS' involvement again. I knew if he made the point in print, the AP and other newspapers would pick it up and the word would get out. Still, I was amazed that it had not been apparent to the media from what I had said at my press conferences the day before. On the other hand, the media, like everyone else, was concentrating on the record-breaking number of deaths—twenty-three victims in addition to Hennard—and on its traditional quest for a generally unattainable answer to a simple question: Why?

Most of the reporters engaged in that morning-after effort were in Killeen, getting their information from Killeen police, anyone they could find who knew any of the people involved, and the various agencies, organizations, and institutions working to help the wounded and the families of the victims. The media calls to my office were only moderate to light, though we did get a lot of photographers coming by to shoot driver license photographs of the victims. (In Texas, a driver license photograph of a deceased person is considered a public record. The living are protected, with images available for law enforcement use only.)

I had previously scheduled to take a day of vacation that Friday, with plans to drive to West Texas for a weekend canoe trip down a portion of the Pecos River. Two friends, Glen Ely of Austin and Patrick Dearen of Midland, and I were working on an educational video on the history of the Pecos. I would be standing in front of a video camera again, but under much better circumstances. I considered postponing the trip, but by the close of business Thursday the media calls were at a manageable level, and I needed a break.

Before I left Austin Friday morning, I read the newspaper's extensive second-day coverage of the massacre. My call to Phillips had paid off. He devoted five paragraphs to the DPS angle, quoting me that: "We think they [the DPS and Killeen officers] acted properly and heroically. Given the preliminary reports we have now, DPS is satisfied the actions of our officers saved many lives."

Phillips also quoted Captain Griffith, who said the Motor Vehicle Theft officers would be given some time "to regain their equilibrium" before returning to regular enforcement duties.

On June 2, 1992, Colonel Wilson presented Director's Citations to Sergeants Fore and Cooper in recognition of their "exemplary professional response exhibited during a crisis situation, which resulted in the saving of many lives." Lieutenant Henson and Sergeants Guthrie and Parrack received letters of commendation.

Not until the following spring was I finally able to walk back inside another Luby's. It was a new cafeteria, the first for New Braunfels, but it had the same floor plan as the one in Killeen. The Luby's in Killeen was remodeled and reopened. I have driven by it a few times, but I will never go back inside it. I admire those who can.

* * *

Fast forward to February 19, 1994. It was the Mexican food the night before, Linda later said. Well before dawn on that Saturday, she went into hard labor. We left for the hospital about 9:00 A.M. After Linda had endured contractions for most of the day, the baby still had not come. The monitors were beginning to show our daughter was in distress.

"We're going to have to go ahead with a C-section," the doctor said. "I'll see you in OR."

Linda and I had attended Lamaze classes and agreed that I would be with her when the baby was born.

While the doctor scrubbed up, a nurse found a set of hospital greens big enough for me to get into. With face mask, a French milk maid-looking head piece, and blue paper covers over my shoes, I joined Linda in the operating room. The surgical nurse moved a stool to the head of the operating table and gestured toward it.

"You better sit down here," she said. "We lose a lot of fathers during these."

"That's okay," I said. "A couple of months ago during hunting season my arms were up to my elbows inside a dead deer. And besides, I was at Luby's in Killeen."

At 5:50 that evening, our daughter Hallie Dorin Cox, eight pounds, four ounces and nineteen-and-a-half inches, was born.

Wackos in Waco

On the weekend of February 27-28, 1993, not only was I not in the loop about was what going on in Waco, I didn't even know there was a loop.

As my friend Larry BeSaw later put it, a spokesman often is "first to get called, last to know." That certainly was my experience at the beginning of this crisis.

Linda and I were in Houston, trying to sell Texana at a rare book and paper show. Over coffee on Sunday morning, I read with moderate interest a story in the *Houston Chronicle* about some religious nut in Waco, a guy named David Koresh who supposedly thought it was his divine right to whip children as young as eight months old and had fathered children with up to fifteen women, including some who were not of legal age. The story was an Associated Press rewrite of an investigative piece by two staff writers for the *Waco Tribune-Herald*, Darlene McCormick and Mark England. That copyrighted story had run Saturday morning in the Waco newspaper, the first of a seven-part series called "The Sinful Messiah."

The story, though it foreshadowed trouble, did not indicate any DPS role. The concern raised in the story that Koresh and his followers might possibly possess illegal automatic weapons was a federal matter. Questions dealing with the welfare of children were primarily an issue for the Texas Department of Protective and Regulatory Services.

Sunday mornings are slow at book shows. The doors usually open to the public at 10:00, but except for die-hard bibliophiles, potential customers don't start trickling in until after

38

church and lunch. That gives me a couple of hours to peruse the stock of my fellow book dealers, looking for titles I might want for a customer or for myself.

I was wandering the aisles, enjoying looking at other people's books, when my pager went off. I figured some Trooper somewhere had stopped a vehicle and seized a bunch of dope, or some reporter was having trouble finding a report on some cowboy who got drunk and tried to fly a pickup truck. Those are the kinds of calls I usually get on Sundays, assuming I get any at all. Despite Texas' large population and immense size, sometimes I go a whole on-call shift (a week) without a single after-hours telephone call from the media or from our communications center.

So, with no great rush and certainly no premonition of trouble, I moved toward the door leading to the outside hall and a bank of pay telephones. I was devoting much more thought to getting another cup of coffee than making a phone call to Austin.

The communications operator sounded flustered. When she hadn't found me at home and when I did not instantly answer the page, she had called Laureen Chernow. In January 1992, when I was promoted from my status as acting head of PIO to chief of media relations, I had asked that Laureen be promoted from her position as PIO for our Division of Emergency Management to my assistant PIO. Lieutenant Colonel Thomas called me "Newsy One" and Laureen "Newsy Two."

"Sorry it took so long to get back to you," I said. "What's up?"

"They raided that place in Waco this morning," the communications operator said. "Did you see the story in the paper? Several officers have been shot and there's still shooting. We're already getting media calls."

"Is this something we're doing?" I asked.

"It's the ATF [Federal Bureau of Alcohol, Tobacco and Firearms], but we've got people there and SWATs [Special Weapons and Tactics team] en route," she said.

"Any DPS officers down?"

"I don't think so," she said.

I thanked her and asked her to keep me informed. My next call was to Lieutenant Colonel Thomas.

"I'm hearing several ATF agents are dead and a lot more are wounded," he said. "It's probably going to be worse than that."

He told me that Rangers, Highway Patrol Troopers, and our SWAT team were either already on the scene to help out or en route.

"I'm in Houston," I said. "I guess I need to get to Waco as quick as I can. Linda could drive the car back to—"

"No, this is a federal deal," he interrupted. "They've already got their PIOs there. Let's let them handle it."

Of course, that didn't stop me from getting media calls about it. The ATF public information officers on the scene (there were two) might be talking to local reporters, but they obviously were too busy to return calls from out of town and out of state. I could judge that by the number of calls I was getting.

Throughout the rest of the morning and into the afternoon, I spent a lot of time on the pay phone telling reporters: "The DPS is there to offer assistance, but was not involved in the raid or the shooting."

We had not been there early on, but some of the media had been. The *Waco Tribune-Herald* and KWTX Television each had staffers in the area when the raid went down. Dodging bullets, the TV photographer got incredible and horrifying footage throughout the gun battle.

By shortly after 5:00 that evening, Linda and I had loaded our unsold books and were on I-10, headed back to Austin. Listening to the continuous radio coverage on Dallas' KRLD Radio, I realized this was ballooning into a very big story. Four ATF agents were dead, the most federal officers ever killed in a single criminal incident. Sixteen other officers were wounded. The stand-off had begun and the news media was already playing a part, allowing Koresh to express his views to the world. Claiming he had been wounded in the morning shootout, Koresh did a live telephone interview that evening with CNN, a long interview with a reporter for the *Dallas Morning News,* and later released written statements to be read on KRLD in exchange for the release of some of the children inside the compound.

After Linda and I got home that night I saw for the first time the striking KWTX television footage that would become as familiar over the next several months as a recurrent bad dream: The helmeted, blue-clad federal agents on the roof of Koresh's compound going into a window some of them would never come out of alive, the gunfire from agents taking shelter behind cars and the muffled pops as bullets from the inside drilled through the sides and roof of the structure, the war-like images of stunned agents—bloody and dirt-covered, dragging away their dead and wounded. These images became part of our collective national memory.

Special Agent Sharon Wheeler, one of the ATF PIOs, had collected after-hours telephone numbers for Dallas television stations prior to the raid in anticipation of announcing its successful conclusion. When I saw Wheeler being grilled by the media after the raid, I began to feel a little less guilty about not having been on the scene. On the other hand, I felt bad about what she was going through. I believe I could have helped, since my office already had experience in crisis situations.

But my boss was right. This was a federal deal.

The next day, Monday, March 1, the FBI took over as the lead agency in the stand-off. Its Hostage Response Team (HRT) had flown in from Washington at 10:00 the night before. The DPS continued in a support role, primarily using Highway Patrol Troopers to man checkpoints on the roads leading to the compound. One of our Public Safety commissioners later put it this way: We were merely "working security."

Koresh had demanded to make a statement over the radio, and KRLD had agreed to run it. His fifty-eight-minute broadcast aired at 1:30 on the afternoon of Tuesday, March 2. I couldn't pick up the Dallas station on the radio in my office, so I went out to my car to listen to it. Not that I could understand much of what Koresh was saying, but it was interesting.

Meanwhile, though Koresh got some free air time for his religious ramblings, the media relations situation in Waco only worsened.

"I am absolutely disgusted with the way the media is being mishandled by the authorities through misinformation or no information at all," David Overton, the news director for Dallas' Channel 5 told the *Dallas Morning News*. "I think they're doing an abysmal job. . . .People want to know what's going on out here. We're just a conduit. This is for the public."

The FBI did not begin holding daily news briefings until noon on Wednesday, March 2. But as the media settled in outside Waco, they zeroed in on the ATF and FBI, and calls to my office from news organizations returned to their normal level. When we did get calls, they usually were from journalists needing DPS press identification cards so they could get past our roadblock to the media encampment dubbed Satellite City that had sprung up about two miles from the compound.

A master's degree or maybe even a doctorate of philosophy in communications awaits the graduate student who can talk his advisor into letting him study what happens at media encampments during a protracted news event.

I had my first experience with this phenomenon during the 1974 prison siege at Huntsville, but that was before satellite trucks, video production vans, and cellular phones. At Huntsville, the media set up camp on the ground outside the prison administration building, immediately across the street from the prison where the hostages were being held. Southwestern Bell started stringing phone wire for many of the news organizations. CBS News had a telephone installed under a tree. Correspondent Ed Rabel sat under that tree in a lawn chair until prison officials called a briefing. After the press conference, he would come back to his "office" under the tree and call in a report to the radio network. When it came time for his report to be aired, he would go listen to it on the radio in his rental car. Film had to be driven or flown to Houston to be developed and distributed. Print reporters dictated their stories over the portable bank of pay phones Southwestern Bell had trailered in. Most of those print reporters had two major sets of deadlines a day (back then big cities still had afternoon papers).

Now, nearly two decades later, the media encampment in McLennan County featured dozens of satellite trucks, production vehicles, travel trailers, power generators, rental cars and vans, tents, and portable toilets. Long-lens video cameras mounted atop scaffolding kept an around-the-clock electronic eye on Koresh's compound. Still photographers toted around lenses long enough to photograph the planets. Other scaffolding served as broadcast platforms for TV correspondents, enabling them to be high enough to have the compound show up behind them when they were on camera, offering the illusion of nearness to the scene.

The journalists couldn't gather and report news all the time. For one thing, there was not that much news to gather, especially as the siege dragged on. Frisbees flew, suntans began, golf swings were perfected. Practical jokes helped combat boredom and relieve stress, and not all the beverages consumed were coffee and soft drinks. The Salvation Army provided food, but backyard barbeque grills began showing up to supplement the free fare. On Saturday nights the more convivial journalists gathered for the weekly "ditch dance," as in bar ditch, the drainage area on either side of the roadway. Yard art flourished. CNN staffers spread Astroturf in front of their trailer, adding homey touches like a white picket fence, flowers in planters, and a plastic duck with three ducklings, their heads appropriately stuck in the sand.

A city by definition has a government. Satellite City had two mayors, one presiding over the north side of the two-lane farm road that cut through the encampment, and one presiding over the south side. The south side mayor was backed by his newly born newspaper, *The Satellite City Daily News*: "If It Happens, It's News To Us!"

The Troopers manning the checkpoint closest to Satellite City were not immune to the monotony. Soon, a M*A*S*H-like scrap wood sign-tree began growing outside the DPS tents. Each time a group of Troopers rotated in from a particular area, they added a sign pointing out the distance to their hometown. The DPS was keeping some eighty Troopers in the area, rotating in a new contingent each week. The regional liaison officer for the Department's Division of Emergency Management, Steven Vaughn, worked with Danny Smith, the Waco-based Highway Patrol captain, to arrange for logistical support for DPS personnel. Vaughn contacted officials at the Texas State Technical College in Waco to secure dormitory rooms for Troopers. He obtained portable generators, heaters, tents (donated by a Waco tent and awning company), water containers, portable toilets—all the things needed for an extensive, extended operation.

At the intersection of Farm Road 2491 and Loop 340, two miles west of Satellite City, a spot known as Woodie's Hill evolved into a retail center of sorts. Entrepreneurs hawked everything from photocopies of various court documents pertaining to Koresh to T-shirts and souvenir hats. The spot became a tourist destination. Troopers, journalists, and people drawn because of all the publicity spent money at Woodie's Hill. My favorite T-shirt slogan: "My parents went to Mount Carmel and All I Got Was a Lousy AK-47."

While the DPS, as I continued to tell reporters, was not directly involved in trying to resolve the stand-off, the Rangers were quietly investigating the so-called second shooting, a gun battle between ATF agents and three followers of Koresh outside the compound on the evening of the raid. The Rangers also were looking into whether the media presence in the area of Mount Carmel before the raid had the effect of warning Koresh of the impending raid.

Extensive media coverage draws kooks like bugs to a porch light on a sticky summer night. Though Laureen and I referred the serious media questions to the feds, we dealt with the openly crazy callers ourselves. One helpful citizen called our office to suggest an innovative solution to the crisis:

"I'm sure the University of Texas would have the equipment you will need," the man began.

"What equipment is that?" I asked, interested.

"Something that will generate microwave energy," he said. "Thing to do is beam that intense energy into the compound."

"What will that do?" I asked, still interested.

"Slow cook them from the inside out," he responded matter-of-factly. "If that doesn't work, get a howitzer," he continued. "Blow their roof off and they'll come crawling out like ants."

I thanked the man for taking time to call us. "I've got a call on hold," I said. "I have to go."

Laureen took a call that rivaled the one I'd gotten. At first, the man's request had seemed routine. He was in Waco, calling from a pay phone, and needed us to issue him a press card as soon as possible.

"Who are you with?" Laureen asked.

He was the author of two books on how to put the romance back into relationships, he said, "The King of Romance." He needed the press card, he continued, so he could join the media gathered near Mount Carmel and start hitting reporters and producers up for appearances on their shows to promote his books.

He could hardly contain his excitement. This exposure could cut five to six years off his time line to becoming internationally known. He needed the DPS press card as quickly as possible. He was a man on the move.

Actually, Laureen concluded, he was a man on the make. She explained our criteria for the issuance of press cards and said he did not meet those criteria.

As she later reported to me, "I could not be sweet-talked, even by the King of Romance."

A lot of the media inquiries we received during the standoff were from other countries, particularly Great Britain and Australia. Some foreign nationals were among Koresh's followers. These callers had a bit of trouble understanding the American judicial system, especially the difference between state and federal law enforcement. It was a little difficult to explain to them that a Texas law enforcement agency was not the lead agency with such a serious situation taking place only a hundred miles from the state capital.

Evidently lacking any other information source, one reporter for the venerable *London Times* apparently resorted to fiction writing in his coverage of the events in McLennan County. On April 7 his readers were treated to a feature story about Texans and their well-known affinity for guns.

"What you wear is what you are in Waco, Texas," the reporter wrote, "although what you are is also accurately reflected by what you drive and what you shoot."

A lot of that shooting, the reporter continued, happened

at Linda's Happy Time Tavern, which "boasts some of the town's more exciting brawls."

When the *London Times* piece came to the attention of *Dallas Morning News* state editor Donnis Baggett, he decided to learn more about Linda and her Happy Time Tavern, an establishment that had not cropped up in any of the domestic coverage of the stand-off. So, hoping to get the inside story from Linda herself, Baggett called directory assistance for Waco to get a phone number for the tavern.

"*Hmm*," the operator said, "I'm not showing anything under the name Linda's Happy Time Tavern."

Baggett, figuring maybe the place was outside the Waco city limits, asked her to check again.

"Checking the entire area code, I show nothing," she said.

At one point during the siege, Koresh's followers hung from their watch tower a banner bearing this message:

God help us
Send in the press

Soon I would come to believe that Koresh had that all wrong. Within a few weeks, resorting to gallows humor in an effort to cope with what had become the most stressful situation of my career, I suggested those two lines should be reversed to: "Send in the press . . . God help us."

The siege went on and on with only minor developments. A few more children were released, a few adults left, Houston lawyer Dick DeGuerin negotiated, the FBI began employing psychological techniques including playing mournful music, tapes of dying rabbits, and Nancy Sinatra over loudspeakers. The number of reporters had become vastly disproportionate to the amount of news. Beyond that, maintaining a presence at Satellite City, especially for the television stations, was tremendously expensive. The mega-media coverage began to wane.

When Passover passed with no apocalyptic shootout or surrender, and when the biggest thing that happened on Easter was a media Easter egg hunt, the Mount Carmel story was obviously losing altitude rapidly. The worst one-liner making the rounds was the phrase "Christmas in Waco." As the media population declined, Satellite City began to lose its boomtown feel.

Still, the FBI agents looking through the scopes of their sniper rifles and the electronic eyes at the end of the long lenses kept up the vigil at Mount Carmel.

"Welcome to Koresh World"

Eating frozen yogurt from Dairy Queen, I was watching death on a live shot—an arrangement of words as contradictory as what I was seeing: Hell on a nice spring day.

Television has given us Baby Boomers numerous opportunities to witness history as it happened, in what it later became popular to call "real time." But due to various circumstances, I had missed several of those epochal events. On November 24, 1963, millions of Americans saw accused presidential assassin Lee Harvey Oswald gunned down by Jack Ruby in the basement of the Dallas Police Headquarters on live television. I wasn't watching TV when Ruby pulled the trigger, but my granddad saw the shooting. With the surging instincts of an old reporter, he rushed out and said excitedly: "Someone's just filled Oswald full of lead!" I did see the July 20, 1969, moon landing live, but on January 26, 1986, when anyone watching CNN would have seen the space shuttle *Challenger* explode on live television, I was at work.

On Monday, April 19, 1993, the fifty-first day of the Waco stand-off, I was home in Austin for lunch, watching the noon news on one of the local TV stations. Near the end of the half hour, the station returned to one final live shot of the Branch Davidian compound before the newscast ended.

The anchor said, "Something seems to be happening."

Actually, it had been evident all morning that something was going to happen. Watching television while getting ready for work, I'd learned that FBI-driven armored military vehicles had begun punching holes in the walls of the compound at 6:00. "This is not an assault," the FBI agents assured the Davidians over loudspeakers. They would not be hurt. All they needed to do was come out and surrender. But the Davidians, wearing gas masks, started shooting at the tanks.

At 10:30 that morning, the FBI held its regular press briefing and explained that CS tear gas had been "introduced" into the compound.

I later read reports that a friendly DPS Trooper had alerted the media shortly before the gassing began, but no one in the Public Information Office got the word in advance.

Now, as I watched this live feed from McLennan County during the noon hour, I recalled the old joke about the guy caught red-handed doing something he shouldn't. The fellow in the wrong denied everything, saying, "Are you going to believe me or your lyin' eyes?"

Normally, when a television station shows video—or airs something live—some news reader tells you what you are seeing, usually based on his or her script and occasionally on actual perspective and interpretation. With a live shot, however, you are seeing the same scene the commentator is and, depending on the circumstances, hearing the same sound. Without any filtering, you can reach your own conclusions.

The moment I saw a slight wisp of smoke coming from a corner of the structure, I realized something was much more amiss than did the newscaster, who went on with the standard promise of "full coverage this evening at six." A few seconds later, when the smoke began to darken, I knew the situation was moving quickly out of hand. Not for what seemed like a minute or more (though maybe it was only seconds) did the newscaster finally realize that something bad was happening in McLennan County even as he spoke and we watched.

I'll chalk up my quick assessment not to greater intellect but to experience. As a police reporter, I had covered a lot of fires and I learned a lot from firefighters. Dark smoke means live fire. Lighter smoke, gray to white, means water's reaching the flames and the fire's about to be under control. I saw no white smoke, only more and more black smoke. Then, suddenly, eruptions of orange billowing into the blue sky. The fire was wildly out of control. The way the wind was blowing that day, I knew that fire was not going to be contained. The only uncertainty that I had at that point was whether Koresh and his followers were bailing out on the other side of the structure, out of view of the long-lensed television camera. Soon, however, it became evident that no one was leaving, or at least, only a few.

I switched to CNN, hoping they were more informed than the local television news reader. Not having a cable connection in my office, I phoned my secretary and told her what was happening. "I'll be at home for a while to see what's going to happen," I said. "Call me here if you need me for anything."

Though I had appreciated the gravity of the situation at Mount Carmel the moment I saw the smoke, what happened the next day would surprise me as much as the fire had surprised the FBI and the rest of the nation.

FBI Agent Bob Ricks had been handling most of the briefings during the siege. On Tuesday, April 20, at the end of the 10:30 A.M. briefing, Ricks announced to the media—on live television—that the Texas Rangers would be doing the follow-up investigation into the fire. Any further questions should be addressed to the Rangers. The FBI would not be conducting any more press conferences.

Laureen Chernow and I had been watching the briefing on the television in our office. Now we looked at each other in stunned disbelief. For fifty-one days, we had been politely referring any media calls we got about the stand-off to the U.S. Attorney's Office in Waco, the FBI, or the ATF. No one had given us a heads-up that the DPS would now be handling the investigation or that we would be fielding the media calls from here on.

Our phones began ringing almost immediately. And kept ringing. Some of the calls were from reporters still standing in the room at the Waco Convention Center, where the daily briefings had been held. By the end of the day, my office had received 117 calls (and we probably had more we didn't have time to write down) from various media organizations around the world.

These are some of the questions we logged:

- AP, Dallas: "Why is media being kept so far back? It's ludicrous. Request the air space restriction be lowered. . . ."
- ABC News, New York: "Wants info on Waco. Wants to go live with Texas Rangers."
- *Austin American-Statesman*: "Are y'all going to take over? ATF & FBI referring everything to Texas Rangers."
- *Los Angeles Times*: "Was DPS taken off-guard by FBI turning situation over to Rangers?" (No, only the Public Information Office was.)
- CBS, Dan Rather's office: "Wants to do interview."

After conferring with Colonel Wilson and the head of the criminal law enforcement division, Chief Bill Pruitt, I prepared a basic statement for the media. Actually, there was not much we could say. No one, except perhaps the people who had died in the fire, could have answered the questions we were being asked that day. But the media—and through them the world—did not want to settle for that. They wanted to know why so many people, including innocent children, were dead. How had the fire started? Reporters were asking me that and they were asking Attorney General Janet Reno and even President Bill Clinton.

These were the points I made in the one-page, double-spaced news release:

- The DPS had begun the most complicated investigation in its modern history. With a seventy-eight-acre crime scene and several score victims, the only comparable situations since the creation of the agency in 1935 were the deaths of 293 students and teachers in the March 18, 1937, natural gas explosion at the New London consolidated school, the April 16, 1947, Texas City disaster—in which nearly 600 people died when two tankers carrying anhydrous ammonia exploded—and the May 11, 1953, Waco tornado, which killed 114 people. But those had all been natural disasters, acts of God. The undertaking at Mount Carmel was a criminal investigation, based on the actions of a man who thought he was the son of God.

Colonel Wilson estimated it might take the DPS up to two weeks to complete its work at the site.

• In an unprecedented action, more than thirty Texas Rangers, nearly a third of the whole force, had been deputized as federal officers. This was for evidentiary purposes in the federal judicial system. The Rangers, however, would remain under the direction of the DPS.

I showed Chief Pruitt a draft of the statement before I released it. He read it and handed it back to me with a broad smile—one of the few smiles, if not the only one, I saw that day. "You didn't say anything," he told me, "and it didn't take you long to do it."

At the bottom of the release was a note to editors: "Texas Rangers will not be available for interviews. Additional media statements will be issued as information becomes available. Evidentiary information cannot be released."

The media, of course, was not happy with this at all. Calls for more information—and in complaint over our brief statement—started going to Governor Ann Richards' office. The media wanted someone on camera to explain what was going on and to answer their largely unanswerable questions.

I was in Colonel Wilson's office again when Governor Richards called him early that afternoon. She did most of the talking. When he got off the phone, Wilson told me to get to Waco as soon as I could and put together a press conference. Someone from the governor's press office, Chuck McDonald, would be coming up from Austin to help me.

Since I was going to be in Waco, I needed some help answering the calls coming to my office. Laureen and Alicia, our secretary, didn't have enough arms or ears to handle the deluge. Since my wife had a background in public information, I asked for her help. Actually, I asked her boss for Linda's help. But he readily agreed, and she came over from the DPS' Motorcycle Safety Bureau, where she worked as a program coordinator, to PIO to lend a hand with the calls.

Colonel Wilson told me to meet Senior Ranger Captain Maurice Cook at the motel in Waco where the Rangers had been staying. A planning session had been set for 5:00 that afternoon. I knew what dealing with Captain Cook was going to be like, but like a good trooper I drove to Waco to meet with the captain and the prosecutors from the U.S. Attorney's Office, Ray Jahn and his wife, LeRoy.

I approached this meeting with a certain lack of enthusiasm because I knew from previous encounters that Captain Cook had no use for the news media, and by extension, little or no use for me or for my office.

His Rangers had standing orders not to do news media interviews, with the exception of talking to local reporters, unless he gave clearance. If I called a Ranger anywhere in the state to ask even the most basic questions about a particular case I'd gotten a media call about, I could usually count on a call from Captain Cook reminding me that all information about the Rangers had to come from him. That would have been fine, but he never had much information to share. Any time I argued for more information, or merely for his consent for a Ranger to do an interview, the captain would listen politely, like the experienced police officer he was, but my plea had about as much effect as some college kid protesting to a Trooper about to write him a speeding ticket.

Even when reporters wanted nothing more than a general interview for a neutral-to-positive story on "What modern Texas Rangers do," the Ranger commander generally turned them—and me—down. I could offer them interviews with a Highway Patrol Trooper or narcotics investigator or virtually anyone else in the agency, but not a Texas Ranger. Sometimes an appeal to Colonel Wilson for intervention worked, but eventually I pretty much quit trying. For insight into the Texas Rangers, the public had to rely on the bearded, karate-kicking Chuck Norris as "Walker, Texas Ranger" on Saturday night television.

When I got to Waco, I went straight to the motel where the strategy meeting was to be held. Within minutes, Cook and I were sparring over information—more accurately, the absence of information. Just as I had expected, he was not telling me much of anything.

"Remember, I work for the DPS," I told him, my frustration building, "not the news media. You and I get our paychecks from the same place. I'm not going to release anything I shouldn't. I could show you a stack of letters commending me for the way I handled the media at Killeen," I threw in.

"Yeah," he shot back, "from the media."

Incredibly, I came out of the meeting with two pages of notes. I went from the motel room to the Waco Convention Center. The press conference began at 8:30 that night.

Probably twice the number of reporters and photographers that had been in Killeen were waiting for me at the Convention Center. The press conference would be carried live on many stations and CNN.

As I squinted in the glare from all the lights and looked down at my six-point outline, I found only one thing worth chuckling inwardly about. In the spring of 1992, I had started taking night courses to finish the undergraduate degree I had abandoned work on as a junior in 1970. One of the classes I was taking at Southwest Texas State University in San Marcos that semester was a required freshman level speech course I had never gotten around to taking during my first college career. I had already made a speech or two to my fellow classmates, none older than twenty. Grading me was the professor's teaching assistant, a graduate student all of twenty-three or twenty-four. I hoped the TA and my professor were tuned in. Maybe I'd get extra credit for the little talk I was about to make to the world.

"The DPS deeply regrets the loss of life yesterday," I began. "We are going to do everything we can to determine what happened inside that compound. We will move as fast as we safely can."

The bodies would be taken to the Tarrant County Medical Examiner's Office in Fort Worth for identification and autopsy, I said. Rangers had seen numerous bodies in the ruins, and the ones they could see all appeared to be charred, but it was not yet safe enough to begin removing the remains. Only one body, found outside the still hot rubble, had been removed so far.

"Our number one concern right now is safety," I continued. An ATF Explosive Ordnance Disposal (EOD) team would have to clear the debris of any grenades and any other potentially dangerous devices before some forty-five DPS crime lab-

George Hennard emptied this pistol inside Luby's and discarded it onto a plate of chicken.

— Photo by Missey Micheletti, Courtesy
Texas Department of Public Safety.

Serving line at Luby's.
— Photo by Missey Micheletti, Courtesy
Texas Department of Public Safety.

A bullet removed this restroom icon's leg at Luby's. During the massacre, two women hid inside.
— Photo by Missey Micheletti, Courtesy Texas Department of Public Safety.

A small drop of blood contradicts the message on this gift cup on the floor inside the Luby's cafeteria at Killeen.
　　　　　— Photo by Missey Micheletti, Courtesy Texas Department of Public Safety.

Laureen Chernow conducting press conference at Waco during the siege.
— Courtesy Texas Department of Public Safety.

"Satellite City," Waco, a boomtown in the spring of 1993.
— Courtesy Texas Department of Public Safety.

Signs point to the way home from Waco.
— Courtesy Texas Department
of Public Safety.

TV cameraman gets footage of search for evidence in ruins of the Mount Carmel compound.
— Courtesy Texas Department
of Public Safety.

The daily media tour at site of Koresh's compound.
— Courtesy Texas Department
of Public Safety.

A practical joke helped relieve tensions during DPS investigation in the aftermath of the fire. The sign on the post says, "Ranger Hitching Post."
— Courtesy Texas Department of Public Saftety.

Ranger Clayton Smith talks to family members of the compound fire victims.
— Courtesy Texas Department of Public Safety.

The U.S., Texas, and ATF flags fly at half-staff over the remains of the compound.
— Courtesy Texas Department of Public Safety.

CNN President Tom Johnson and author outside Koresh compound.
— Courtesy CNN.

Author outside DPS command post at Koresh compound ruins.

oratory workers and Rangers could begin work at the scene, I said.

Once the scene was considered safe, law enforcement personnel would be photographing and videotaping the scene, marking and collecting evidence, and doing a detailed diagram. All evidence collected would go to the FBI crime laboratory in Washington.

Since a federal search warrant was still in force for the scene, the Rangers had been deputized as U.S. marshals under federal criminal procedural rules to protect against any future challenges on the admissibility of any evidence gathered.

Finally, I said, because of the safety concerns I had already discussed, no press pools could be allowed into the area.

As soon as I had worked my way through my outline, a barrage of unanswerable questions followed. I tried to handle some of them, but I finally had to have a Trooper escort me out of the building or I would have been there all night.

After the press conference, I headed back to Austin, about a ninety-minute drive. I had to be at the local NBC affiliate, KXAN-TV, before dawn the next morning for an interview on "The Today Show." Then I had to teach a previously scheduled media relations class at our training academy. When the class was over, I would return to Waco.

The class, a component of a week-long "Effective Communication" school the DPS offers, usually runs from 9:00 in the morning until noon. Normally, I give an overview on the news media and go through suggestions on how to deal with the media effectively. Laureen shows a video demonstrating what not to do when confronted by reporters. Then, after a break, we reconvene the class in the Training Academy video studio for some role-playing in front of a camera. But the people signed up for this day's class did not get their nickel's worth.

During a break, I checked with Alicia to see what the call load was like. Dozens of messages were piling up, she said. I located my friend Captain Mark Warren, assistant commander of the academy. "Sorry, Mark," I told him, "I'm going to have to cancel the rest of the class. I've got to get back to Waco."

I left almost immediately. Laureen would be going, too,

but she had to go home and pack and would join me there later. It would be nearly two weeks before we got to return to our homes in Austin.

My pager went off as I drove north on I-35. The display showed it was my office calling. When I got Alicia on the cell phone, she said, "John Lumpkin with the AP in Dallas says he's got to talk to you right now." I knew Lumpkin was head of the AP's Dallas bureau and that it must be important. I thanked her for relaying the message and called the AP.

Lumpkin was furious. The DPS had arrested one of his photographers and a photographer for the *Houston Chronicle* after Troopers spotted them trying to sneak through a wooded area to get a better view of the crime scene. Both photographers were in the McLennan County Jail, Lumpkin said. He wanted his staffer to be released immediately and assured me the management of the *Chronicle* felt the same way.

I promised Lumpkin I would see what I could find out about the arrests and get back to him. Colonel Wilson also was en route to Waco. I called him on his car phone and ran the situation by him. He told me to tell the press that we were merely trying to protect the integrity of the crime scene. He wanted to make the point to the media that the DPS was serious about keeping people away from the ruins of the compound until it was safe, but he said he'd see to it that neither photographer would be filed on. In other words, as the old expression goes, the photographers were going to beat the rap but not the ride.

The two trespassing arrests underscored the worst problem I faced that afternoon. The media, despite my patient explanation the night before of our safety concerns, was pushing hard for better access to the site. They still could get no closer than Satellite City, which was more than two miles from the burned-out compound.

I was not overjoyed having someone sent in from the governor's office to assist me in dealing with the media, but Chuck McDonald, with the clout of the governor behind him, was helpful in working out an arrangement with the Rangers and the U.S. Attorney's Office to allow a press photo pool to get close to the site on Thursday.

McDonald's help on that issue freed me to gather information for the briefing that night. Also that afternoon, we arranged for the rental of a room at the Convention Center that we could use as a media center. We ordered three phone lines and hired a secretary through a local temporary service. McDonald told me the governor's office would gladly pay for all this, but the bills eventually went to the DPS and the agency ended up cutting the checks.

At the briefing, I assured the press that the DPS took no pleasure in the arrests of the two photographers, but that we had to keep the crime scene secure during the evidence-collection process. Safety remained a big consideration, I said. Koresh had had thousands of rounds of live ammunition inside the compound. With the ashes still smoldering there was a very real possibility some of that ammunition could explode from the heat. "Cook off" was the term the Rangers used. A high-powered rifle round could kill at more than a mile away. Too, there were reports that Koresh's arsenal had included hand grenades.

Back in Austin, Linda was still handling the media calls to PIO and scheduling interviews. She had me set up to be on ABC's "Good Morning America" Thursday morning.

After the press conference, Waco police PIO Sergeant Malissa Sims, who had been helping referee the FBI briefings and had offered me the same service, was standing nearby when one of the "GMA" producers came up to talk to me about my interview the next morning.

"Where are you staying? I'll pick you up at your room and drive you out to our trailer," she said. "I know it'll be early, but I'll have some coffee and orange juice."

"Could I talk to you in private for a minute?" Sergeant Sims asked, grabbing my arm.

I excused myself and walked with her out of hearing range. Laureen came with us.

"If I were you, I wouldn't have anyone come by your room," the sergeant said. "When the FBI was here, one or two females in the media were doing anything to get information, if you know what I mean."

Stunned, I thanked her for the insight and went back into the crowd of reporters.

"I'll be in the lobby at 5:30," I told the producer. "I think Laureen will ride out with us."

I never heard any specific details of what had happened—if anything—between any federal officers and female journalists in Waco prior to the beginning of the DPS investigation and my daily briefings, but nothing out of line ever occurred during my time in Waco, despite the intense competition for information. As one writer later put it, the media quickly exhausted all primary, secondary, and even tertiary sources for news. Indeed, during slow periods before the fire, which were frequent, they had even resorted to interviewing each other.

That summer I was asked to talk to a group of reporters at a seminar, sponsored by Sam Houston State University in Huntsville, on covering crime news. Among the speakers were a couple of women journalists who had been in Waco. At one point, giving advice to these young reporters on how to get reluctant sources to talk, one of the women said, "If nothing else works, you can always 'skirt 'em.'" But if anyone tried to "skirt" me at Waco, I must have been too tired to notice.

Laureen and I had booked rooms at the same motel where the Rangers were staying. When we went there to check in, I noticed something different. No Ranger cars were parked outside the motel. I soon learned that was because Rangers were no longer staying at the motel. They had decamped—all of them.

I never heard an explanation, but I had a theory: Captain Cook thought having two PIOs staying at the same motel with the Rangers was a security risk. Laureen and I no doubt would be having reporters in and out of our rooms at all hours and, these journalists being near so many Rangers, they might see or hear something they shouldn't. What the captain didn't realize was that Laureen and I were not interested in socializing with reporters and darn sure weren't operating a hospitality suite. In fact, if the media had found out where we were staying, we would have moved. If a reporter needed to talk with one of us, we wanted them to contact our office at the Convention Center, or, after hours, to call the DPS communications center in Austin.

I was up well before dawn for the "Good Morning America" interview. The producer met Laureen and me on time outside the motel's entrance and, true to her word, had coffee, orange juice, and doughnuts.

I would be on live for viewers in the Eastern time zone, and an hour later in Texas and the rest of the Central time zone. When I asked how many people would be watching, the producer said, "Oh, around seven million."

They sat me on a stool with an open field in the background. Two miles behind me, in the dark, were the still warm ashes of Mount Carmel. Host Charlie Gibson asked me the questions. The producer and I had gone over what they would be in advance. In other words, it was not a hard-hitting probe for information. It was merely the appearance of reality and the latest news, though it was neither.

Among those seven million viewers, I later learned, were my two young nieces in Columbus, Ohio, then four and six. When their mother, Linda's sister Sara Livingston, spotted me on the tube, she said, "Look, Rebecca, there's Uncle Mike!" The four-year-old studied the screen for a second, then asked, "Where's Aunt Linda?"

When Sara noticed me on TV again the following day, six-year-old Rachel happened to be the nearest to the screen. "Look," her mom said, "it's Uncle Mike. He's famous." The little girl thought about that for a minute and then asked, "Is he rich?"

The GMA folks gave us souvenir lapel pins that said "Good Morning America" and the producer drove us back to the motel.

After breakfast, we went to the Convention Center to meet our new temporary secretary and get our office organized.

Though I had not minded appearing on "Today" and "Good Morning America," I was smart enough to say no to a couple of other requests. Producers with CNN's "Larry King Live" and NBC's "Face the Nation" both pressed hard for me to go on their shows the first week after the fire. Had I consented to be a guest, I would have been pitted against Koresh's lawyer, Dick DeGuerin. It would have amounted to a debate, with me—merely a spokesman for the DPS—representing the side of "the government." I said no thanks and never regretted it.

It's fascinating how fast a routine develops during an ongoing crisis situation. I suppose it's basic human nature to strive for order in chaos. Within a day or two, Laureen and I had settled into a set schedule that held up fairly well through the rest of our stay in Waco.

This was a typical day, though many days were still marked by atypical situations.

After an early breakfast, we went to our office at the Convention Center to check the morning papers, take care of any planning we needed to do, and catch up on any pending phone calls. At 9:00 or 9:30 A.M., I would leave for the DPS command post at Mount Carmel. As soon as I could find him each morning, I would meet with scene commander Ranger Captain David Byrnes for a rundown on what had happened so far that day and what was planned. Laureen would come out at about 10:45 A.M. At 11:00 A.M., we would meet that day's pool at the media checkpoint. We had quickly learned to let the media fight among themselves over who would go in each day. Our role in that process was only as referees. We each had a state car, and we'd load both with reporters and photographers and then escort them past the DPS checkpoint to the gate leading to what was left of the compound.

Laureen would usually return to our downtown office after lunch and handle any pending media calls. I would meet again with Captain Byrnes, and anyone else I could find who knew something newsworthy, and then leave about 1:30 P.M. for the Convention Center and our daily 2:30 P.M. briefing.

I would normally open the briefing, referring to a handwritten outline to remind me of the points I needed to make. Then I would introduce any "guest stars" I had. Tarrant County Medical Examiner Dr. Nizam Peerwani, along with colleague Dr. Rodney Crow, described the gruesome process of body recovery. Paul Gray, assistant chief investigator for the Houston Fire Department, spoke for a team of arson investigators from across the country which had been assembled to look into the cause of the fire that leveled the compound.

The real star, however, was Onyx, a dog with the

Allegheny County (Pennsylvania) Fire Marshal's Office trained to sniff out traces of accelerants—flammable liquids used to start fires. Laureen and I arranged a photo opportunity for the fittingly named dog, a black Labrador retriever. The super-sniffer had flown to Texas with Fire Marshal John M. Kaus and other team members in her own first-class seat, happily eating a first-class meal.

The fact that Onyx was a particularly big hit with the media showed how desperate they were for news and how little they had to settle for. We had an internationally known anthropologist from the Smithsonian Institution scheduled to appear at one press conference, but at the last minute, for reasons they did not offer to explain, the U.S. Attorney's Office told me to cancel him. This guest star who never made it before the media had been brought in to assist in the body identification process.

After our guests said what they wanted to, we would take questions together, with either me or Laureen serving as umpire in case the questions started coming in outside the reasonableness zone.

We tried to keep the briefings to no longer than a half hour. As whatever news we had offered hit the wires, we would get a flurry of telephone calls at our temporary media office and in Austin. When the phones quieted, and all the calls had been returned, I would drive back to the command post to observe operations for the rest of the day. I continued to return media calls from one of the phones in the command post trailer.

After 5:00 P.M., Laureen would return to the command post until work ended for the day, usually around 7:00 P.M. Media calls usually continued into the evening, though we generally "put the lid on" and accepted only emergency media calls after 10:00 P.M.

"You look beat," Laureen told me one night. "I'll tell Communications to call me tonight if anything happens. You get some sleep."

The next morning, Laureen was the one with circles under her eyes. A prison riot had broken out in Limestone County overnight. Dozens of Troopers and Rangers as well as the DPS

SWAT team were rushed to nearby Groesbeck to quell the disturbance. Some 130 prisoners were in an open yard trying to wreck the privately operated facility. Laureen had taken dozens of media calls throughout the night and into the morning.

I put myself back on call that night so she could get some sleep. Luckily, the state stayed quiet and we both got some rest.

In addition to the Waco and non-Waco related media calls, our Austin office—which now consisted of our secretary Alicia with backup as needed from Linda, who was now back in her own office—began referring calls from the general public with questions or comments about Waco. One caller from Arizona, obviously a discriminating collector, had a simple enough question: Could he buy Koresh's 1966 black Camaro? Koresh would not be needing it anymore, he said, and the car was a real piece of history. We told him since the vehicle was parked on Branch Davidian property, it probably was considered evidence, but suggested that he contact the U.S. Attorney's Office for a definitive answer.

One of the more unusual, and touching, incidents I was involved in after the fire never got much if any publicity on this side of the Atlantic. Because of the circumstances, that was just what I wanted.

It began with a call from a British television producer who had an unusual request. He had traveled to Texas with two British subjects who had lost family members in the fire. One of the men had lost his wife and five children, the other his sister and a niece. They had with them medical and dental records that the Rangers needed. He would be happy to turn over the records, he said, but he did want a little something in return: One, video of the two Brits handing over the records to a Ranger, and two, someone to escort the two men, plus his camera crew, to the compound so the grieving men could lay flowers on the roadway and say a prayer.

I contacted Ranger Sergeant Clayton Smith, one of two Rangers whose primary assignment was to locate medical records to aid in the identification process, and ran the request by him. We could get eight sets of medical records for one bit of flexibility on our part. When I assured him that the video would only be aired in the United Kingdom, he agreed.

Of course, seeing to that was going to be a problem. Laureen and I had driven through Satellite City enough times for the media to be familiar with our car. It would be hard to slip past, especially if the reporters saw someone with a video camera in the car. It could create a riot, since they would think—correctly—that we were playing favorites by letting in non-pool members.

To get the swap accomplished as discreetly as possible, I set up a handover of the records in the parking lot outside the Convention Center. Though that's where we had our briefings, the media preferred to stay at Satellite City until shortly before each press conference. The place usually was relatively reporter-free, unless someone from the media came by looking for me or Laureen to ask a specific question.

Sergeant Smith did a great job. He patiently posed for the video, receiving the records and warmly shaking hands with the family members as the camera rolled.

The exchange completed, I loaded the men and the camera crew in the state car and drove them to the front of the compound, the same place I took the daily pool.

When we got to the gate leading onto the Davidian property, I parked the car and stayed back respectfully as the two men, each with a small bouquet of flowers, walked slowly down the road to a point where they could easily look over at the rubble where their loved ones had died.

The two men took in the scene. Yellow wildflowers dotted the grass between them and where the compound had been. Big bass occasionally slapped the water of the stock tank on the property as they rose to devour a hapless bug that made the mistake of landing on the surface.

Three flags at half-staff whipped in a south wind over the debris in the distance: The U.S. Stars and Stripes, the Texas Lone Star flag, and an ATF flag with four gold stars on it, one for each of the dead agents. The men, women, and seventeen children who had died on April 19 had their own little flags—a field of small plastic Day-Glo orange ones, each marking the spot where a body had been found. Eight of those tiny flags marked the last known location of the family members of these two men.

They stood there, silently looking on as Rangers and crime lab personnel collected evidence that might eventually explain what had happened when Koresh's compound went up in flames. But these men, I knew, had questions no one could ever answer.

I limited the amount of time media could stay in the road and take pictures, but I decided to let the two British men have as long as they wanted. It was the least that the State of Texas—and I—could do. Finally, they gently laid their flowers down against the barbed-wire fence surrounding the property and knelt in prayer.

As I watched the men wipe away tears, I thought of how some of the reporters complained and argued about getting access to the site just to take pictures and make notes. In the face of the profound grief of these two men, the concerns of the media seemed petty.

So did some of their behavior.

Mark Potok, a Dallas-based reporter for *USA Today*, reinforced for me the value of one of the points I make when I do media relations training: Never say anything around a reporter that you wouldn't want to see on page one of the next morning's newspaper or hear repeated on the evening network newscast.

One day Potok made the media pool and got in the state car I was driving. When all the other reporters were in the car and the cameramen had their gear stowed, in the spirit of being both friendly and witty, I said, "Welcome to Koresh World." Everyone laughed and I soon forgot the remark.

The next morning, sitting with a fresh cup of coffee in our Convention Center office, I opened that morning's edition of *USA Today*, circulation two-plus million. I was not surprised, of course, to see a story from Waco on the front page of this national daily, since the investigation and ever-rising body count was still big news. But I was incredulous when I read the first paragraph of Potok's story: "'Welcome to Koresh World,' shrugged a DPS spokesman as he began the daily media tour to the charred ruins of David Koresh's compound at Mount Carmel." Or something like that. Potok may or may not have used my name in his lead, but I was the only DPS spokes*man* giving the media special access to the area immediately outside the crime scene. What I do remember clearly is that Potok gratuitously sandbagged me with that quote, which he and everyone else in that car clearly recognized as a bit of gallows humor not intended for quotation, a little levity from one old reporter to a group of younger guys still in the business. Potok quoted me with total accuracy, no question. But it was a cheap shot, even though it was a stupid thing for me to have said, and one that earned him lasting fame. Since then, I have told the story to hundreds of communicators and police officers I've trained in media relations. I use his name every time I tell the story and will continue to do so.

The next time Colonel Wilson visited the command post, I confessed my lapse—a classic case of being hoisted by one's own petard. The colonel just laughed.

I can think of at least two other incidents involving the media at Waco that weren't so funny.

One evening, on my way back to the motel after a long day, I became involved in a bizarre pursuit. Normally, the DPS chases people, not the other way around. Of course, not being a commissioned police officer, I don't do chases; I just talk to the media about the results of the occasional high-speed chase involving the Highway Patrol. But as I drove through Satellite City, a reporter in a marked KXAS-TV unit pulled up behind me and started flashing his headlights, indicating he wanted me to stop. There was no new news to talk about, I had done my last briefing for the day, it was late and I was exhausted, and I didn't like the idea of being curbed by a reporter. He knew perfectly well that I was not a police officer, so he couldn't have been trying to pull me over to report a crime or to seek my help in performing a Heimlich maneuver. So I ignored him. Apparently thinking that I simply wasn't paying attention, the reporter pulled up alongside of my DPS car, driving in the oncoming traffic lane. Again, he motioned for me to pull over.

Furious, I got on the two-way radio and told Laureen, who was behind us in her state car, that if he didn't stop I was going to call for a Trooper to stop him for reckless driving. We must have driven on for a mile or more before he finally got the idea that I wasn't going to stop and, as the police would say, "discontinued his pursuit."

Over dinner that night, I was still livid. Looking back on it, it wasn't that big a deal. I suppose I should have pulled off the road and answered the TV journalist's question, but I had been available to answer questions all day long. My reduced patience was symptomatic of the growing fatigue, compounded by stress, caused by our twelve-to-fourteen-hour days.

I was definitely growing testy. One day at the Convention Center, I was having a private conversation when I got a funny feeling that someone was slipping up behind me. I whirled around and found myself looking into a video camera. The cameraman, someone from the UK, had been recording my conversation. When I realized what he had been doing, I broke another media relations rule: I used a short, four-letter word with a heritage tracing back to the Anglo-Saxons of his homeland to suggest what course of action I felt the photographer should take. He got that on tape, too, and kept rolling as I stormed off.

Again, this was not the real me. I am usually a relatively easygoing sort. At least that's how I see myself. But the situation was getting to me. The daily procession of body bags. The seemingly endless and unanswerable questions. Reporters chasing me on the highway and slipping up behind me with sound and video rolling. The daily struggle to get a handle on what was going on.

Another part of the stress had been in trying to coordinate our work with Chuck McDonald of Governor Richards' office. The best example was what happened on Saturday, April 24. I was running late to that day's press conference, headed toward the Convention Center from the command post with the latest information on the progress of the DPS investigation. CNN would be carrying the briefing live. Rather than wait for me, McDonald decided to go ahead and open it. As Laureen watched in growing horror from the sidelines, looking at her watch and wondering where I was, McDonald began a rambling monologue about his children and the children killed in the fire. When he broke into tears, someone in Atlanta mercifully pulled the plug. I got there a short time later and took over. Clearly, the stress had taken its toll on McDonald as well. He went back to Austin that afternoon. After that, Laureen and I were on our own, which in many ways made our job much easier.

On Friday, April 30, Laureen and I decided to shut down our Waco operation. Seventy-two bodies had been transported to Fort Worth. The concrete bunker had been bulldozed. Most of the evidence had been collected, though some work would continue over the weekend.

By this point, even many in the media were begging us to leave. As one reporter put it, "As long as you are holding press conferences, we've got to be here." Which raises a version of the classic question, "If a press conference was held in the woods and no one came, would it make a noise?"

Laureen and I were packed and on our way out of town when one last crisis developed. The media seemed to feel that the only event that would bring the tragic story of Mount Carmel to closure, at least until the trials of any indicted survivors, was the positive identification of whatever was left of Koresh's body. Everyone we had talked to who was in a position to know about that said a positive identification of Koresh was not expected until sometime the next week. Fine, we thought, the four local justices of the peace (whose statutory role includes the duties of coroner) or the Tarrant County Medical Examiner's Office could handle that.

Laureen was following me as we drove toward I-35 and home when I heard CBS correspondent Rita Braver report on Dallas' KRLD Radio that a Justice Department source had confirmed that Koresh's body had been identified.

I radioed Laureen to pull over so we could talk. If Braver's report was true, we had been misled by the people we had been dealing with every day for nearly two weeks. We called Judge David Pareya's office. The justice of the peace, a former broadcast journalist, had taken over the bulk of the media interviews concerning body identification and autopsy results. No, his secretary said, Koresh had not been identified. I had talked to Attorney General Janet Reno's press secretary shortly after the fire and had his telephone number in my notes. Since it was getting close to 5:00 in Washington, I quickly called him to find out what was going on. I told him what I'd heard Braver report. "Unless you know something we don't know in Waco, I'd appreciate it if you'd get in touch with her and tell her she's wrong," I said. He thanked me and said he'd take care of it.

As I drove toward home, I heard the story corrected on the next CBS radio newscast. But Sunday, I got a call from Judge Pareya's office. Koresh had now been identified. Could we help set up a press conference so the judge could make the announcement?

I notified Laureen of this unexpected development and we met as soon as possible at our office. From there, we drove to Waco for one more briefing. The remains previously known only as MC (Mount Carmel) Doe No. 8, found on Thursday, April 22, had been identified from dental comparisons and body x-rays as David Koresh. He had died of a single gunshot wound to the head.

* * *

Only four months after Mount Carmel, I was the one being x-rayed.

Back in Austin after ten days in Waco, the number of questions to my office concerning the DPS investigation into the fire and stand-off had dropped off steadily. But my mind, especially at night, kept wandering back up the highway to Waco. I saw those skulls all over again. I answered and reanswered questions at phantom, middle-of-the-night press conferences.

For the first time in my life, I began experiencing insomnia on an ongoing basis. I'd go to sleep at my regular time, about 10:30 on a normal night, but by midnight or so, I'd be wide awake. Not wanting to bother Linda, I'd get up and go into the living room. That summer I watched a lot of "Perry Mason" reruns, enjoying the temporary escape to simpler, black-and-white times.

The DPS, at Lieutenant Colonel Thomas' instigation, had provided debriefing sessions and counseling opportunities for everyone who had been in Waco, plus stress management training. I took advantage of all of that, but I still was having trouble sleeping. Another reason, in addition to the stress of those ten long days in McLennan County, was a chronic condition I suffered from: indigestion.

The heartburn was nothing new. I'd been diagnosed with a hiatal hernia back in the 1970s. The doctor told me that if I watched what I ate, which would include forsaking coffee and other acid-stimulating beverages and foods, and kept my head elevated at night, I could live with the condition.

But if I was not careful, which was more often than not, burning stomach acid would slosh up into my esophagus. A couple of times, in the dead of night, I nearly choked from the sudden reflux. Stomachs are designed to handle the strong acid needed for digestion, but not the esophagus.

Now I know—too late for me but maybe not for you—that the constant irritation from stomach acid reaching the esophagus can lead to cancer. Back then I did not, or I would have been a lot more careful with my diet.

My indigestion had steadily been getting worse. I went through a giant, economy-size bottle of antacids every month or so. In addition, my energy seemed to be waning. Linda was urging me to go to the doctor. She reminded me that I had not had a checkup since before we were married. Reluctantly, I agreed to make an appointment.

After several weeks of testing and nerve-wracking uncertainty, I finally had a diagnosis: cancer in my esophagus.

When a CT-scan showed no sign of metastatic disease, my oncologist said I had a good chance of beating it. He recommended radiation and chemotherapy. "You probably won't need surgery," he told me. The treatment was fatiguing, but I did not even lose any hair.

In April 1994, one year after Waco—and only two months after the birth of our daughter Hallie—a checkup showed that the cancer had come back. This time, the doctor said, most of my esophagus had to go. The operation was May 4.

I woke up from a long procedure with new plumbing but a paralyzed right arm. The doctor did not know for sure why or whether I'd ever be able to use it again.

Then, to compound a bad situation just a bit more, the

pathology report, delivered by my surgeon as I still lay in the intensive care unit, showed that one of my lymph glands had been cancerous, as well as the portion of my esophagus that had been removed. I would have to undergo another round of chemotherapy. And this time, my oncologist said, I would lose my hair. He was going to have to use some harder stuff, so to speak.

Of course, I couldn't have cared less about my hair. Being bald for half a year saved on shampoo, haircuts, and time. My interest was in getting use of my arm back and in living long enough to see my daughter grow up, not whether I had any hair.

My arm was back to normal in less than three months. Still kicking nearly five years past my first diagnosis, I like to tell people that David Koresh probably saved my life.

A brief history of the first Republic of Texas

> *"Well, there she is—Texas. A man keeps movin' around his entire life lookin' for his particular paradise. I reckon I found mine. There's plenty of room out there for every dream I ever had."*
> —Fess Parker as Davy Crockett in "Davy Crockett, King of the Wild Frontier," 1955

It's been more than forty years, but I still remember those lines and most of the words to the ballad that accompanied Walt Disney's version of the life of Davy Crockett:

> "Davy, Davy Crockett, King of the Wild Frontier.
> Born on a mountaintop in Tennessee . . ."

And so on, for twenty verses. (I also recall parts of the spoof version of this song, a tune equally popular among my fellow first-graders: "Baby, baby Crewcut . . . Born on a tabletop in Tennessee . . .")

As he was for most of us Baby Boomers (the Census Bureau says there are 80 million of us born between 1946 and 1964), Disney was my first history teacher. I was a regular viewer of his Sunday night television show. I read his comic books and went to his movies. I saw the first national broadcast of "Davy Crockett at the Alamo" on February 23, 1955. This was the final installment of Disney's Crockett trilogy, which, though primarily intended for the black and white of television, Disney had the foresight to film in color. The TV series, seen by an estimated 30 million people, was so successful that later in the year Disney combined the episodes and released them on the big screen in color. I soon saw that version too.

My reaction to the final scene of the movie, when Fess Parker—I mean Davy Crockett—goes down in a swarm of Mexican soldiers while swinging Ole Betsy, his trusty flintlock, triggered my first serious reflections on, and vague understanding of, death.

I pestered my mother and grandparents for Davy Crockett toys. I had a Davy Crockett rifle, a Davy Crockett shoulder pouch (real frontiersmen called this a possibles bag), a Davy Crockett powder horn, two styles of Davy Crockett hat (a coonskin cap my mother bought for me at a long-since closed downtown Austin department store, as well as a sort of fringed cowboy hat), and probably some other paraphernalia I don't remember. For indoor enjoyment, I had an Alamo play set, which included tin walls (my grandmother always told me to be careful and not cut myself on the sharp metal edges, an event she assured me would result in a fatal case of "lockjaw") and molded plastic defenders and attackers. Considering the value of all that mass-produced Crockett-ana today, I sure wish I still had it. The Alamo set alone would be worth several thousand dollars to today's collectors.

Thanks to Davy Crockett and other productions, from "Twenty-thousand Leagues Under the Sea" to "Old Yeller," the impact of Disney on my own life and many others almost is beyond measure. Factoring in a reading and storytelling family that already had an appreciation for history, and passed it on to me, I had a more severe case of Crockettitis than most other kids. At the age of five, I used plastic modeling clay to build a miniature Alamo and was ever prepared to start swinging Ole Betsy at the drop of a coonskin cap while playing "Alamo" with my neighborhood friends. Walt Disney was as much a part of our young lives back in the mid-1950s as measles, chicken pox, the loss of baby teeth, the fear of polio, and the beginning of elementary school.

The first time I visited the real Alamo, it had not yet been air-conditioned. We stayed at the nearby Menger Hotel, a venerable San Antonio hostelry opened only twenty-two years after the siege and still in business today. I have a picture my granddad took of me standing next to one of the old cannons on the oak and palm-shaded Alamo grounds. I know now that there were no oak trees or rustling palms anywhere near the Alamo during the battle. Nor were there any goldfish in a nice, rock-lined pond.

Before I understood that the familiar facade of the modern Alamo hardly resembles the structure as it looked during the siege, or knew much of anything else about life, I hounded my grandparents and my mother with seemingly endless questions about the Alamo. Granddad, particularly, always had an answer. I realize now that his answers were not always the right answers, but I don't recall him ever sloughing off one of my questions with "I don't know," or "Because, that's just the way it was."

The only one of his wrong answers I distinctly remember was when I asked him what the Mexican Army uniforms looked like. "They were green," he replied with authority. "Well, olive drab," he added. That was wrong, of course. Now, as the middle-aged parent of a bright pre-schooler whose favorite question is a simple "Why?", I can understand Granddad's willingness to at least try to answer all my questions. We adults like to think we have all the answers, even if we have to make some of them up as we go along. Of course, sometimes we don't even understand the question.

In my era, Texas history was a required area of instruction for fifth- and seventh-graders. In the fifth grade, I got my first copy of a little publication that was almost as powerful as Disney in shaping my generation's concept of Texas history: "Texas History Movies." This booklet, produced and distributed for free to Texas schools by the old Magnolia Oil Company (which later became Mobil Oil), had already been in print for thirty-five years by the time I received my first copy. Now, just like any surviving Davy Crockett paraphernalia, "Texas History Movies" has become a collector's item. The original version, the one I read, is by today's standards off the scale in terms of being politically incorrect. A kinder, gentler version was reissued by the Texas State Historical Association in the 1980s, but it has not reached anywhere near the number of eager young readers that the original did.

So, strongly influenced by Disney, "Texas History Movies," my granddad and even the state-approved textbooks of my era, I reached young adulthood before I began to realize the Texas Revolution was a bit more complicated than my original perception: a downtrodden group of freedom-loving patriots who violently overthrew Mexican oppression.

I now understand that the revolution which made Texas an independent republic, while it was a colorful part of Southwestern history and had a big impact on the overall Texas myth, was not the simple struggle of virtuous, God-fearing Anglo-Saxons over despotic, cruel Hispanics who weren't even very good marksmen. The Texas Revolution was born of a clash of ethnic identities, cultures, religions, and political systems, along with a fair amount of misunderstanding, happenstance, and hunger for land. The truth is usually gray, not all white or all black.

This is not to say there were not good men and women involved in Texas' struggle for independence. Most of them, I think, did believe they were fighting for freedom. In 1850 Dr. John Shackelford, a survivor of the revolution, wrote one of his old comrades: "I feel as though Texas has half my heart; for under its soil lie the bones of a gallant son and nephew, and others who were dear to me. They fought—they bled—and they died to establish her independence." But the revolution was more involved than that, as most aspects of history are.

Ethnicity certainly did not determine good and bad. Some Mexicans fought on the Texas side (some of them dying in the Alamo), and some Anglos, most notably Kentuckian John Bradburn, who figured in some of the pre-revolutionary disputes, were on the Mexican side. A Mexican named Lorenzo de Zavala was the first vice-president of independent Texas. He was considered a traitor by Mexico. Juan Seguin was the Texian military officer who respectfully buried the ashes and charred bones of the defenders of the Alamo, yet he later found it expedient to live in virtual exile in Mexico.

But most people don't know about these complicated

nuances of the Texas Revolution and its aftermath. To them, the conflict boils down to the fall of the Alamo, the triumph of Sam Houston at the Battle of San Jacinto, and the glorious birth of Texas as an independent republic. The old saying that a little knowledge is a dangerous thing rings particularly true here.

In the early-1960s, Richard Lance McLaren, a third-grade pupil in Ohio, was assigned to do a book report on the Alamo. Whether his scholarship went beyond copying the dust-jacket blurb from a library book on the Alamo, I do not know. But I know how I used to write book reports. McLaren later said this school assignment is what got him interested in Texas history, particularly the part about an independent republic resulting from the revolution.

If McLaren (of the latter day Republic of Texas) had delved deeper into Texas history while a student, he might have saved himself and others some trouble. What he apparently never learned was that there have been numerous events in Texas' history that we today would label as a "separatist movement." All of them failed. The Texas Revolution, that portion of borderlands history which so inflamed McLaren, was the only such movement that accomplished its purpose. And it barely succeeded. The message of history: Most of the time, with the notable exceptions of the American, French and Russian revolutions, the presiding governmental authority is better organized and better armed than the would-be separatists.

One of these ill-fated Texas separatist efforts was the Fredonia Rebellion in 1826. Haden Edwards, who had worked with Texas colonizer Stephen F. Austin, the Father of Texas, got to thinking that maybe he should be at least the Uncle of Texas. He applied for and received his own land grant from the Mexican government in 1825. Edwards' land was in East Texas around Nacogdoches, a community dating back to Spanish colonial time. The only problem was that Edwards' grant was checker-boarded with old Spanish and Mexican land grants. Edwards did not exactly know where these tracts were, because the Spanish, and later the Mexican, government did not keep deeds on file in a courthouse, as was the Anglo tradition. The landowner had the only document, often a parchment signed by a representative of the king of Spain and sometimes by the king himself, giving him legal right to his holdings.

To sort out who owned what, and maybe increase the amount of land he could parcel out to new settlers (for money), Edwards spread word that anyone with an existing grant within the borders of his large new grant had to come to him and prove ownership. Naturally, this had a rankling effect among those settlers who felt they didn't have to prove a darn thing. They had been there first and they had a deed. Of course, some of them did not. Pieces of paper, even ones bearing a royal seal, are easy to lose, not to mention loss associated with the occasional flood, house fire, or Indian attack.

The settlers whose land ownership was called into question by Edwards protested vigorously to the distant Mexican government. Eventually, Edwards' *empresarial* grant was revoked. The governor of Coahuila and Texas ordered Edwards and his brother Benjamin to leave the land.

Benjamin had another idea. Instead of packing up and moving on, he proclaimed the forfeited grant to be an independent state, Fredonia. He found willing allies among the nearby Cherokees, who had already been run out of their traditional home in the southeastern United States. Though the Mexican government had agreed to let these Indians settle in Texas, they, too, were having trouble getting title to what they now felt to be their land.

On December 16, 1826, a red-and-white flag went up over a Spanish colonial structure in Nacogdoches called the Old Stone Fort. The banner symbolized the newly forged bond between Anglo and Indian. Sewn on the flag in big, bold letters were the catchy words "Independence," "Liberty," and "Justice."

As soon as the Mexican authorities heard of this, the governor dispatched a military force to put down the rebellion. The goal was accomplished without the shedding of blood. In fact, when word reached "Fredonia" that Mexican soldiers were on the march, most of the followers of the Edwards brothers quickly set aside their concerns for independence, liberty, and justice in favor of life. Their own. The Edwards brothers fled to Louisiana and two of the Cherokee leaders were hanged by other, more level-headed members of their tribe. What could have been one of Texas' first stand-offs was averted.

This incident, while something of a comic opera with some aspects reminiscent of McLaren's 1997 stand-off, was important because it contributed to Mexican distrust of Anglo settlers. And the word Fredonia would come up again in Texas during the late twentieth century.

If the Fredonia Rebellion was news to you and you don't know a whole lot about the first Republic of Texas (actually, it wasn't even the first), don't feel too bad. Several years ago Archie P. McDonald, a history professor at Stephen F. Austin State University in Nacogdoches, developed a fifty-question "Texas History Diagnostic Quiz" for his students. What he found was that many of them, and other individuals he surveyed, suffered from what he termed historical amnesia. Forty-nine percent did not know the defeat of the Texans at the hands of Santa Anna on March 6, 1836, was called the Battle of the Alamo. Sixty-seven percent did not know that the Battle of San Jacinto was the turning point of the Texas Revolution, and fifty-six percent of his sample were not aware that Sam Houston became the first president of the Republic of Texas. So, for the historical amnesiacs or those who can at least fall back on the excuse that they didn't grow up in Texas, this is the short version of what happened:

The "Lexington" of Texas was what came to be known as the "Come And Take It" incident at Gonzales. In October 1835, a detachment of Mexican cavalry was sent from San Antonio to Gonzales, an old settlement about sixty-five miles to the east, to reclaim a cannon that had been provided the local citizens for their protection against hostile Indians. The citizens did not want to give up the weapon. Under a flag bearing the words "Come And Take It" they prevented the soldiers from doing just that. Some shots were fired, but Mexican casualties were light—only one or two killed—and one Texian suffered a bloody nose.

In December, Texas forces took San Antonio, defeating the troops of General Martin Perfecto de Cos, brother-in-law of General Antonio Lopez de Santa Anna, military dictator of

Mexico. Cos retreated to Mexico and the Texians began digging in, knowing the Mexican Army would be back in force.

From all accounts, Santa Anna, like most dictators, was not the sort of person likely to be singled out as humanitarian of the year. On the other hand, from the Mexican perspective, he was doing the right thing: Attempting to put down a rebellion.

By February 1836, the general was moving north toward San Antonio at the vanguard of some 6,000 troops. The first elements arrived on February 23, sending 180 to 200 Texans (the exact number has never been established, though the best estimate is 189 with another eleven listed as possible defenders) scurrying into the fortified ruins of an old Spanish mission, San Antonio de Valero—better known as the Alamo.

Most historians agree the Texans made a stupid mistake by holing up in the Alamo. Sieges—"stand-off" is the trendy word for lesser sieges, though a siege is a siege is a siege—are almost always won by the besiegers, not the besieged. From Troy to Corregidor, the outcome has been the same, no matter how just the cause of the besieged. Sooner or later, those laying the siege come up with a Trojan horse, or its equivalent. In a stand-off, taking hostages is the only potentially equalizing factor.

The Texans in the Alamo had no hostages.

Sam Houston, possessing both a solid knowledge of the classics and a good deal of common sense, had ordered the Texans to destroy the Alamo and pull back east, where most of the Anglos lived. Though the largest community in Texas at the time, San Antonio was on the far western frontier. It had no real strategic value to the Texas cause. The provisional government of Texas and most of its citizens were in the more populated eastern half of the province. Unfortunately, Houston's order was ignored.

The Texans managed to hold the Alamo for thirteen days. But before dawn on Sunday, March 6, 1836, some 1,500 Mexican troops, after an initially unsuccessful assault, succeeded in storming the old mission. All the defenders were killed, though the battle over how Crockett died—whether using Ole Betsy as a club as Disney had it or executed on orders of Santa Anna after he was found in hiding and tried to surrender—continues today.

Houston, meanwhile, had gathered all the Texas citizen-soldiers that he could and was on the march—away from Santa Anna. Most of the rest of the Anglo settlers in Texas also were in flight, a panicky exodus that came to be known as the Runaway Scrape. Historians have debated for years whether Houston was trying to lure Santa Anna and his army into a trap by pulling farther and farther to the east, or whether he was headed for sanctuary across the Sabine River in the United States. Only the result is incontrovertible: On April 21, 1836, Houston's army defeated Santa Anna in the Battle of San Jacinto. In eighteen minutes of mostly hand-to-hand fighting that turned into a slaughter, some 650 Mexicans were killed. The Texans lost two outright and six more who later died of their wounds.

The Texans had faced only a third of Santa Anna's army. But they had captured the Mexican commander-in-chief, and his subordinate generals chose to march back to Mexico rather than keep up the fight and try to rescue the man who fancied himself as the Napoleon of the West.

Anyone who thinks Texans fought to create their own independent nation needs to know this: Shortly after the end of the revolution and the landslide election of Houston as the Republic's first president, the people by a vote of 3,277 to 91 heartily approved the notion of Texas seeking annexation to the United States. It just took nearly a decade for it to happen.

Some other truths about the original Republic of Texas:

• No cohesive spirit existed among its citizens. President Houston could hardly control his army, a body swollen with "soldiers" who came to Texas after the fighting was over specifically for the free land the government was offering to anyone who shouldered arms in its behalf. Two men vying for command of the military fought a duel over the matter. In 1843, Edwin Moore, commodore of the Republic's Navy, was court-martialed by the Texas Congress. Among the charges was piracy.

• Strong leadership was lacking. If everyone involved in the Republic's government had been as charismatic and savvy as Sam Houston, maybe an independent Texas would have had some show. On the other hand, if all Texian officials had been as vain and headstrong as Houston, they would have been fighting all the time. The Texas Constitution did not allow the chief executive to serve a second consecutive term, which further hampered the young Republic's efforts to accomplish anything for its citizens. The other Texas presidents, Mirabeau B. Lamar, David G. Burnet, and Anson Jones, were not as capable as Houston.

• The Republic of Texas government did some dumb things. Near-mutinous invasions of Mexico in 1841-42 almost precipitated a second war that Mexico might have won. The so-called Santa Fe Expedition, by which President Lamar hoped to establish real, as opposed to paper, control over New Mexico, was a bust.

• The Republic had no money. The currency the Republic produced during President Lamar's administration, called "redbacks," was virtually worthless. At one point, Texas money brought only twelve cents on the dollar in exchange for U.S. currency.

• Geographically, the Republic simply was too large for its government to control. On December 19, 1836, the Texas Congress declared that its boundaries began "at the mouth of the Sabine River and running west along the Gulf of Mexico, three leagues from land, to the mouth of the Rio Grande, thence up the principal stream of said river to its source, thence due north to the forty-second degree of north latitude, thence along the boundary line as defined in the treaty between the United States and Spain, to the beginning." This took in roughly half of what is now New Mexico, plus portions of the present states of Oklahoma, Kansas, Colorado, and Wyoming.

• Never having anything of value other than plenty of land, the Republic of Texas left behind no great edifices (the first Texas capitol was a log cabin and the last was only a one-story, white-washed frame building), no enduring monuments to its heroes or the events that made them heroes, no improved roadways, canal systems, developed harborage or navigational aids, no institutions of higher learning, no great works of literature or music. The

Republic's government even turned down an offer from a gentleman named Samuel Morse for a free system of communication via a newfangled thing called a telegraph.

Still, historians can point to a few bright spots reflected from the Republic's Lone Star, including the five-point star itself, which continued as the state's principal icon. The Texas Rangers, established by Stephen F. Austin in 1823 to "range" his colony and protect it from Indians in exchange for free land, came into their own during the days of the Republic. John Coffee Hays, the best known of the early Ranger captains, did much to establish the Ranger legend and some of their traditions during his service to the Republic in the 1840s.

Also, the Republic's Constitution established a General Land Office to parcel out its public land and keep records and detailed maps showing who owned what. This unique office was continued after statehood and evolved into a state agency involved in everything from overseeing low-interest land loans for veterans to keeping Texas' beaches clean. Today its collection of maps is integral to the understanding of the state's history as well as its land ownership.

But if a government should be judged on the basis of its accomplishments, which is the standard put to most things and people, the Republic of Texas was a singular failure. Essentially, all that Texas got for its revolution and short-lived status as an independent nation was its oil-rich tidelands and an attitude. Annexation to the United States continued as a major issue, with only intermittent lapses, throughout the brief existence of the Republic.

Even after Texas was formally admitted to the Union on February 19, 1846, the urge on the part of some Texans to tamper with the status quo continued to break out occasionally. The joint resolution of Congress which enabled Texas to become a state contained this provision:

New States, of convenient size, not exceeding four in number, in addition to said State of Texas, and having sufficient population, may hereafter, by the consent of said State, be formed out of the territory thereof, which shall be entitled to admission under the provisions of the federal constitution.

Those forty-nine words have been the basis of numerous attempts to subdivide Texas into two, three, four, or five states. Counting some of the pre-annexation efforts, there have been at least twenty-four such efforts. In addition, at least eight tries at shrinking Texas have been made, including a suggestion that part of East Texas be ceded to Arkansas. And only two years after Texas joined the Union, someone proposed that it secede and try again as an independent nation. Most of the time, these separatist movements were founded on a belief by folks in one part of the state (usually West Texas) that they were not getting as much governmental attention (i.e, their portion of the revenue pie) as the rest of the state.

Other than its secession from the Union at the beginning of the Civil War in 1861, Texas' most serious partition crisis was in 1868. This was during Reconstruction, when a group of West Texans who came to be called "coyotes" howled loudly, but in the end unsuccessfully, for a separate state of West Texas. Other notable separatist movements occurred in 1915, 1921, 1969 (state Senator V.E. "Red" Berry of San Antonio wanted Texas divided into North and South Texas, with gambling legal in the state of South Texas), and in 1975. In all of these cases the movements were peaceful, the only fighting being rhetorical.

Not since the Civil War had someone in Texas taken up arms in support of a separatist viewpoint. Not until Rick McLaren and a few others started reading up on Texas history. But McLaren and his colleagues didn't want Texas cut up into separate states. They wanted Texas once again to be an independent republic—a prosperous, enlightened nation that never was. They were willing to fight, they said, and die if necessary, to make that happen.

Old Fort Davis didn't have log walls

Rick McLaren was not the first eccentric attracted to Fort Davis, and he probably won't be the last.

The land itself has a lot to do with it. Jeff Davis County is high, rugged, yet beautiful. Its mountains, rising above the grassy prairies of the Chihuahuan Desert, are the piled remnants of ancient volcanic explosions. Before pollution blowing in from a large, un-scrubbed coal-fired power plant in Mexico began cutting into the clarity of the air, old-timers used to say a person could climb one of those peaks and see all the way to tomorrow in one direction and clear back to yesterday in the other. Much of the time in the Big Bend, a person can still see at least as far as tomorrow morning, if not the whole day. At 5,050 feet above sea level, Fort Davis, the county seat, used to be called the "Mile High Town" by Chamber of Commerce types not concerned about being 230 feet short of actually measuring up to that boast. But Fort Davis is the highest town in Texas, with the highest paved road east of the Rocky Mountains leading to it, even if it's not quite a mile high. These days the Chamber's slogan is "From Fort Davis the rest of Texas is all downhill."

Maybe it's the remoteness that lures eccentrics. Once a place of relative safety and cool water for westward-bound travelers, Fort Davis hasn't really been on the way to anywhere important since the Southern Pacific Railway bypassed it in the early 1880s because of the mountains. Instead, the tracks went through Alpine, a town then called Murphysville about

83

twenty-five miles away, and from there to Marfa, south of Fort Davis. Though you can still catch an east- or west-bound Amtrak passenger train at Alpine, it's a three-and-a-half-hour drive from Fort Davis to the nearest commercial airline connections at Midland-Odessa. The nearest large city is El Paso, 220 miles to the west. Even with the 70 mph speed limit, it still takes a long time to get to Fort Davis. It's so far from what most people consider civilization that a person has to drive eighty-eight miles to get to the closest Wal-Mart! At night, with no urban lights to spoil the view, the moon and the stars of the Milky Way seem nearer to Fort Davis than anyplace else.

Maybe it's the sparse population the eccentric find appealing. The deer, antelope, mountain lions, wild turkeys, and quail far outnumber the human beings. Fewer than 2,000 people live in Jeff Davis County, which at 2,264.5 square miles is Texas' third largest county—smaller only than neighboring Brewster and Presidio counties, respectively the state's first and second largest counties. Jeff Davis County is bigger than either Rhode Island or Delaware. Fort Davis, with 1,212 residents, is the largest community in the county. The only other town in the county is Valentine, a semi-ghost town of 236 inhabitants. Valentine's biggest claim to fame is its name, which every February brings its small post office a flood of mail from lovers across the world wanting a Valentine, Texas, postmark on their valentines.

Maybe the eccentric are attracted by the lingering frontier spirit. The hostile Indians are long gone, as are most of the outlaws. Fort Davis does not even have a jail. It used to, but the four-cell facility built in 1910 was remodeled as a public library when the lockup no longer met state standards. Still, Texas west of the Pecos River is as close as it gets to the Old West. The last three call letters of the only commercial radio station in the area, Alpine's KVLF, stand for Voice of the Last Frontier. Ranching remains the predominant economic factor, though tourism, much of it fueled by the enduring fascination with the Old West myth, is the other mainstay. With their close ties to the land, most of the people of Jeff Davis and surrounding counties are politically conservative. They prefer their government close to home and in small doses.

Ironically, the town of Fort Davis owes its very existence to the federal government, which established a military post named in honor of then-Secretary of War Jefferson Davis at the mouth of Limpia Canyon in 1854 to protect westbound travelers from the Apaches. The Army stayed a decade past the last Indian threat, finally abandoning the fort in 1891.

By that time, a small community had developed adjacent to the post. There was a church and a school, but most of the people were what modern economists would call service providers. The soldiers knew them as shopkeepers, saloon men, and prostitutes. Not everyone lived off the Army, though it was the protection afforded by the fort that allowed ranchers to move into the rich highland. Despite the loss of the military payroll, the community of Fort Davis managed to survive as the old fort slowly crumbled into ruin.

One of the first eccentrics drawn to Fort Davis was Nick Mersfelder, a blue-eyed, mustachioed, Meerschaum pipe-smoking German who came west to the fort in 1881 as a Texas Ranger. After one year's service as a gun-toter for the state, he left the Rangers, settled in Fort Davis, and stayed the rest of his long life. He cut hair, took studio portraits, repaired guns and other items, played a variety of wind and string instruments, loaned money at usurious interest rates, served as justice of the peace for forty-nine years, angled for catfish in the Rio Grande, raised cattle and goats, and had a passion for the color blue. Even the stock of his shotgun was painted blue.

Like another famed old-time West Texas jurist, Judge Roy Bean of Langtry—the crusty character known as the Law West of the Pecos—Mersfelder had his own interpretation of both the letter and the spirit of the law.

"Don't you go quoting any law to me!" Mersfelder once thundered to an out-of-town attorney haplessly trying to argue a legal point in Mersfelder's court. "I don't care what your law is. *I'm* the law in this town."

When Mersfelder died in 1939, his successor as JP, and to some extent as town character, was a former newspaperman and Western writer from Missouri named Barry Scobee. County commissioners figured they might as well appoint him to replace Mersfelder—after all, he already had an office in the courthouse. Believing that the articles Scobee wrote about Fort Davis were good for tourism, the court had let him have a free office on the second floor of the courthouse back in 1927, only a couple of years after he'd moved to town. Scobee went on to write what remains the definitive history of the old cavalry post that gave the town its name and was the moving force behind the preservation of the fort's ruins and its development as a National Historic Site. In 1964 a mountain overlooking Fort Davis about a mile north of town was named in his honor. Fittingly, Scobee's last book was a biography of his predecessor, Mersfelder.

A close friend of Scobee's was a Western history buff named Ed Bartholomew. A Houston-born pilot who evolved into a writer, publisher and bookseller, Bartholomew moved to Fort Davis in the early 1950s. He managed the old fort for a Houston entrepreneur who had plans to turn it into a resort. But when the scheme died with the entrepreneur, Bartholomew stayed, publishing a newspaper, running a book publishing company, and selling old books by mail. He moved to New Mexico for a while, but he returned to Fort Davis and settled there for good.

Though he did not succeed Scobee as a Jeff Davis County JP, Bartholomew followed his trail in a literary sense and as one of the town's more interesting and mildly eccentric characters. His specialty is research on Western gunmen, particularly the bad boys—and a few bad girls. He researched and wrote an excellent two-volume history of Wyatt Earp that is now quite rare and expensive and numerous other books and booklets on various well- and lesser-known shootists. Bartholomew is the person who first told me about Rick McLaren.

I beat McLaren to Fort Davis by more than a quarter of a century. One evening in 1954 I was sitting on the polished wood floor of my grandparents' house in Austin, happily generaling a fight between blue plastic cavalrymen and red plastic Indians outside my Fort Apache set, when Granddad, a writer and former newspaperman, asked, "How'd you like to see a *real* old fort?" I was ready to go right then, but I think it was a week or so before we went.

This was before cars had air-conditioning, and it was a hot

trip. I remember my grandmother dipping a washcloth into the green metal ice chest Granddad kept in the trunk, and then wrapping it around my wrist to help keep me cool. Though I was excited about getting to see a Real Old Fort, being stuck in the backseat for hours at a time was not hugely fun.

At Ozona, about the halfway point between Austin and Fort Davis, Granddad took my picture next to the statue on the courthouse lawn honoring Davy Crockett and his famous credo, "Be Sure You Are Right Then Go Ahead." The colorful frontiersman, a good hand at storytelling and shooting, never got any farther west than the Alamo, of course. But Crockett County, an oil-rich area just east of the Pecos, was named in his honor. I still have a picture of me looking up at Davy's motto, but I can't say that over the years I haven't occasionally gone ahead without being sure I was right.

The first thing I remember about old Fort Davis was wondering why there were no log walls around it. I knew from watching Westerns that all cavalry posts were protected by palisades of sharpened logs, though back then I didn't know the word "palisade." My Fort Apache set certainly had log walls (albeit of snap-together plastic) and that's what I expected of a Real Old Fort. My mother and granddad patiently explained to me that old Fort Davis had never had log walls, an early lesson to me that the truth is not always what you think it is.

Walking across the old parade ground with Granddad, still wondering why Fort Davis hadn't had high walls to protect its soldiers from the Indians, I picked up a dirt clod to throw. It broke open to expose an old buckle.

"That's probably an old saddle cinch," Granddad said when I handed it to him. "When we get home, I'll fix it so you can wear it as a belt buckle."

As we started to walk into the museum at the fort, Granddad warned me not to show my parade ground find to the elderly woman collecting the modest admission price. That's the first thing I did, of course, but she didn't try to claim my buckle for the museum, as Granddad had feared. Back then it was perfectly legal to keep such a find. Today it would be a crime to keep an artifact found at a federal cultural landmark like old Fort Davis. I still have that old buckle and consider it one of my most prized possessions. It bears a file mark where Granddad started to follow through on his promise. For some reason, he never completed the project. But it was the first historical artifact I ever found and an early milepost in a lifelong interest in history. In addition to that old buckle, I have several crinkled black-and-white 8x10 prints of a chubby little boy in faded blue jeans and a white T-shirt wearing a cowboy-style Davy Crockett hat at the ruins of old Fort Davis.

Ten years later, in the summer of 1965, as a teenager by then even more interested in history and Real Old Forts, I got to meet Scobee on my second-ever visit to Fort Davis. My grandparents and I were on our way back to Austin after visiting my aunt and uncle in El Paso. I think Granddad knew everyone of consequence in Texas back then, including Scobee. When we stopped by the judge's cluttered courthouse office for a visit, I persuaded Granddad to buy me a copy of Scobee's book on the history of the fort. Granddad, with only a slight bit of theatrical hesitation, peeled off a $10 bill to pay for the book, which Scobee autographed to me. Only a thousand copies of the book had been printed, and within two years and two weeks of its publication all had been sold. These days the book, which has never been reprinted, goes for $100 or more when you can find one. Mine is not for sale.

A couple of years later, in the summer of 1967, I started working as a reporter for the *San Angelo Standard-Times*. I talked with Scobee almost every day as I made my way down what we called the "call card," a list of the correspondents we checked with daily by telephone. By this time, the seventy-seven-year-old Scobee was too deaf to hear thunder, but he could still read his rain gauge and knew that someone from the *Standard-Times* would be calling every evening.

"No, we didn't get any rain," he'd yell into the phone and hang up, skipping any small talk. In West Texas, if rain falls somewhere, that's news. Scobee seldom had any other news to report—just an obituary about once a month—but he continued to provide the newspaper with occasional feature stories he'd mail in. In 1974 Scobee and his wife moved to Kerrville so that he could be close to the Veterans' Hospital there. He died in 1977 at the age of ninety-one and was taken back to Fort Davis for burial.

Most of the outsiders drawn to these mountains over the years were content with the relative seclusion they afforded and were not bent on being catalysts for sweeping change. If they had offbeat ideas, they made no effort to convert others to their way of thinking.

All Richard McLaren wanted to do when he first moved to Fort Davis was to grow the perfect grape.

A native of St. Louis, Missouri—the same state that produced Barry Scobee—McLaren grew up in Wilmington, Ohio, raised by his mother and grandmother. His father had left when McLaren was three. He graduated from high school in 1972, having established a reputation as a good tennis player and a finicky eater. He would not eat the cafeteria food and got permission to go home every day for lunch, the first time he bucked the system and won.

Three years later he married his high school sweetheart. In 1977 the couple decided to move to Texas. They went to Fort Worth, where McLaren did everything from carpentry work to selling insurance. He did not go to college, but he was a quick study, if mercurial in his interests.

Reading *Texas Monthly* and *Texas Highways*, McLaren learned about Fort Davis and something new—the state's nascent wine industry. With financial support from a woman in East Texas, McLaren decided to move to Fort Davis and start a vineyard. Apples had been grown successfully in the high, cool climate for years. Why not grapes? he thought. He and his first wife moved to the Davis Mountains Resort in October 1979.

Living in a lean-to heated by burning wood in a fifty-five-gallon drum, McLaren and his wife fell a bit short of turning the 6,000-acre resort into another Napa Valley. They managed to produce one batch of wine, but the organic vineyard scheme withered on the proverbial vine.

Outsiders have almost as tough a time taking root around Fort Davis as McLaren's grapes did. Most of the land has been in the same families for generations, and people tend to look on strangers as, well, strangers. Tourists who spend money are thought of a little better.

McLaren's efforts to become a landowner in Jeff Davis County started him down the trail that would lead him to his faceoff with the DPS. He was buying some owner-financed lots in the resort, owned by Larry Stewart of Rockport, Texas. Occasionally, McLaren would be late on a payment, but Stewart was understanding, even though he easily could have foreclosed on the lots. Sometimes Stewart loaned McLaren money for food.

Inspired by a court case in California involving old Spanish land grants, McLaren told Stewart in 1984 that he didn't have to pay for the lots he'd been buying. When Stewart disagreed, McLaren said he would pay him anyway, out of friendship and because it was the right thing to do. But four months later, the payments stopped and Stewart was forced to institute foreclosure.

McLaren's response was to file suit alleging that the subdivision, and all of Jeff Davis County for that matter, had been improperly platted. Finding faulty surveys is not a new way of acquiring free land, and though it took a decade-long legal fight, it worked for McLaren.

In 1994 McLaren created what he called the Davis Mountain Land Commission, his first step toward a separate government. McLaren also tangled with the resort's home-owners association over how fees it collected were spent. Joe Rowe was president of the association, the beginning of the friction between the two. McLaren's research into land issues, begun because of his lawsuit, led him to his belief that Texas had been illegally annexed to the United States.

McLaren found in the course of his research that fights over boundary lines in Jeff Davis County were nothing new. Neither was the notion of separatism an altogether novel concept in the area. The story goes back to 1875, when the Texas Legislature created Presidio County. The new political subdivision covered 12,000 square miles and was the largest county in the United States. Fort Davis was named county seat, since the military post was there. A decade later, however, the citizens of Marfa thought that since they had the railroad, they ought to have the county seat. The matter was placed before the big county's small electorate, and by a vote of 391 to 302, Marfa became the new county seat. Two years later, Fort Davis partisans asked the Legislature to whittle down Presidio County and let them have a little land for their own county. The Legislature went along with this "secession" effort and created a new county with Fort Davis as the seat of government. Most of the residents around Fort Davis were Yankees, having come to the area with the military or because of it. Some say that just to spite them, the lawmakers named the new county after the former president of the Confederacy.

That version of how the new county got its name may not be anything more than legend, but ill will continued between Jeff Davis and Presidio counties for years. Not until 1905 was a lawsuit over county boundary lines settled.

McLaren's lawsuit with Stewart was settled out of court in 1995. McLaren got twenty lots (all the unsold ones in the subdivision), two buildings, and $87,900 from the sale of some land to the Texas Nature Conservancy. The legal success convinced McLaren that other victories were possible if you just dug deep enough into the records and carefully sifted all the dust fallen between the cracks of history.

In the small town of Fort Davis, McLaren's favorable outcome in his fight with Stewart, even though it was in the form of a settlement, was big news locally. But anywhere else in Texas, Richard McLaren was far from being a household name.

Outlaw and lawman history is one of my major interests. Whenever I'm in Fort Davis, I try to go by and see Ed Bartholomew, always a font of good stories. Over the years, I have interviewed him on audiotape and in front of a video camera.

In July 1995 I was on my way back to Austin from Tucson, Arizona, where I had given a talk on the Texas Rangers at that year's convention of the Western Outlaw and Lawman History Association (WOLA). I detoured slightly to Fort Davis and stopped by Bartholomew's place. Knowing that he does not hear very well, I banged hard on his door and yelled. His old Volkswagen van was in his driveway, but no one answered the door.

Fortunately, it does not take long to find someone in Fort
Davis. Knowing he likes to take his meals and coffee at the
Fort Davis Drug Store, I drove over there—the social center of
the Dairy Queen-less town. The place was busy, but that afternoon Bartholomew was not one of the customers.

Stepping back out into the dry air, which was hotter than
it felt, I looked down the main drag and noticed a tall, thin
man on a bicycle. I drove in his direction and pulled up alongside him. Sure enough, it was Bartholomew. I rolled on ahead
of him, got out of my Explorer, and waved. He was on his way
to dinner at a Mexican food restaurant.

"It's the best in town," he assured me. "You're welcome
to join me."

Over dinner, we talked about Indians, Rangers, and outlaws. Back at his house, we sat outside in the cool mountain
air under a bright moon, enjoyed after-dinner cigars, and
talked until nearly midnight.

I don't remember how it came up, but at some point
Bartholomew mentioned that "a bunch of nuts" had settled up
in the mountains on the old "Skinny" Friend Ranch—the
Davis Mountains Resort—and were claiming they weren't part
of Texas.

"All they're really trying to do is get some free land,"
Bartholomew said. "But they are going to be trouble one of
these days." The person behind it all, Bartholomew said, was
Rick McLaren.

I hadn't planned on spending the night in Fort Davis, but
Bartholomew's stories had been too good to pass up. By the
time he had begun to wind down a little bit, I was too tired to
drive as far as Alpine, much less Austin, which was 450 miles
away. Bartholomew insisted I stay in one of his guest bed-
rooms. The next morning, I was up before dawn. I had to get
back to Austin.

Bartholomew was already up. Old-timers in West Texas
stir early. They know they can get more work done in the cool
of the morning. When I walked into his kitchen, he handed me
a cup of instant coffee and a baloney sandwich. I thanked him
profusely, knocked down the warm coffee like a shot of tequila
so it would be safe for me to get behind the wheel of my

Explorer, and then discreetly slipped the sandwich into his refrigerator. Bartholomew was not running a bed and breakfast. I'd get something to eat in Alpine, along with a big cup of fresh-brewed joe to go.

One person who drinks more coffee than I do is my boss. A few days later, when Lieutenant Colonel Thomas and I ran into each other at the coffee pot outside his office, I brought up Bartholomew's forecast of trouble in Jeff Davis County. Texas has had plenty of kooks over the years. So far as I know, no one at the DPS took McLaren and his colleagues very seriously. I had all but forgotten the conversation with Bartholomew about McLaren until I got a phone call from a reporter the following January.

A brief history of the second Republic of Texas

I've always felt a little proprietary about Texas' pink granite Capitol, which at 309 feet, eight inches, stands seven feet higher than the one in Washington, D.C.

The huge statehouse, completed in 1888, belongs to all Texans. But my great-grandfather Adolph Wilke, the son of a German wheelwright who immigrated to Texas in 1850, was one of the laborers who helped build it. As a little boy, I'd go with my granddad when he went there to check his Capitol Station post office box. That was so long ago that the mail was put up twice a day and even on weekends.

Once, when I was about four, I got lost. That was the first time I realized just how big that building really is and how empty it is when all the offices are closed. Wandering those halls with the wide, shiny tile floors and shadowy recesses, hearing only echoes as I cried out for my granddad, was scary. Fortunately, he found me before too long.

As a teenager, my first job was as an assistant sergeant-at-arms in the Texas Senate. I was a "go-fer" during two legislative sessions, in 1965 and in 1967, the year I graduated from high school and began full-time work as a newspaper reporter.

Over the years, I covered a lot of news stories in the Capitol, including the 1974 Constitutional Convention, the first such gathering in the state since Reconstruction. Sitting through that convention, which came within only three votes of placing a new state charter before the electorate, taught me a lot about local and state government. In fact, I learned more about such things as home rule than I ever wanted to know or have needed to know since.

Though the convention was a perfectly legal attempt to revamp—and modernize—some aspects of Texas government (the Texas Bill of Rights, similar to the U.S. Bill of Rights, had not been under consideration and would not have been changed), others have come to the Capitol openly espousing less orderly change. In 1969 thousands of young people protesting the Vietnam War marched on the Capitol. DPS officers and Austin police used tear gas to get the unruly mob out of the building.

I was in Lubbock working for the *Avalanche-Journal* at the time of the anti-war riot, but I later covered other anti-war demonstrations and two notable Ku Klux Klan rallies at the Capitol. Both KKK gatherings got ugly, and one nearly ended in a gun battle. An Austin police lieutenant, who never got the credit he deserved for what he did, threatened to shoot some Klansmen if they opened their car trunks and pulled out weapons, which is what they were preparing to do as a hostile crowd of anti-Klan protesters closed in on them. I believe the lieutenant would have followed through with his threat, but no one ever got the chance to find out. The Klansmen, perhaps envisioning another kind of shroud in their immediate future, decided to remove their sheets and retreat instead of finding out if the lieutenant with the pistol pointed at them was bluffing.

Less than a year after this close call, "my" Capitol nearly burned down. Before dawn on Sunday, February 6, 1983, fire broke out in the apartment of Lieutenant Governor Bill Hobby and quickly spread through the east wing. A friend called and woke me up to tell me that a two-alarm fire had been reported at the Capitol. I pulled on a gray jogging suit and, without benefit of caffeine, sped toward downtown. From several miles away I could see black smoke pouring from the building in the glare of the lights illuminating the dome. I knew this was no ordinary two-alarm fire. I was the first newspaper reporter on the scene, and I stayed on the story for the rest of the day.

The Austin Fire Department finally contained the fire, but just barely. Acting Fire Chief Brady Pool told me later that morning that at one point he'd thought the fire was going to win. In fact, he recommended to Governor Mark White, who along with other worried state and city officials stood outside the burning building, that papers and furnishings should be removed before the fire spread further.

The fire, which started in a television set, had been the catalyst for an extensive refurbishing to the building and addition of an underground annex—a $200 million project. The newly remodeled Capitol was rededicated on April 21, 1995—appropriately, San Jacinto Day.

The following January, I learned that members of a separatist movement felt that the nicely redone Capitol should be the seat of government not for the State of Texas but for an independent nation.

A group calling itself the Republic of Texas had requested and received a permit from the State Preservation Board to hold a rally at the Capitol on Tuesday, January 16, 1996. Soon after word of this got out, a reporter called my office and wanted to know what security measures the DPS planned to take and what did we think about the claim that Texas was still a republic and that the people planning the rally were its rightful government officials?

Both questions were easy to answer: The DPS never discusses details of the security it provides for the governor or other state officials nor for state property. And under the First Amendment, any group has the perfect right to express its opinions, no matter how bizarre. To protest at the Capitol, all a group needs is a permit. The DPS' only interest was that no one break any laws in support of their views.

For assistant PIO Laureen Chernow and me, being on hand at a gathering of folks calling themselves officials of the Republic of Texas, which they maintained was the true government of Texas, was a welcome change from what had become a January DPS tradition of providing security for Ku Klux Klan rallies at the Capitol. Because of the well-demonstrated potential for violence, KKK appearances always draw the media, which is exactly what the Klan wants. When the media is there in force, I need to be there to answer questions if things get out of hand. Laureen and I had stood by at several KKK rallies, one of which had resulted in several arrests.

The DPS did not expect trouble at the Republic of Texas gathering, but after the Oklahoma City federal courthouse bombing, a law enforcement agency can't take anything for granted. Enough Troopers were on hand at the Capitol to handle things if something happened, but all was peaceful—if weird.

Laureen was at the DPS Command Post in an office on the second floor of the Capitol overlooking the south entrance. While DPS officers looked down on the gathering through the big windows, designed to let in lots of air in a pre-air-conditioning era, I chose to mill discreetly around in the crowd and listen to the speakers. Compared with the tired racist ranting of the Klan, what the Republic of Texas people had to say was interesting. Downright history-making, if you took them seriously.

"Ladies and gentlemen, Texas is no longer a part of the United States of despair," announced John C. Van Kirk, a well-dressed, heavy-set man with a mustache and thinning gray hair who had just been introduced as provisional president of the Republic of Texas.

His supporters, somewhere between 100 and 200, clapped and cheered heartily. Van Kirk was a good speaker, I had to admit. Maybe not as good as historians credit Sam Houston as having been, but a lot better than some of the duly elected officials whose orations I had covered over the years as a reporter.

Following his address, Van Kirk introduced his chief ambassador, Richard McLaren.

Thin and balding (the way his hair flared out from the sides reminded me of the TV cartoon character Krusty the Clown on "The Simpsons"), McLaren seemed both intense and intelligent. And yet he was standing on the steps of the Capitol seriously arguing a point that anyone with even a nodding familiarity with Texas history or law would see as ridiculous.

Texas' admission to the Union in 1846 was illegal, he said, because the people never were offered the opportunity to vote on the issue. Beyond that, he said, after Texas seceded in 1861, its readmission to the United States was never legitimized after the end of the Civil War.

"We never had any intention of leaving the United States

until we discovered that none of this [the manner in which Texas was admitted to the United States] was legal," he said. (Indeed, I later learned that McLaren's first thought had been the creation of a new state, not a new country.) "Legally, we never ceded the soil of the Republic of Texas to any foreign nation."

Though this argument can be summarized in a few sentences, McLaren said ten pounds of paperwork had been filed with the International Court of Justice in the Netherlands, sometimes also referred to as the World Court.

When I saw a woman distributing a half-inch-thick sheaf of papers labeled "Press Pack," I sidled up and asked for a set. She looked at me suspiciously. I had a coat and tie on. Most print reporters no longer wear coats and ties, and I am not ruggedly handsome enough to pass for a television "correspondent." I don't even blow-dry my hair.

"Are you with the media?"

"Yeah," I said, "I write for the paper," which was absolutely true. My book review column runs once a week.

Fortunately, she handed over the packet without asking to see my press card.

Meanwhile, someone else with the Republic of Texas had handed over an even bigger set of documents to the DPS for delivery to Governor George W. Bush. Accepting on behalf of the state was then Chief of Traffic Law Enforcement George King, the highest ranking uniformed officer with the DPS. King handed the papers over to someone to examine to make sure that's all they were—papers. Once it had been determined the material was safe, it went to the governor's general counsel.

Before the rally broke up, Van Kirk delivered an ultimatum: State officials had thirty days to vacate the office.

Laureen and I jokingly speculated on whether the new government of Texas would still need spokespersons on its payroll.

"Maybe they'll give us a raise," I offered. If the Republic couldn't afford to pay more, perhaps a cabinet post could be considered: Minister of Public Information sounded impressive.

Back in my office, I went through the ROT press kit and had my secretary Lisa Hunter make a copy to send over to our

Special Crimes Service. Based on this document, and other sources, here's a chronology of the group's activities up to that point:

April 12, 1994: Inspired by a Texas legislative act that specifically allowed Harris County to control growth in unincorporated areas by creating land planning entities, McLaren created the Davis Mountain Land Commission. He saw the commission as something of a separate county—his own. When the Jeff Davis County Commissioner's Court passed a resolution in March 1995 that it did not "recognize the Davis Mountains Land Commission as a political subdivision of the county," McLaren, twisting logic, interpreted that as official support of his extralegal commission.

September 18, 1995: McLaren wrote Governor Bush to notify him that "the Republic of Texas is moving forward with reestablishing its standings under the Laws of Nations" and requesting that "you appoint a Special Committee to work with the Delegates of the Republic of Texas in accomplishing these goals."

October 18, 1995: McLaren filed with the Texas Supreme Court a "brief" advancing his argument that Texas was illegally annexed into the United States.

November 16, 1995: The Texas Supreme Court dismissed that filing (Case Number 95-1002 "In RE: The People of the Republic of Texas") for "want of jurisdiction." McLaren and others in the movement interpreted this judicial brush-off as a positive development. Though the dismissal only meant that the procedural formalities necessary to get a matter properly before the court had not been met, McLaren saw it as an admission by the court that the ROT was beyond state government.

December 1, 1995: McLaren wrote U.S. Secretary of State Warren C. Christopher "to Legally notify you that the Supreme Court of Texas has Certified by its notice . . . that it is without Domestic or international standings involving the Citizens, their government or eminent domain on the Soil of Texas involving the Republic of Texas," and that "the provisional government of the Republic of Texas is now being reformed."

December 13, 1995: This was the day the ROT later claimed the new Republic of Texas began its existence. The rebirth occurred in a meeting hall in Bulverde, a community in Bexar County.

January 5, 1996: Van Kirk wrote Governor Bush a polite but direct two-page letter that "it is now resolved at law that the Republic of Texas is re-instated as its own free and independent Nation among nations, and is subject only to its treaties authorized by its Constitution."

January 7, 1996: A twelve-point "Proclamation of the Transitional Plan of the Republic of Texas," adopted by the "General Council of the Government of the Republic of Texas," was signed by Van Kirk and Ruth E. Klause, Council secretary. The three-page, single-spaced document outlined "the transitional operations of the provisional government of the Republic of Texas for an interim period until a constitutional convention shall be held. . . ."

January 10, 1996: Van Kirk issued a "Formal Announcement" to "All the people living on the soil of Texas who cherish liberty, freedom, law and order" to gather in front of the Capitol at 10:30 A.M. January 16.

January 13, 1996: Officials of the "provisional government" met at an Austin motel with some seventy representatives of various militia groups and discussed what they termed the militia groups' "peacekeeping role" in the new government.

Though the Republic's officials were talking separatism, nothing in any of their rhetoric up to that point implied the possibility of illegal actions. In fact, the "Formal Announcement" from Van Kirk specifically said, "We will not play a role in adversity to law or judicial process. . . . One errs to think this is an action to secede from the union. . . ." But there was this ominous line as well: "There are many fringe factions who want civil war or martial law in Texas so they can remain in power in order to continue the depletion of assets of the People of Texas."

March 1996: Others in the ROT movement apparently were not as peacefully inclined as Van Kirk. At a meeting on March 9 in Lubbock, ten of the twelve members of the Republic's cabinet voted Van Kirk out of office. The point of contention was whether militia groups should be welcomed into the Republic's fold.

"They're crazy idiots," Van Kirk said of the Republic's pro-militia faction in a newspaper interview a few days after his ouster, a vote of impeachment he did not accept. "I can't stand them. I hate what they stand for."

In addition to his comments in the media, Van Kirk wrote the DPS to warn that some of the militia members were "likely to pull stupid stunts." He urged the agency to be particularly cautious on March 18, when the Republic planned another Capitol rally. "Certain individuals, with militia-type mentality, have coerced weak individuals on the general council [of the ROT] to act in a way that advocates violence and reckless endangerment to the good people of Texas."

Laureen got the call from an *Austin American-Statesman* reporter needing a comment on that from the DPS. "We are cognizant of our responsibilities to protect the Capitol complex," she answered.

Again, the DPS assigned extra Troopers to the Capitol for the rally, just in case. In addition to Van Kirk's letter, tensions were heightened by an "order" issued on March 6 by a Republic of Texas common law "court" in Tarrant County. The "Notice to Vacate Notice of Eviction," addressed to the "State of Texas" and Governor Bush gave him five days to "vacate" (what the governor was supposed to vacate was not mentioned in the "order") or "face further legal action under the law of nations and the laws of the Republic of Texas."

McLaren and a couple hundred ROT supporters—minus Van Kirk—showed up for the March 18 event. They waved Lone Star flags and shouted "God bless the Republic of Texas," and, after making some speeches, marched four blocks from the Capitol to the Internal Revenue Service office at the federal building. There, the Republic's "secretary of defense" ordered the IRS to get out of Texas within thirty days.

"We don't want to create chaos," McLaren said. "But we got to reclaim our rights."

As I had during their first rally, I kept on the edge of the crowd, listening and watching. ROT security people milled around, nervously talking into their radios and looking up at nearby high-rise buildings as if expecting snipers to begin raining fire on them at any moment.

To this point, media coverage of the Republic of Texas movement had tended toward the tongue-in-cheek. But on March 26, the FBI found itself locked in a stand-off with another group who believed they were citizens of a foreign nation—Montana. More than a hundred federal agents were surrounding a 960-acre farm near Jordan, Montana, where an anti-tax group that called itself the Freemen were holed up following the arrest of their leaders, LeRoy Schweitzer and Daniel E. Peterson.

Documents filed in federal court in San Antonio showed that Schweitzer had sent a one-million-dollar bogus money order to a man who claimed to be an ROT "citizen." Before the siege, the Freemen held classes in Montana offering instruction in their phony money order scheme and some 800 separatist-leaning individuals from thirty states (including Texas) had attended.

The scam worked this way: Legal documents would be filed that created a non-existent debt on a piece of property. Then this "credit" would be used to write millions of dollars' worth of worthless money orders. "Its value [was] created out of thin air," Assistant U.S. Attorney William Harris told a reporter. "That is fraud."

Fraud presumes an effort to get something, usually money, for nothing. But fraud can serve political aims as well. With increasing frequency, ROT members were filing bogus liens and other official-looking documents—paper issued by common-law "courts" with no legal standing—with county and district clerks all across Texas. These extralegal documents, aimed at everything from circumventing taxes to separatism, were tying up property rights and clogging the court system. Texas Attorney General Dan Morales, whose office began receiving requests for opinions from bewildered governmental officials, began calling the ROT filing blitzkrieg "Paper Terrorism."

As I read and watched news accounts of the stand-off in Montana, some of them hauntingly similar to reports that had come from Mount Carmel during the siege there, it was obvious to me that the Republic of Texas situation was only the Lone Star version of a much bigger movement.

The people involved in the Texas movement—McLaren

claimed there were 2,000 in Texas with membership growing rapidly—seemed to think the right combination of common law, biblical citation, legal mumbo-jumbo, and their own peculiar interpretation of history could do what four years of bloody Civil War had not been able to do in the 1860s: wrest a state from the Union.

On March 25 McLaren wrote then DPS Director Colonel James Wilson, enclosing a sample of the "official documents of identification that the Citizens of the Republic of Texas will be carrying with them [on] Texas highways . . . including identification cards.

"We expect you to notify all city police, county sheriffs and their departments, and all members of your department of the documents that will be used by our Citizens in accordance with international law and the common law of the nation of Texas," the letter said.

McLaren continued in the letter that ROT members would be surrendering their driver licenses, which are issued by the DPS, for certificates issued by the Republic of Texas. But Texas law is clear: Driving is a privilege, not a right. If you drive a vehicle in Texas, a driver license is required—one issued by a recognized government.

Copies of McLaren's letter were placed on the windshield of every car at the law enforcement appreciation dinner in the West Texas town of Snyder on April 11, an event attended by both Attorney General Morales and Colonel Wilson.

April 15, 1996: A certified letter was sent to all 254 Texas county sheriffs from ROT "Secretary of Defense" Archie H. Lowe of Rice, Texas, informing them that they would be replaced if they did not pledge allegiance to the ROT.

April 20, 1996: Some 350 ROT "citizens" met in the ballroom of the swank Grand Kempinski Hotel in Dallas the day after the third anniversary of the end of the Waco siege and one day before the 150th anniversary of the Battle of San Jacinto. They decided to undertake a Republic of Texas "grand jury" investigation of the Waco incident. In the hotel lobby, ROT members sold Republic of Texas license plates for $50 and official ROT identification cards for $25. To get one, people had to renounce their current citizenship and provide thumbprints—in triplicate.

Texas law enforcement officers began handing tickets to any driver of a vehicle with ROT license plates instead of the plates issued by the state through county tax assessor-collectors. On May 3 a deputy constable in Harris County arrested a fifty-three-year-old man for driving with an expired vehicle registration and not having a driver license or proof of liability insurance. The old van he had been driving bore ROT license plates, not valid Texas plates. When the driver refused to say whether he had any weapons or explosives in the vehicle, a bomb squad was called in to check it. No explosives were discovered, though officers did find plastic pipe, wires, batteries, and what they believed was a detonator.

May 1996: In response to the letter from Lowe, Nacogdoches County Sheriff Joe Evans decided to have a little fun. He announced the resurrection of Haden Edwards' Fredonia Republic.

"We're not going to be intimidated by these people," he said. "So a group of us decided it might be a good idea to form our own republic. After all, the Fredonia Republic predates this fly-by-night [original] Republic of Texas by ten years."

Senior U.S. District Judge Lucius Bunton III of Midland did not think the Republic's activities were all that funny. Stewart Title Company of Houston had sued McLaren in federal court and won a judgment ordering him to stop placing meritless liens against the property of various of his neighbors, and companies they did business with. When McLaren said he refused to recognize the jurisdiction of a federal court, the judge held him in civil contempt.

May 2, 1996: Attorney General Morales released Opinion DM-389, holding that district or county clerks should not file any document issued by a "court" not named in the Texas Constitution or statutes.

May 4, 1996: McLaren was arrested by deputy U.S. marshals on the contempt citation issued by Judge Bunton. The "ambassador" was on his Jeff Davis County property, operating a tractor, when arrested.

May 9, 1996: In a hearing in Pecos, Judge Bunton

ordered McLaren to stay in jail until he changed his mind about refusing to obey federal law. "I don't want to make a martyr out of you," the judge said, "but it is my duty to uphold the judgment of this court. I can't allow you to thumb your nose or maintain federal courts don't have jurisdiction." McLaren said he was willing to stay in jail indefinitely. "The Republic of Texas is a living, breathing entity," McLaren told the judge. "People will react. Things are fixing to get out of hand."

May 20, 1996: Attorney General Morales mailed letters to fifty-five ROT members telling them to "cease and desist engaging in any and all unlawful or illegal activity under the purported authority of the Republic of Texas." While anyone had a right to protest the government, he said, no one had the right to violate its laws. No exception existed "for those who profess political or philosophical disagreement with our government." The letter was more than unsolicited advice: It was a necessary precursor to a civil suit and a warning that criminal prosecution also was possible.

June 7, 1996: McLaren was released from the Ward County Jail in Monahans, where he had been held on the contempt citation since May 4, after finally agreeing in a hearing before Judge Bunton to stop filing bogus liens.

June 13, 1996: The eighty-one-day Freemen stand-off in Montana ended peacefully.

June 25, 1996: The Attorney General's Office sued McLaren and twenty-four ROT members, alleging restraint of trade, retaliation, intimidation, and falsifying government documents. In the suit, Morales sought to be named temporary receiver of the Republic of Texas organization, which would give him authority to dissolve ROT-filed liens or other orders issued by ROT common law "courts." State District Judge Paul Davis signed a temporary restraining order enjoining ROT members from issuing liens.

July 9, 1996: State District Judge Joe Hart extended the temporary restraining order issued by his colleague the month before, but said he had no authority to name the Attorney General's Office as receiver for the Republic of Texas and the defendants in the lawsuit. McLaren ignored a subpoena to the hearing, saying at a press conference that he would "only obey the orders of Mr. Bunton, and those will have to be on a diplomatic basis."

July 12, 1996: In Letter Opinion No. 96-066, Assistant Attorney General James E. Tourtelott held "the Republic of Texas does not exist. Texas has not been a republic for over 150 years. The so-called Republic has no sovereignty, no authority, no part in the political apparatus of this state."

August 20, 1996: The ROT placed classified ads in some Texas newspapers announcing it was ready to begin transferring state assets into its accounts. Those assets, McLaren said, would belong to all citizens of Texas. "We have not had time to notify them but everyone who is in Texas now is a citizen of the Republic." Attorney General's spokesman Ron Dusek told the media: "The Republic of Texas has no more authority than the Moose Lodge."

October 15, 1996: The Attorney General's Office filed a motion for contempt sanctions, maintaining that the ROT and the defendants in the state civil suit had violated the court's order by continuing to file bogus liens and other ROT documents. McLaren now claimed a $93 trillion lien against the State of Texas, the United States, and the Roman Catholic Church.

October 18, 1996: At 10:50 A.M., fifty-five-year-old Archie Lowe, then ROT president, was arrested following a routine traffic stop by College Station police after he refused to sign a ticket for driving with an expired inspection sticker and not having proof of liability insurance. Richard Lee Ray, Jr., thirty, a "captain" in the ROT "police" force and a passenger in the car Lowe had been driving, was arrested for unlawfully carrying a weapon, a handgun. Both men could have bonded out of jail for a few hundred dollars, but they refused to do so. McLaren called the police "kidnappers, privateers and pirates" and issued a statement that the ROT's "defense forces" had been placed on "high alert" and that "an act of this nature will be dealt with by the use of force, if necessary." As a precaution, the DPS sent three Troopers to stand by outside the Brazos County Jail, but after spending one night in the lockup, the two men decided to pay their bonds and get out. No incidents occurred.

October 28, 1996: Judge Hart found twenty-eight ROT members in civil contempt of court on two counts for sending notices to 175 banks and 750 public officials that state assets had been transferred to a newly created public trust controlled by the ROT. The judge gave the group seven days to rescind their "order" or face a fine of $10,000 on one of the counts. On the other count, he said, the fine would double for each day that order was ignored.

November 19, 1996: Compounding daily, the ROT's contempt of court fines had reached $1.3 billion. Morales said it might be necessary for the court to seize property of ROT members to satisfy the fines.

Also in November, the ROT, never a tight-knit organization, impeached McLaren, stripping him of his title as ambassador. This action was pushed through by Darrel Dean Franks, ROT treasurer. McLaren had accused Franks of embezzlement, and Franks maintained McLaren had usurped the powers of the ROT's General Council. Several other officers also were relieved of their official ROT status, and a new provisional council was elected. McLaren ignored the ROT action and continued to speak for the movement.

December 19, 1996: McLaren failed to appear before Judge Bunton to explain why he had continued to issue bogus liens and documents. Once again finding McLaren in civil contempt of court, the federal judge issued a warrant for his arrest. From his "embassy" in the Davis Mountains, McLaren told a reporter for the Associated Press: "If they [officers trying to serve the warrant] enter the embassy, they'll be in violation of international law. We have the right to remove them with bodily force, if necessary." U.S. Marshal Jack Dean, based in San Antonio, said the warrant would be served, though there was no timetable and no assault on McLaren was planned. "We'll take it easy and it will get served," Dean said.

December 20, 1996: Though federal authorities intended to deliver the arrest warrant to McLaren, he would not be getting any late Christmas cards. The day after Judge Bunton's contempt citation was issued, the U.S. Postal Service ceased mail delivery and pickup at the Davis Mountains Resort, citing safety concerns on the part of the mail carrier. The community's mail boxes were located at a small general store. Behind the store, on property owned by McLaren, was the ROT "embassy," though McLaren soon relocated the diplomatic post to his trailer farther up the canyon. The building had served as the community's volunteer fire hall prior to construction of a new facility up the canyon. On December 23 a postal inspector picked up mail that had been in the box since the previous Friday and sealed it.

McLaren had never been reluctant to talk to the press, but late in 1996 he began what can only be called a concerted public relations campaign. Within two months, McLaren granted lengthy interviews to the *San Antonio Express*, the *Austin American-Statesman*, the *Fort Worth Star-Telegram*, the *New York Times*, and *USA Today,* as well as readily agreeing to be interviewed by assorted radio and television stations.

The *Star-Telegram's* Barry Shlacter even noted the media attention in his profile of the "ambassador," writing that the ROT movement and McLaren's defiance of a federal judge "has attracted much media attention, in which McLaren clearly revels."

In support of that, Shlacter quoted forty-six-year-old Robert "White Eagle" Otto, whom he identified as McLaren's "guard and chief of communications": "He's got NBC-TV, three other interviews today and a live radio show tonight."

Visitors to McLaren's property found the "embassy" to be a 1950s vintage trailer with a wooden lean-to attached. A rectangular white sign resting over a double-pane window proclaimed the structure as the Republic of Texas' embassy. Though the surrounding scenery—tall pines and rocky cliffs— was impressive, the "embassy" was far from a stately diplomatic post. The Republic's flag—a single gold star on blue— flew from a modest staff in front of the trailer. Nearby was a tent where Otto stayed. Behind the embassy was a ridge. A dry creek bed cut across the road leading to the trailer, then flanked the property, winding farther up the canyon.

1997: One of the points McLaren had made during his media blitz was that he planned to convene a public "hearing" in the Capitol rotunda to expound on the ROT contention that Texas "was and still is unlawfully held as a captive nation."

But on January 2 the Attorney General's Office said the group could not be granted a permit to use the statehouse because they lacked an official state sponsor. Also, an assistant attorney general noted, public events at the Capitol were limited by State Preservation Board rules to forty-five minutes. McLaren had wanted to conduct six hours of "hearings" over five days.

By the time the Attorney General's Office announced that the planned event could not be staged in the Capitol, McLaren said he had decided to hold the "hearings" in Fort Davis instead. He would accomplish his goal of getting the issue before the public by videotaping the proceedings and selling copies for $25 each, he said. Besides that, since there was a warrant for his arrest, he wasn't making any public appearances. From Fort Davis he warned, "If they arrest me, we will fire upon them. A civil war will erupt."

In his reaction to the state's denial of the group's planned use of the Capitol, ROT President Lowe was more pacific in tone: "We are not going to force our way into our own Capitol . . . endangering Texians and provoking armed conflict."

Despite Lowe's statement, the attorney general told his employees to stay home on January 7, the day the ROT "hearings" were to have begun. That gave several hundred state employees who worked in the Price Daniel Senior and William P. Clements buildings an unexpected day off. Department of Criminal Justice employees and some court employees who worked in the two buildings also were told not to report to the office.

The DPS stepped up security at the Capitol Complex, but the day went by without incident.

Three days later, state Representative Will Hartnett of Dallas filed a bill that would make it illegal to file false liens. A first offense would be a misdemeanor. Anyone convicted of filing false liens three times would face a felony charge. On January 17, 1997, Governor Bush, at General Morales' request, declared the issue an "emergency." That enabled the Legislature to take up consideration of the bill immediately.

On February 17 ABC's "Nightline" weighed in with a program on McLaren and the ROT movement. That show prompted an Ohio man, evidently a fan of CBS' Saturday night drama series, "Walker, Texas Ranger," to write the Austin newspaper: "My advice to the esteemed Texas attorney general is to contact Texas Ranger Walker and his counterparts, and let them clean up that West Texas mess."

In addition to the federal contempt citation, authorities now held another arrest warrant with McLaren's name on it. He had been charged with burglary in connection with the forced entry into a house in the Davis Mountains Resort that had been sold at foreclosure. Though he was free on $1,000 bond, the warrant for his arrest was issued after he failed to appear for a pretrial hearing on February 21.

On March 4 newly elected Jeff Davis Sheriff Steve Bailey faxed a letter to McLaren, urging him to turn himself in on the state failure to appear warrant. "Rick, I am requesting you take a small step back toward reality," the sheriff wrote. "You are way out in left field when you think that local, state or federal authorities are scared of a confrontation. . . .Do not let this situation escalate." If McLaren or any of his supporters seriously injured or killed an officer, the sheriff continued, "you will be filed on for capital murder or attempted capital murder."

McLaren responded to Bailey's letter with a double-barreled blast of rhetoric: "There is a vast amount of international support from outside militias that have been put on alert and if you make such a violent attempt [to serve the warrant], it will not end here; it will only be the beginning." Should officers try to arrest him by force, he continued, they could be held accountable by an international war crimes tribunal. "You can be tried and hung [sic]."

In an effort to counter some of this unfavorable publicity concerning the Republic, President David Johnson of Odessa, the head of another ROT faction, embarked on a statewide media tour to spread the movement's message. "People want freedom," he said at a San Antonio news conference. "They want the government out of their lives. We're going to pull it off. It's just a question of when."

The siege begins

It will be years, if ever, before April 19 is considered just another spring day. First Waco, then Oklahoma City. What next?

"Clearly, this is a day that lives in infamy in the movement," Ken Toole, president of the right-wing Montana Human Rights Network, told a reporter for *USA Today*. Toole and others in the right wing movement refer to April 19 as "Patriots' Day." At least April 19, 1997, would fall on a Saturday and most state office workers would be gone for the weekend. The media calls began as the anniversary approached: "Is there more security at the Capitol this week? Is the DPS worried something might happen this April 19?"

Although the DPS never discusses what measures it takes to provide security for the governor or other state officials and state buildings, there certainly was a heightened awareness that particular week. Two years earlier, on April 19, 1995, the federal building in Oklahoma City had been blown up, supposedly in retaliation for the events outside Waco. One hundred sixty-eight people died. Now the accused bomber, Timothy McVeigh, was on trial in Denver. But would some other disturbed person seek to make retaliatory terrorism an annual or biennial event?

As another "Patriots' Day" neared, the federal government certainly was taking no chances. The FBI sent an advisory to federal agencies reminding them of the coming anniversary. The Justice Department instructed its employees to keep office blinds closed as a safeguard against flying glass. The U.S. Space

Command and North American Aerospace Defense Command canceled tours at its Colorado Springs center.

In short, a lot of people were edgy.

But much to my relief, when April 19 finally came, my pager stayed quiet. The day passed without incident in Texas.

Three days later, on April 22, 1997, Austin police and Travis County sheriff's deputies arrested the Republic's former "secretary for intergovernmental coordination," Jo Ann Canady Turner of Austin. She was jailed on two contempt of court citations issued by Judge Hart after she filed a lien against an Austin moving and storage company in violation of the judge's order. Though no longer an officer of the ROT's "provisional government," Turner was one of the twenty-five ROT members named as defendants in the lawsuit filed by the Attorney General's Office. Turner and her husband had been evicted from their Lake Austin home on March 11, 1996, after failing to pay taxes on it for two years. A constable had contacted the moving company to remove her possessions from the house and place them in storage. When she did not pay the moving bill, the items were sold to cover costs. Turner had then filed a lien on the company.

News of Turner's arrest brought an immediate reaction from McLaren in Fort Davis: "When they arrested her," he said, "they enacted a declaration of war."

In response to Turner's arrest, McLaren said "warrants" had been issued by the Republic for various "foreign agents," including "the unlawful state legislature, all United States federal judges and all IRS agents on Texas soil."

I was about to leave the office for the day on Wednesday, April 23, when an operator in our underground communications center called with a strange report: An 18-wheeler loaded with .50-caliber machine guns, 81mm mortars, and assorted weapons parts—but no ammunition—was missing. The truck had disappeared from a defense contractor's satellite tracking system near the little town of Hye in Blanco County, west of Austin.

A short time later, I started getting media calls. But not, to my surprise, about that missing truck. The FBI, a reporter told me, was looking for a truck last seen near Fairfield on I-45 in

East Texas, headed for Houston. That tractor-trailer rig carried four unarmed Air Force missiles. They were supposed to have been delivered to an airbase outside Albuquerque but had not shown up.

Word of the missing missiles propelled the story onto the wires and soon CNN. Before long media calls were coming in from all over the nation. When the media learned that two trucks were missing, the story really went ballistic. Had the trucks been hijacked by a terrorist group stocking up armaments for a major attack? Was Denver and the coming Oklahoma City bomber trial the target?

The story soon flared out, like an empty booster falling from a rocket pushing its payload toward earth orbit. The truck with the machine guns was found at a truck stop in El Paso. Its two surprised drivers did not even know they and the military weapons they were hauling had been missing. A DPS Trooper checked the truck and found its cargo undisturbed. Their satellite transponder had failed.

The missing missiles turned up the next day at a junkyard in Eastland County, in West Texas. The driver of the truck apparently had gotten a little strapped for cash and had sold his load, which turned out to be harmless training missiles, not anything that could have been used by terrorists. He was arrested by the FBI. The only thing this short-lived incident did was demonstrate the jitteriness of the news media in the wake of Oklahoma City, and the rapidity with which a news story—even a non-story—can take flight.

The following Friday, April 25, if any members of the Legislature or federal judges had been whisked off to Republic of Texas custody, or if any other missiles were missing, I had not heard about it. I was on my way to Dallas, my only worry being the unusually heavy rains we were having. But the drive was uneventful, if slow.

My Ford Explorer was loaded with books I'd be trying to sell at the Dallas Book and Paper Show that weekend. Linda and Hallie would be driving up to join me later in the evening. After unloading the books and setting them up on our display table, we would be dropping by a drinks-and-dip party hosted by one of our fellow used and rare book dealers.

Our life was fairly well back to normal, at least for us. For a while, ours had been anything but typical. The same week in November 1994 that I was to have my final round of chemotherapy, Linda had detected a lump in her left breast. At first she dismissed it, presuming it to be a problem associated with nursing nine-month-old Hallie. But when she had the lump checked, the diagnosis was cancer. Linda began chemotherapy the same week and had five rounds during the next four months, followed by a mastectomy, then high dose chemotherapy with stem cell rescue at San Antonio's Methodist Hospital, and finally, radiation. In an ironic twist, her stem cell transplant fell on the second anniversary of Waco, April 19, 1995. That day, of course, also was the date of the Oklahoma City bombing, and she watched the media coverage from her hospital bed, surrounded by doctors and other medical personnel involved in a procedure to save her life. Now, two years later, she was doing fine.

After the book show closed for the day on Saturday, we drove back to Fort Worth, where we were staying with friends. In appreciation for their hospitality, we took them to dinner that night at an Italian restaurant near the Texas Christian University campus. Right after we ordered, my pager went off.

I left the noisy dining room and went outside to one of the empty red-and-white checkered sidewalk tables and called Austin. The cold front that had brought the rain I drove through on the way up had cooled off things just enough to make sitting inside preferable to being outside. As I waited for the call to go through, I wished I had a hot cup of coffee to warm me up. The communications operator said a television reporter in Austin needed to talk to me. The reporter had left a cellular phone number for me to call.

"I'm here outside the Board of Private Investigators," she said as if she were beginning a live broadcast. "The DPS has sealed off the building, but nobody will tell me what's going on."

The news caught me by surprise.

"I'm in Fort Worth and I don't know anything about it," I told her, "but I'll try to find out and call you back."

Linda, Hallie, and our friends were well into their pasta before I finally got back to the table.

The DPS, I had learned, had confiscated documents and changed the locks at an office building occupied by the State Board of Private Investigators in connection with an investigation into the agency's record-keeping. It had taken me quite a few telephone calls to gather what little information I could release to the media. By that time, other TV stations had learned of the situation and started to call in. After I handled those calls, hoping to preempt any more interruptions that night, I called the Associated Press and the Austin newspaper to let them know what was going on.

The brief flurry of after-hours activity, while not the way I would have liked to spend my personal time, had become easier than it was when I first went to work for the state in 1985. Back then, I had no cellular phone and my pager was a semi-antique that worked off our radio system, which is to say it had a range of only twenty to thirty miles outside of Austin. Now, with a satellite pager and a good cellular phone, I can travel and still be on-call. In effect, I carry my "office" with me.

When my pager went off during the noon hour the next day, I assumed it was headquarters with another media call for me about the Board of Private Investigators matter. I'd already had one follow-up call on that subject from the Texas State News Network earlier that morning. But that short-lived story was about to go off the media radar screen. Something was happening outside Fort Davis involving Republic of Texas members.

Our DPS office in Pecos was reporting that shots had been fired and two people taken hostage, and that Highway Patrol Troopers and Texas Rangers were responding to a general call for assistance from the Jeff Davis County sheriff. My hastily scribbled notes, written on a used Day Runner page I found at the pay telephone where I made my first call to Austin, said: "Pecos—hostages—husband & wife—car on driveway—Republic TX Ft Davis—11:52 am—DPS on scene."

I knew any incident involving the Republic of Texas folks would be a news story, but I wondered if the reported hostage situation was truly a sudden outbreak of separatist terrorism or just a spat between a husband and wife or boyfriend and girlfriend that had overheated into a shooting. Even people involved in what they believe to be noble causes sometimes don't get along. Domestic violence can be just as deadly as terrorism, though usually not as newsworthy. I sure didn't have enough information to call it either way, and neither did anyone else, or least not anyone I could get by phone. Lieutenant Judy Altom, the Safety Education Service supervisor based in Midland, was sending SES Trooper Lucila Torres to the scene from El Paso to handle any media that showed up, but Torres was several hours away. The lieutenant did not know anything more than I did at that point.

On a Sunday, the slowest news day of the week, anything even slightly unusual is going to get a lot of media attention. Within a short time after the initial call from the DPS, I returned calls to CNN, NBC, ABC, KTRH Radio in Houston, WBAP Radio in Dallas-Fort Worth, Channel 4 in Dallas, WOAI Radio in San Antonio, and National Public Radio. Ron Dusek, my counterpart with the Attorney General's Office, also called to find out what was going on.

The first Ranger to reach the scene was Sergeant Dave Duncan, stationed in nearby Alpine. He is a modern Lone Ranger, the only Ranger assigned to the sprawling Big Bend Country and one of only three Rangers located west of the Pecos River. As soon as Duncan assessed the situation, he called his boss, thirty-nine-year-old Captain Barry Caver of Midland. A native of Dallas, the brown-haired, brown-eyed six-footer had been promoted to Ranger captain in November 1996.

Caver had just walked into his house from church when the phone rang. When he got off the phone with Duncan, Caver—a nineteen-year DPS veteran and a Ranger for seven of those years—called pilot John Brannon and asked him to get the Midland-based helicopter ready.

As it became clear that I would be spending most of the afternoon on the telephone, I called the DPS and told one of the communications operators to get in touch with Laureen and Sherri Deatherage Green. Sherri, a native of Roxton in East Texas, and a former *San Angelo Standard-Times* reporter, had been hired as our third public information officer in January 1995. I told the operator to ask them to go to the office as soon as they could and start helping with the media calls.

We've learned to expect a shock wave of media calls in the first few hours after big news involving the DPS breaks. Communication occurs at the speed of light, but it still takes time for reporters and TV camera crews to reach the scene of a breaking news story, assuming there is a scene to reach. Until the media gets to wherever the action is, if the DPS is involved, they depend on us for the initial information. If the immediate scene is not accessible to them, or the situation is tightly controlled (such as it was in Waco), the flow of media calls might slow slightly but stay fairly constant. My state credit card bill showed I made twenty-seven telephone calls from that pay phone in a three-hour period that Sunday afternoon.

During a break between telephone calls, I jokingly told a fellow dealer that maybe I'd better quit going to book shows, recalling how Linda and I had been at the Houston book show when shooting broke out at Mount Carmel four years earlier. That was on a Sunday. Now, it looked like the Republic of Texas situation had finally boiled over—also on a Sunday.

ABC News was insistent that I go on camera for them that afternoon. I patiently explained that I was in Dallas—more than halfway across the state from Fort Davis—and that I knew very little about what was going on.

"No problem," the caller said. "We just need someone on camera."

"Okay," I said, "I'm at a book show at the Market Hall here on the Stemmons Freeway. Tell your crew to check in where they're selling tickets and someone will come get me."

The network crew made it within a half hour or so. The cameraman did a tight shot of my face to de-emphasize the background of big buildings and traffic. A light rain was falling. As the camera rolled, Hallie watched the process and wandered around beneath the view of the video camera. Suddenly, we heard the screech of a car braking and skidding, followed by the crunch of bending metal and the tinkle of broken glass. Someone driving by had been watching the interview as well, instead of keeping his eyes on the car ahead of him.

On the way back to Austin, I managed to drive a bit more carefully than that rubbernecker in Dallas had. But though I kept my eyes on the road, my mind was on Fort Davis. Judging

from the news I was hearing over the radio, the deal amounted to more than a family spat. I began thinking of Waco.

McLaren, like Koresh, was already on the radio, making
demands. The only difference was that Koresh had been
allowed air time in the hope he would give himself up or at
least release the children in his compound. McLaren talked on
WOAI Radio in San Antonio, a clear-channel, 50,000-watt AM
station that can be heard over much of West Texas during the
day and over a large part of the nation at night. He told
reporter Tracee Evans that the "prisoners of war" would be
released if Republic of Texas prisoners were freed. These prisoners, he said, were a captain in the Republic's defense forces,
Robert Jonathan Scheidt, and Jo Ann Turner, the former ROT
official arrested in Austin the week before. Scheidt had been
arrested earlier Sunday in an incident that apparently had
escalated into the hostage situation now at hand.

But the release of the ROT members was not all McLaren
wanted: "We want them [the state] to . . . agree to a referen-
dum to allow Texans to vote on the independence issue."

Out in West Texas, Captain Caver also was thinking about
Waco. He had been there the day of the fire. If Koresh had
come out, Caver would have been in on his arrest. As it was,
Caver spent the night of April 19, 1993, on one of the grim-
mer assignments of his career—guarding with other Rangers
the still smoking remains of the compound and scores of
charred bodies.

No one working this Sunday afternoon, however, had
much time to dwell on their memories. In Austin, Laureen and
Sherri were busy trying to learn a little more about what was
going on. The couple being held was Joe and Margaret Ann
(known to her family and friends as "M.A.") Rowe, residents
of the Davis Mountains Resort.

McLaren and "White Eagle" were not the only ROT members talking to the media.

"The Rowes are prisoners of war," Richard Franklin Keyes
told a *Dallas Morning News* reporter. Keyes identified himself
as a "Defense Force officer" for the ROT. "They are not
hostages. This is a military operation. I was ordered to move
on this location, so I did."

Though only twenty-one, Keyes was cagey enough not to go into too many more details. Like a good soldier, or spokesman, he referred the reporter to "Ambassador" McLaren for answers to any further questions.

From the media standpoint, this was a dream story: Everyone was talking—the bad guys (with plenty of threatening rhetoric), the good guys (we weren't saying as much, of course), and virtually everyone else reporters could get in touch with who had some kind of take on the situation. Neighbors and various other county residents freely offered their comments.

Obligingly, McLaren faxed out a media release that night. The Rowes, he said, were "two state of Texas agents." The Davis Mountains Resort "has been sealed off by units of the Republic of Texas Defense Forces."

As Napoleon Bonaparte said, an army travels on its stomach, and out in Fort Davis, the ROT soldiers were getting hungry. The older of the soldiers, forty-six-year-old Gregg Paulson, asked Mrs. Rowe to fix them some lunch. She heated a plate of leftover lasagna.

Paulson was a tactician, not particularly interested in the exacting details of McLaren's legal-historical argument for Texas' return to its former status as an independent nation. But he certainly supported the general concept.

"If you're not willing to die for your freedom," he liked to say, "you don't deserve it."

He'd earned a GED (general educational development, recognized as the equivalent of a high school education) in the Army. After his separation from the service, he'd toured the country on a motorcycle, doing drugs. He married in 1975 and had four children, but got a divorce after having an affair. He drove a truck for a living and eventually turned to religion, later declaring: "I'm an old-fashioned Christian." He'd remarried in 1992. He and his wife, a tall, thin woman with short hair and round-lensed glasses, had drifted to Texas from New Mexico to join up with McLaren.

Now he considered himself a sergeant in the Republic of Texas Defense Forces, but he wore a long, very unmilitary beard. He was still a stickler for military discipline, however.

When Keyes responded to an order, he snapped out "Sir, yes *sir!*" And when he addressed his wife, it was as "Private Paulson."

After they ate, thirty-three-year-old Karen Paulson observed to Mrs. Rowe: "Boy, my mother is not going to be happy with me."

"I have daughters close to your age," Mrs. Rowe replied, "and let me tell you, no mother would be proud of what you're doing."

The third and youngest member of the occupation team was Keyes, wired up and agitated, just like McLaren. The Rowes felt he was dying to shoot someone.

"Boy, wait till they see this in Kansas," Keyes said at one point as they watched on CNN the news they were making. "They thought I was some kind of a nut, and I showed them."

The twenty-one-year-old was referring to the folks back in St. Marys, Kansas, population 1,700. Keyes was born in Traverse City, Michigan, the oldest of seven children. The former altar boy had been a good student but did not have very many friends. He was impressionable and got caught up in the militia movement. In February 1997 he had filed a document at the Shawnee County, Kansas, courthouse asserting that a portion of the state actually was part of the Republic of Texas. He had worked in a toilet manufacturing plant until quitting to move to Texas in early April to become one of McLaren's "soldiers."

Mrs. Rowe was beginning to think that Keyes wanted to kill her. Except for when she was allowed to go upstairs, he kept a pistol trained on her most of the time.

At one point that afternoon Mrs. Rowe came downstairs and found Keyes with his back to her, talking on the telephone. Her husband's 9mm was on the kitchen counter, within easy reach.

For an instant, she considered grabbing the gun. She might have an advantage over Keyes, but there were two other people with guns inside her home. She decided to leave the weapon where it was. Later, she learned that her instincts had served her well. The pistol had been unloaded by one of the intruders. If she had picked it up, she realized, Keyes might have used it as an excuse to shoot her. The tempting placement of the pistol might have been a setup.

While the Paulsons and Keyes held their position at RoweVista, McLaren and "White Eagle" kept talking to the media.

McLaren told a reporter for the *Houston Chronicle* that he had ordered militia members across Texas to start "picking up federal judges, legislators and IRS agents for immediate deportation. It's a blanket order for any foreigner found on the soil of Texas. . . ."

Even without all this willingness on the part of the participants to be quoted, the events alone made it a catchy story: A separatist group claiming it had taken military action. Two citizens being held captive after an armed attack on their home. Orders issued to "deport" federal judges. Law enforcement officers from all over that part of West Texas rushing to the scene. Was it the beginning of another Texas Revolution? The ROT people seemed to think so. I knew this was a story that had legs. It could end up being another Waco or a ready-made screenplay for a made-for-TV movie. At least no one had been seriously injured—yet.

Fittingly, considering how much I'd been thinking about Waco, on the way back to Austin from the book show Linda and I stopped there for supper. We ate at the venerable Elite Café on Waco's famous traffic circle, one of the few such early-day highway interchanges left in Texas. Elvis Presley once ate there.

If Elvis had not already been dead when the Cable News Network began around-the-clock coverage of major news events in 1982, someone at CNN would have come up with a screen graphic giving his death a handy title. At 11:22 P.M. EDT, CNN posted an illustrated story about the West Texas hostage-taking on its Website. Beneath the headline "One injured in separatist stand-off" was an image of the Republic of Texas seal with the word "Stand-off" partially superimposed over it. The event now had a name: The Republic of Texas Stand-off.

The plane leaves at 7:00 in the morning

Monday, April 28: Day Two

Nothing like a miserable night's sleep before a really big day. If there's ever a time a person needs seven or eight hours of blissful unconsciousness, it's the night before something important. But it seldom works out that way, at least not for me.

As soon as I was back in Austin Sunday night, I went straight to the office to see how things stood and to help Laureen and Sherri with calls. Laureen said Lieutenant Colonel Tommy Davis wanted me to call him at home. Davis had been promoted to second-in-command of the DPS when Colonel Thomas was named director of the agency in September 1996. He said the DPS plane was leaving for Alpine early the next morning. When I finally got home a little after 11:00 that night, Linda had repacked my bag.

"I've given you five days of clothes," she said. "If you're there longer than that, you'll have to find a laundry or I'll get some more clothes to you."

At the moment, though, I had more to worry about than what I'd be wearing. For one thing, I hadn't yet written my weekly book review column, which runs in the Austin newspaper and several others across the state. Normally, if I don't get a column finished during the weekend, I'll work on it early Monday morning and wrap it up when I come home for lunch. But in the morning, I would not have much time to work. At 7:00 I had to be at the State Aircraft Pooling Board, where the

DPS keeps its Austin-based Turbo-Commander. I knew if I wasn't at the airport on time, I'd be driving to Fort Davis instead of flying.

I've read somewhere that people actually get more sleep than they realize even when it seems like they tossed and turned all night. I hope that's the case, but I did not feel like I'd had any sleep at all. I was worried about the column. How could I get something written in the morning and still get to the airport on time? In my sleeplessness, I got an idea and started "writing" the column in my mind.

When I did doze off, I dreamed about being late for the flight to West Texas. Lateness is not a part of the DPS' culture. Several years earlier, after getting a call that a young Trooper had been shot in the head by a drunk outside Waco, I had raced to the airport from a Christmas party on the other side of town to fly there with then Lieutenant Colonel Wilson. Not having a cellular phone, I stopped somewhere and called the communications operator at our district office to have her relay that I was en route, but running a little late. When she passed on my ETA, I heard Wilson say over the radio: "Tell him to get his ass here in a hurry or we're leaving." Obviously upset over the critical injury of one of our Troopers, he forgot he was not talking over a Criminal Law Enforcement voice-privacy radio. I made the flight.

Around 4:30 Monday morning, I gave up on trying to get any more sleep, got out of bed, and went to the kitchen to flip the switch on the pot of coffee I'd built the night before. Out in my home office after the first cup, the words came easily. I liked what I had "written" during the night. Now, it was merely a matter of typing what I had composed in my head. I was through in a half hour.

I got to the Pooling Board shortly before 7:00. Even so, I was the last one there. Standing outside the twin-engine plane, a prize seized several years earlier from drug smugglers, were Chief Pilot Bill Isbell, Senior Ranger Captain Bruce Casteel, and Narcotics Lieutenant Doug Vance, newly named commander of the DPS SWAT team.

I stowed my bag in a compartment on the side of the plane, the agency's biggest and fastest aircraft, and went inside for one last pit stop before we took off. The coffee pot inside the Pooling Board building sure looked tempting. I definitely could have used another cup. But I remembered another DPS flight several years before and decided against it.

On that earlier occasion, a gas pipeline had exploded near Brenham in East Texas. Several people were injured and killed. I flew from Austin to Brenham in one of our single-engine planes, then transferred to our Houston-based helicopter on the tarmac. Right before leaving my office for the Austin airport, I had gulped down a freshly poured cup of coffee in what seemed like one swallow.

Not too long after takeoff from Austin, I had begun thinking about going to the bathroom—just a mild awareness of need, nothing that couldn't wait. After the transfer to the helicopter, during which there had been no time to duck inside a flight service building, my situation grew from awareness to desperation.

As my bladder filled to the point of urgency, I considered the possibilities: Losing control and achieving a permanent place in the agency's folklore as the first employee to wet his pants on a DPS helicopter or, to avoid embarrassment and to get relief, simply opening the door and jumping. That choice somehow seemed less horrible than the first. At least I'd feel better before I hit the ground.

The moment we landed, I unsnapped my shoulder harness, opened the door, ducked my head, and ran under the swirling rotors to the nearest cedar tree.

The media had been told that I was coming, and when they saw me get off the chopper in such a purposeful run, they figured something big was happening and gave chase. A close call, but I made it to the bush before ending up in an impromptu press conference with my pants unzipped. If any of the cameramen got any embarrassing video, they never tried to blackmail me with it.

"You should've said something" the pilot later shrugged, a note of surprise in his voice. "I would've landed in a field. Do it all the time."

But this morning, I didn't think it would go over too well with my fellow passengers for me to ask our chief pilot to put the plane down just so I could make a pit stop on the way to Alpine, the closest airport to Fort Davis. I would tough it out and do without coffee for a while.

"Where do we stand this morning?" I asked Casteel after he got buckled in.

The senior captain filled me in on the night's developments as we taxied toward the main runway.

"They got those hostages out early this morning," Casteel said.

Casteel, who'd gotten a rundown on the incident around 2:00 that morning, passed on what he'd learned from Caver.

The Midland Ranger captain had been in Jeff Davis County since about 2:00 Sunday afternoon. He'd flown in with Highway Patrol Captain David Baker. When they got to the scene, Caver found that law enforcement officers who had rushed to the area from surrounding counties had sealed off the road leading to the Rowes' house. A volunteer firefighter trained as a paramedic had walked up the road to drop off a medical kit so Mrs. Rowe, herself a trained emergency medical technician, could provide first aid to her injured husband. But no other action had been taken. At the request of Sheriff Bailey, Caver took charge.

A command post was taking shape in the guest house on the Paradise Mountain Ranch, an 11,000-acre working cattle and goat ranch 1.4 miles past the stone gate Davis Mountains Resort entrance off Highway 166. Mary Lynn (Rusty) Wofford, whose family has had the ranch for four generations, and her husband John, a Border Patrol supervisor, also operate a bed-and-breakfast at the ranch.

Though the midday attack had come at the Rowes' residence, the Woffords knew their ranch also was on McLaren's short list of military targets. The Woffords and McLaren had already been fighting for years—at the courthouse. It had cost the couple $100,000 and twelve years of worry to fight off claims by McLaren that their ranch had been incorrectly surveyed and should in fact belong to him, not them. On September 17, 1996, the Woffords had finally prevailed in state district court, but McLaren had ignored a judgment ordering him to pay the Woffords' legal fees.

From the guest house command post, Caver telephoned the Rowe residence.

Keyes, who in a couple hours' time had already made more than two dozen long distance calls from the Rowes' phone to various militia members across the country, answered the phone.

"We're here, we've got these people and we're not mistreating them," he told the Ranger captain. "Their injuries aren't serious."

"What do you want for the hostages?" Caver asked.

Keyes did not like the word "hostages."

He blustered: "They're prisoners of war. You've got one of ours. Now we've got one of yours."

Their discussion continued through the afternoon and into the evening. Though Caver was solidly in command of the law enforcement officers on the scene, no one inside the Rowes' house seemed to want to be in charge. Despite that, it began to look like swapping Scheidt—the man arrested earlier that day by Sheriff Bailey—for the Rowes would be acceptable to the ROT. Caver sent two Rangers to the jail in Marfa to get Scheidt and bring him back to the command post at the Wofford Ranch.

At first, however, Scheidt declined being exchanged.

Jake Brisbin, Presidio County judge, spent about twenty minutes talking philosophy with the prisoner. "I suggested to him," the judge later recalled, "that there are a few times in people's lives that they can step up and do the right thing."

Scheidt finally agreed, saying that he did not want to see the Rowes get hurt. He was driven to the Wofford Ranch by the Rangers. Taken into the command post with a hood over his head so he could not see anything that might later prove useful information for his colleagues, he said he wanted his knife and guns returned. The Ranger captain said no, he could have his impounded van and other possessions back, but not the weapons.

Caver consulted with Casteel, Lieutenant Colonel Davis, and the FBI. They all agreed that swapping Scheidt for the Rowes made sense. Given Rowe's medical history, everyone was concerned that he might have another heart attack.

Late that night, the details were finally worked out. Scheidt was free to go if the Rowes were released. Since the Rowes already were in their own home, their "release" amounted to the gunmen leaving the residence. Scheidt drove up in his van from the Wofford Ranch.

Caver kept the Rowes on the phone line so they could alert him if the ROT "soldiers" went back on their agreement and stayed in RoweVista despite Scheidt's release. But the three intruders soon left the Rowes' house and got in the Volkswagen.

Followed by Scheidt, they drove away from the house, presumably heading back to McLaren's trailer. Left behind was the white ROT station wagon, its tires flattened by Keyes' gunshots. Then Sheriff Bailey and an FBI agent, followed by an ambulance staffed by two volunteer fire department emergency medical technicians, drove up to the house. Covered by Rangers and other officers, they got the Rowes out of their house. Rowe, his wife by his side, was rushed by ambulance to Big Bend Memorial Hospital in Alpine.

I took notes on all this and then read that morning's *Austin American-Statesman*. The banner story was the standoff. A striking color photograph showed a Trooper, a rifle slung over his shoulder, standing at a roadblock. When I finished reading the stories, I passed the newspaper on to Lieutenant Vance, who studied the schematic map of the resort produced by the newspaper's graphics department.

Though Casteel was relieved that the hostages had been freed, he worried that an even worse situation was developing.

"Barry says we've still got dozens of residents back in that resort," he said. "They're all potential hostages. We've got to get those folks out of there and find out for sure where the Republic of Texas people went after they left the Rowes' house."

Our flight to San Antonio took only twenty-five minutes. At San Antonio International Airport, we picked up U.S. Marshal Jack Dean, retired captain of Ranger Company D and Casteel's old boss. Dean's office held the federal contempt citation for McLaren.

At the flight service terminal, Casteel got a cup of coffee.

The steaming black liquid looked wonderful, but I held firm. I was determined not to be the cause of an emergency landing.

Back in the air, headed west, Marshal Dean told us a federal grand jury in the Northern District of Texas had been investigating McLaren and his fifty-year-old wife, Evelyn, in connection with their issuance of bogus Republic of Texas money orders. He said indictments were anticipated. I remembered reading a newspaper story in January that reported Evelyn McLaren had ignored an order to appear before a federal grand jury in Dallas. Evelyn, the former wife of a friend of McLaren's, had become McLaren's common-law wife in 1996. She had two grown children by a previous marriage. A U.S. Postal Service employee, she had commuted between Fort Worth and Fort Davis on weekends until her retirement January 24. Now she lived with McLaren at the "embassy" in Jeff Davis County.

Since the marshal held the contempt citation for McLaren, his deputies had been keeping close tabs on the "ambassador's" activities, hoping for a chance to arrest him without incident. One of the things they had been observing was the shopping habits of the occupants of the ROT "embassy." McLaren did not venture out, but since they had to eat, others did, including Evelyn McLaren. Unless they had stocked up recently, Dean said, McLaren probably did not have enough food for a long siege.

A tired Captain Caver met us at the Alpine airport.

I loaded my gear into the back of a Suburban belonging to Ken Clouse, an investigator for District Attorney Albert Valadez of Fort Stockton. Valadez' 83rd Judicial District covers a huge hunk of the Trans-Pecos, including Jeff Davis County. If any criminal cases came out of the unfolding situation in Fort Davis, he'd be the prosecutor.

We drove to the new Ramada Limited motel on the western edge of Alpine for a scheduled 9:00 briefing and planning session for all the agencies involved. Except during hunting season, I doubt Alpine had ever seen so many men and women with guns at one time—at least not since bandit raids along the border during the Mexican Revolution brought a full American military mobilization in the Big Bend. The motel's

conference room was standing room only: FBI, green-uni-
formed Border Patrol agents, Highway Patrol officers, locals,
and state and federal prosecutors.

I grabbed a muffin and a cup of coffee—finally—and took
a seat in the middle of a long conference table. Except for the
attorneys, I was the only civilian in the crowd. As a DPS
employee, I had every right to be there, but I felt like a
reporter who'd snuck in on a closed meeting and was afraid
someone would recognize him and throw him out. I wanted to
be invisible. Since I couldn't disappear, I stayed as low key as
possible. I figured any second someone would ask me to leave.

An FBI agent from El Paso opened the briefing. The FBI
stood ready to do everything it could to help, he said. The
agent then introduced Jeff Davis County's tall sheriff, forty-six-
year-old Steve Bailey.

Though just beginning his first term as a sheriff, Bailey
had been in law enforcement since 1978. He'd started his
career as a deputy sheriff in Reeves County, where he'd grown
up. Then he'd worked as a deputy and later chief deputy in
Presidio County. In November the voters of Jeff Davis County
had decided he'd make a good sheriff. With only two deputies,
Bailey stayed busy. Being sheriff means more than forty hours
a week, though he'd been around long enough to know that
already. This morning he looked and sounded tired. It had
been a rough weekend.

Bailey took it from the top. The fatigue made his words
come slowly.

On Saturday, the sheriff told us, Joe Rowe had called him
to report that he had seen three people in camouflage and carrying assault rifles on a hill across the road from his house.
Using a rifle scope, they'd been looking directly at his house.
When Rowe and his son, who happened to be visiting, got in
his pickup and drove toward them, the three scrambled off the
hill and drove off in a white van. Rowe suspected they were
Republic of Texas followers, since the van did not have license
plates.

Bailey went to the resort and drove around, but did not
see the van or anyone who looked suspicious. He left the area.
That night Rowe called again, wanting something done about

the encroachment of his property rights. The sheriff explained he'd looked for the people Rowe had described but had been unable to find them.

Sunday morning, Bailey got another call from Rowe. The trespassers were back, walking around on his property and land owned by his neighbor, Dan Alexander. A short time later, Alexander's wife phoned the sheriff and said the people were on her property. She and her husband wanted to file trespassing charges against them. Then, about 11:15 A.M., Rowe called again. A white van driven by one of the trespassers had passed his place, apparently headed toward Fort Davis.

Bailey dressed and drove south of town on Highway 17 toward its intersection with 166, the road that leads to the Davis Mountains Resort. At the intersection, about two miles from town, the sheriff spotted the van that Rowe had described.

"I stopped it for speeding and ended up arresting the driver for trespassing and unlawfully carrying weapons," Bailey continued his account to us. The driver, forty-three-year-old Robert Jonathan Scheidt, had a pistol, a Bowie knife, and an AK-47 in his vehicle. The rifle, a semi-automatic, was legal. The pistol and the knife, which had a blade longer than six inches, were not.

Bailey knew McLaren and his colleagues had scanners which they used to monitor local and state law enforcement frequencies. The driver was using a two-way radio in the van when Bailey first approached the vehicle. What the sheriff didn't know was what response the arrest would trigger.

Up in the distant mountains, the ROT "embassy" had picked up Bailey's radio traffic when he stopped Scheidt. At the same time, in Presidio County, a deputy investigating the discovery of a dead body had called for a coroner. Though the death turned out to be from natural causes—and had absolutely nothing to do with anything going on in Jeff Davis County—someone at the "embassy" connected the two radio transmissions and reached a faulty conclusion: The sheriff had not only stopped a Republic of Texas "captain," but he had killed him!

Texas Parks and Wildlife Department Game Warden Randall Brown had stopped by to back up the sheriff when the

Presidio County dispatcher broke on the air with an urgent broadcast not often heard in that part of Texas: "Shots fired! Hostages. Ten-thirty-three! Davis Mountains Resort."

Ten-thirty-three was not the time of day. It is a law enforcement code meaning "emergency, respond quickly."

The sheriff asked Brown to transport Scheidt to the Marfa jail. The misdemeanor arrest he'd just made was no longer a priority. As soon as the game warden had custody of Scheidt, Bailey sped toward the resort. The Presidio County dispatcher was now putting out a general call for assistance from any law enforcement officers in the area.

Bailey knew that McLaren back in February had faxed militia groups a battle plan that called for taking the Rowe residence, the Wofford Ranch, and the county courthouse. Now it looked like McLaren had started executing that plan.

When Bailey concluded his briefing and sat down, Captain Caver outlined his actions of the night before. Like Casteel, his concern was that McLaren might decide to collect more hostages. Another possibility, though remote, was that McLaren might try to attack the Wofford Ranch. But the easiest thing for McLaren to do, if he were so inclined, was take some new prisoners. The DPS, working with the sheriff, would concentrate on securing the rest of the resort.

The meeting ended with the understanding that the DPS would handle the situation, with assistance from Sheriff Bailey and other area officers. The FBI and Border Patrol also would do all they could to help, from information-sharing to providing officers for additional firepower. The U.S. Attorney's Office, meanwhile, would be looking for a federal "nexus"— possible federal charges in connection with the incident the day before.

I didn't hear anything during the meeting that led me to think I would be able to return to Austin that night, unless the people who had held the Rowes captive decided to surrender. As soon as the meeting ended, I followed Rule Number One for an out-of-town crisis situation, learned years ago when I'd spent a couple of nights getting what sleep I could on the ground in front of the prison administration building in Huntsville: Get a motel room before you do anything else. Of course, the FBI agents who'd flown in that morning had been through a few crises themselves. All the motel had left was a specially equipped room for the physically handicapped. I took it. Other than a wider door and a detachable shower head, the manager said apologetically, it wasn't different from any of the other rooms.

Room key card in hand, I called to check in with my office. Laureen said Lieutenant Colonel Davis needed to talk with me, and she transferred my call into his office. He said that Governor Bush's office was anxious that I do a press briefing as soon as possible, particularly to address questions that had already come up about why the Rangers had traded a prisoner for two hostages. The colonel did not want me to make too big a point about it, but suggested I point out that Scheidt would have been released from jail on bail before long anyway. In effect, all that had been done was move Scheidt's release time up a bit. And possibly save a man's life.

I called Laureen back.

"Put out a media advisory that I'll be having a press conference at two o'clock," I told her. Then I filled her in on the meeting that had just ended.

Casteel told Vance to head his SWAT team toward Alpine. Chief Pilot Isbell would fly back to Austin to pick up most of the team. The rest would drive their van and special equipment out.

After a quick stop for hamburgers, Caver drove Casteel and me out to the resort. I've made the drive many times, and I'm never any less impressed with the beauty of the winding highway between Alpine and Fort Davis. For me, every time is like seeing it for the first time.

Caver took us straight to the Rowe residence, an attractive two-level house with lots of square feet of energy-efficient double-insulated glass overlooking the winding, unpaved road that is the principal thoroughfare in the resort. McLaren's lieutenant, "White Eagle," had supposedly suggested RoweVista would make a fine headquarters for the Republic. After seeing it, I agreed with him—at least to the extent that it was a nice place.

Ranger Sergeant Duncan was wrapping up the crime scene work when we got there. He walked us through the front portion of the house, showing us the path of the three shots and the damage the rifle rounds had caused. The floor around the door was covered with broken glass. If three small pieces of lead could cause this much destruction to glass and wood, I did not want to think what they could have done to a human body. Rowe had been very lucky. The Rowes' uninvited guests had pretty well trashed the place during their twelve-hour stay, but inanimate objects could always be repaired or replaced.

As soon as I had a feel for how the attack had taken place, I told Casteel I needed to get back to the command post. He and Caver were not to the point where they could leave yet, but he asked another Ranger to drive me back to the Wofford Ranch. From there, I rode with one of the Safety Education Troopers to the media checkpoint.

We'd passed through the media encampment on our way in with Caver. It was located at a local landmark known as the Point of Rocks, a roadside park adjacent to a spectacular mini-mountain of boulders off State 166, a little more than three miles from the Wofford Ranch. The collection of satellite trucks and vans was not yet quite as large as it had been outside Waco, but it was an impressive array of high-tech media equipment, particularly superimposed as it was over the beautiful, wide-open landscape. The scene was incongruous, as alien as the Apollo spacecraft on the surface of the moon. Only here there were many "spacecraft," all with their transmission discs trained heavenward. At times over the next few days, I'd wonder whether any intelligent lifeforms were present.

Armed with only three 8½ x 11 pages of notes, I held my promised 2:00 briefing an hour late. It had taken longer than I expected to pull enough information together to make a press conference worthwhile.

The first point I made was that, at the request of Sheriff Bailey, the DPS had taken over as the lead agency. The FBI, Border Patrol, and the U.S. Marshal's Service were lending assistance, I announced, but the DPS would be running things. Remembering Waco, it felt good to say that.

Then I described the attack on the Rowe residence, based on what I'd learned from the sheriff and Captain Caver. I told it pretty much like I'd heard it, leaving out only one choice tidbit: As the ROT members left the Rowe home, they asked the Rowes to videotape them! The ROT "soldiers" apparently thought this would be evidence of the military nature of the action they had taken. I decided not to talk about that because I knew the next question the reporters would ask: Can we have a copy of the tape? The tape and video camera had been collected as evidence, of course, and could not have been released. I later learned the camera did not belong to the Rowes. It had been loaned to them several weeks earlier by the producers of a tabloid television show that needed some video for a story on the Republic of Texas movement and McLaren's refusal to come out of his mountain "embassy."

Felony charges were being readied against at least three people, I told the reporters at the briefing. I promised that I'd release the names of the suspects and the charges as soon as I got the information. Meanwhile, I continued, Caver was continuing to talk with McLaren.

The news media, as the expression goes, abhors a vacuum. Even when there is no solid information to report, air time and newsprint still must be filled. People with a background in whatever the particular area of interest of the moment is —war, terrorism, law enforcement, politics—are sought out to publicly express their opinion on a given situation or action taken. Sometimes these people are paid consultants. (A consultant, the late Texas publisher Frank Wardlaw once said, is someone who knows a thousand ways to make love but doesn't know any women.) Others gladly appear on television or allow themselves to be quoted for free. We saw it during the Gulf War, during and after Waco, after Oklahoma City, during the O.J. Simpson trial, and after the Olympic Park bombing in Atlanta in 1996. Already, the "experts" were being consulted by the broadcast media for their assessment of the DPS decision to swap a man arrested for misdemeanors for two hostages, one of them having a heart condition.

The spin from the Monday morning quarterbacks: The DPS had violated conventional wisdom by acceding to the demands of terrorists.

While I did not want to appear to be criticizing those

who—from a safe distance and after a good night's sleep—
were second-guessing Captain Caver's actions, we wanted to
make sure the public understood why Scheidt was released:

1. Two innocent citizens were being held at gunpoint in
their own home. Saving lives is more important than the
appearance of having given in to terrorists.

2. The person released in exchange for the Rowes had not
yet even had any criminal charges filed against him. As
soon as he was named in any misdemeanor complaints, he
would have been able to get out of jail on bond for a few
hundred dollars.

3. After the exchange, Scheidt returned to McLaren's trailer. Considering the scores of law enforcement officers on
the scene, for all practical purposes that amounted to a
continuation of his arrest. He was not likely to be going
anywhere.

I also announced that more DPS personnel were en route,
including our SWAT team. The plane I'd flown out on had
returned to Austin and was already on its way back to Alpine
with most members of the team. The others were headed west
to Fort Davis in the unit's equipment and communications van.

Casteel and Caver realized there was too much distance
between the command post at the Wofford Ranch and the ROT
property—seven miles. After studying aerial and topographic
maps of the area, they decided to advance up the road to the
Davis Mountains Resort Volunteer Fire Department, about five
and a half miles from the Wofford Ranch. This would be much
closer to McLaren, and would effectively cut him off from all but
about a dozen of the houses in the resort. Though most of the
residents had voluntarily left, some remained and Casteel was
still worried about the possibility of another hostage situation.

With the FBI and Border Patrol SWAT teams standing by
in case of trouble, the DPS SWAT team and a group of Rangers
started working their way up the road that evening. Highway
Patrol Troopers followed to take control of each intersection
they passed.

I sat in the command post and listened to their radio traf-

fic as the officers moved closer and closer to their objective.
By dark, the fire hall had been reclaimed without incident. The
DPS now had officers within a mile and a half of the ROT
property.

At my evening briefing, shortly before 10:00 P.M., I
released the names of six people the DA's office had filed
charges on that afternoon:

- The Paulsons and Keyes had been charged with two
counts of aggravated kidnaping and one count each of
engaging in organized criminal activity.
- McLaren, Otto, and Scheidt had been charged with
engaging in organized criminal activity.

Both crimes, I explained, were first-degree felonies, pun-
ishable by five to ninety-nine years or life in prison and a
$10,000 fine.

As I fielded questions, I could tell that some of the young
television reporters rushed to Fort Davis by their stations did
not know all that much about Texas' criminal justice system.
Some, I suspected, were not even entirely sure what the difference was between a misdemeanor and a felony. Though
anyone who has ever read about a missing child on a milk car-
ton knows about kidnaping, some of the journalists seemed a
bit unfamiliar with the other charge now pending against
McLaren and the others. By filing on McLaren, Otto, and
Scheidt and the three kidnaping suspects for engaging in organized criminal activity, the DA's office was not alleging they
belonged to the Mafia, despite the buzz word "organized" pre-
ceding the word "criminal." All it meant was that the six were
alleged to have jointly engaged in a crime. Three or more people could steal a car and be charged with engaging in organized criminal activity.

The lesson in jurisprudence over with, I announced that
the Red Cross was setting up a shelter for displaced Davis
Mountains Resort residents at the Fort Davis High School
gym. They were unloading enough equipment to handle fifty
to sixty people, I said.

Meanwhile, Captain Caver was continuing to talk on the
telephone with McLaren, though nothing of substance had

come of it. Also, apparently unknown to McLaren, Paulson was talking to the Rangers from another phone. He was acting a bit more reasonable than McLaren, and Caver was hopeful he might decide to give up.

Predictably, the reporters were pressing me to say what the DPS intended to do—take the ROT enclave by force or wait them out. Frankly, the DPS did not yet have any specific plan, other than containment, intelligence gathering, and negotiation. And I certainly wasn't going to publicize that basic strategy.

"We think we can do the right thing," I generalized, refusing to go into anything more specific. "We're hoping we can resolve it peacefully."

Our best estimate at the time was that thirteen people were at the ROT encampment, I said. But the only ones we were interested in were those named in the felony complaints.

Asked if the DPS had any indication that other armed groups were headed to West Texas in response to McLaren's militaristic rhetoric, I said the only people being drawn by that talk were police officers and reporters. "We've had no indication whatsoever that there is any [other] interest in Mr. McLaren's activities."

Not long after I got back to the command post, I heard that two ROT members had surrendered about 9:15 P.M. I figured it might have been the Paulsons, since Gregg Paulson had been talking separately to the Rangers. Fortunately, I didn't rush to a telephone and release that information, because a short time later I learned it was just a rumor. Nothing of the sort had happened.

I stayed around the command post until I felt safe that nothing else was going to happen that night and then went back to Alpine to try to get some sleep.

About the time I left for Alpine, a lawyer from Houston, Terrence O'Rourke, showed up at the media checkpoint. He said he represented McLaren and wanted to talk with him. A Trooper excused himself to check by radio with the command post. While O'Rourke identified himself to the reporters who had gathered around, the command post radioed the checkpoint that O'Rourke should come back in the morning.

O'Rourke told reporters the situation should be settled in court, not "in the mountains with guns." He said that he had talked to McLaren by telephone earlier in the day, and that "he understands that this is a very dangerous situation." Even so, O'Rourke continued, "It's clear to me they are prepared to fight. He did indicate they are well-armed."

With that, O'Rourke left to get some sleep. That was the same thing I had in mind.

Saving America from
New World Order tyranny

Tuesday, April 29: Day Three

The smell of the ashes of Mount Carmel in the figurative sense hung over the Davis Mountains as heavily as the pollution that blows up from Mexico.

I had certainly not mentioned the word "Waco" in any of my media briefings, but the word—and the tragedy it had unfortunately become symbolic of—was on my mind and just about everyone else's, particularly those in the media.

The media's mind-set was evident from their line of questioning:

- "Are there any children in the embassy?"
- "Is the ATF involved?"
- "What kind of weapons does McLaren have?"

"Nobody wants another Waco," O'Rourke had said late the night before, summarizing everyone's thinking.

The number of people involved in this incident was smaller, and so far no one had been killed or even seriously injured. Rowe, in fact, had already been released from the hospital in Alpine. But certainly, there were parallels with the scenario in McLennan County four years earlier. And now another: A Houston lawyer was about to become a central figure in the negotiations.

In Waco, the man with the bar card had been attorney Dick DeGuerin of Houston. Now it was O'Rourke, a colleague of DeGuerin's.

139

The fifty-year-old lawyer, while not as well known as DeGuerin, had an impressive resume. He'd been a Senate page in Washington. As quarterback of his high school football team, he won the nickname "El Tigre," The Tiger. With a master's degree from Houston's prestigious Rice University, he went to law school at the University of Texas at Austin. He worked as an assistant attorney general in Austin and for a time was counsel to the U.S. Department of Energy. After a decade as a prosecutor with the Harris County Attorney's office, O'Rourke moved into private practice, specializing in environmental law.

He'd met McLaren several years before, O'Rourke said, when he went to Fort Davis with former Harris County Attorney Mike Driscoll, who owned property there. When the stand-off began, McLaren called O'Rourke and asked if he'd represent him.

Like McLaren, O'Rourke had political aspirations, but within the framework of the existing government. Though he found McLaren's interpretation of history interesting, he had no separatist leanings. He'd lost three political campaigns, trying unsuccessfully for a post on the Texas Railroad Commission, a district judgeship, and the job as Harris County attorney.

If District Attorney Albert Valadez, the other lawyer who would figure in the stand-off, has a nickname, I never heard it. The youthful looking forty-year-old grew up in San Angelo, where his father was a salesman and restaurant worker. The DA and I hit it off right away. When he said he was from San Angelo, I told him I'd worked for the newspaper there for a couple of years starting in 1967.

"When I was a kid," Valadez said, "I used to go to the *Standard-Times* when Santa Claus would throw candy from the roof of the newspaper."

"Guess who was throwing the candy?" I laughed, explaining that in addition to the person in a Santa suit the whole staff climbed up on the roof to toss candy.

Valadez went to law school at Texas Southern University in Houston, where he graduated in 1983. Nine years later, he was appointed DA when his predecessor became a state appeals court judge. In 1994 Valadez was elected to a full term. He carried four of the six counties in his sprawling district. His opponent was Ken DeHart, now the district judge. Two years later, Valadez was reelected.

I soon realized that anyone who figured Valadez for being a naive, inexperienced prosecutor would be making a bad mistake.

Shortly after 9:00 that morning, O'Rourke was allowed past the checkpoint to meet with Caver and Valadez in the guest house/command post at the Wofford Ranch. The state's position was simple: Felony arrest warrants had been signed for six people believed to be in the ROT enclave. Caver wanted them out of there and in jail. O'Rourke wanted his client to have his day in court, which amounted to the same thing. Neither side wanted any shooting.

Also present this morning was Robert Holt of Midland, a longtime friend of former President George Bush and his son, the governor of Texas. Holt was one of three members of the Public Safety Commission, the policy-setting body which oversees the DPS. The commissioners, appointed by the governor and confirmed by the state Senate, serve staggered terms and are the ones with the power to hire or fire the director and assistant director.

Caver decided to let O'Rourke talk with McLaren. To preserve the confidentiality of the lawyer-client privilege, an old-fashioned communications system was devised. McLaren and O'Rourke began calling it a "diplomatic pouch." Occasionally, over the next few days, I would slip and call it that too. But I tried to stick with the simple description of "packet," since I was constantly repeating my message that the DPS was not interested in matters of international law, only in the service of felony arrest warrants. In reality, the pouch was a United Parcel Service bag turned inside out, made "official" by gold foil bearing the Republic of Texas seal.

While the goal of Caver, Valadez, and O'Rourke was simple, even though each viewed it from different perspectives, McLaren's was not. He wanted something big, some kind of well-publicized hearing on his separatist thesis.

At one point, Commissioner Holt told me McLaren wanted to be taken to Washington to appear before a federal judge in the District of Columbia. Holt even discussed with Judge

Bunton the possibility of a federal judge flying from Washington to meet with McLaren in an Alpine courtroom.

Using the "diplomatic" packet, McLaren had one of his followers leave a "cease-fire" proposal and some supporting documents in the road some distance down from the ROT enclave. Members of the SWAT team picked it up.

As my office worked to keep the world informed of the latest developments in Jeff Davis County, McLaren continued reporting his own take on the situation. At 10:00 that morning, using either a cellular or satellite telephone, he put a three-paragraph message on the ROT Webpage:

> Last night the blood of Texas was warmed by the support of our fellow Americans who have joined with us in a bold move to take back America for the People and not the UN or the One World Government. The word on the shortwave was that if these UN, US, Inc., and STATE OF TEXAS, INC. agents violate this diplomatic mission's sovereign immunity . . . that the People's militia of America will issue a joint declaration of war. . . .

McLaren said he understood "that over 5,000 Texan militia and Republic Defense Force units are in the field [and that] hundreds of support units are moving from all areas of the soil of Texas." Then he sought to place things in perspective, at least his perspective: "Joe Rowe and Sheriff Bailey may go down in history, as having inadvertently set off the liberation of America from New World Order tyranny for a personal vendetta and fictitious speeding charge."

The self-styled ambassador was correct that armed men and women were headed toward Fort Davis. But they were additional law enforcement officers and Texas Army Guard personnel, not ROT sympathizers. It already looked like a law enforcement conference had convened on the Wofford Ranch. FBI and Border Patrol agents in desert camouflage draped with leafy netting seemed to be everywhere. I began to wonder if all the tumbleweeds I was seeing were really tumbleweeds.

"You can't even pee on a bush out here," I jokingly told Laureen when I called the office to check in. "It might be an FBI agent."

Numerous civilian support personnel also were on hand or en route. At the same time, some officers were leaving. Washington had decided there was not sufficient basis for a heavy FBI or Border Patrol presence. Local agents and several members of the bureau's Critical Incident Response Group, Crisis Management Unit, including chief negotiator Special Agent Gary Noesner, would remain. But the bureau's Hostage Rescue Team folks, along with the Border Patrol's SWAT team, were ordered out.

I also was calling for reinforcements. By now, it was clear that the situation was not going to be resolved immediately. I had told Laureen before I left Austin that if the stand-off evolved into a protracted situation, I'd want her to join me in Fort Davis. If it went on for a long time, I'd rotate in Sherri. But Sherri and her husband had a son in kindergarten. Traveling would be harder on her than Laureen, whose family consisted of a husband, a part-Labrador retriever, and four adopted greyhounds. When I saw no signs of a big break on the third day of the stand-off, I called Laureen and told her to get to Fort Davis as soon as she could. She booked a commercial flight to Midland that would leave Austin during the noon hour.

About the time Laureen was on her way to the airport, two large truck-trailers carrying armored personnel carriers drove up to the media checkpoint. This added to the media's— and through it, the general public's—vision of another Waco taking shape. But there were major differences, though the media did not immediately piece them together. For one thing, the APCs were not from the Texas National Guard and certainly not the regular Army, as had been the case in Waco. The thirteen-ton tracked vehicles had been purchased by Sheriff J.B. Smith of Smith County in Tyler with seized drug money. They were civilian law enforcement vehicles, named Bubba One (the words "knock, knock" were painted in white on its front and "Have a nice day!" on its back end) and Bubba Two. And for another, there is a lot of difference between an APC and the tanks which the FBI used at Waco.

An hour and a half after his first Web posting that morning, McLaren put up this short bulletin:

Word just reached us that they are moving APC into our area. National Guard units are now involved so Governor Bush (or his daddy) has issued the order to wipe us out. More later if possible.

"White Eagle" Otto, too, was speaking out to the media. He dictated terms to the Associated Press: "All they have to do is withdraw," he said. "If they withdraw, the defense force of the Republic . . . will stand down. It's very simple. And then there will not be any bloodshed. Surrender is not an option."

Captain Caver and others in the DPS were concerned that the rhetoric of McLaren and Otto might draw some support. The FBI and DPS Special Crimes Service investigators were working hard to gather intelligence on any possible movements of militia toward Jeff Davis County. Several times I noticed Midland-based Special Crimes Captain Larry Benningfield looking worried as he read a freshly arrived fax or took down information over the phone. I didn't ask questions, but I'm a pretty good poker player. I can read faces.

Even if McLaren had reinforcements galloping to his rescue, I knew it would take them a while to reach Jeff Davis County.

The reporters camping out at "Mount Media" could see the mountains and miles of open country as well as I could, but I don't think most of them really appreciated at first just how close to the frontier this part of Texas still is.

For one thing, I doubt if many of them knew that inside of a year, eighteen mountain lions had been killed on the Wofford Ranch in a war much more real than the conflict McLaren was threatening. These big cats—once virtually trapped out but now almost as common as they were in frontier times—live off deer and livestock, particularly young kids. (Note: I'm talking about baby goats, not human children, though mountain lions do occasionally attack children and even adults.) Wofford's son told me they found 150 dead goats in a pen one morning, victims of a rampaging mountain lion. These natural predators are not considered an endangered species, but if a rancher catches one in his rifle sights, that particular cat is likely to lose all nine lives at once.

The only semi-close call anyone with the DPS had with one of the cats during the siege came one night when a Trooper assigned to one of the more remote checkpoints stepped off into the brush to answer a call of nature, no Porta-potty being handy. As he stood in the dark, he noticed two yellow eyes regarding him. The Trooper and the cat held their respective ground with no harm done.

It's not that West Texas ranchers don't think mountain lions (also known as cougars or pumas) are magnificent creatures. It's a matter of economics. Not only do the big cats kill ranchers' livestock, they also hunt and kill mule deer. Though deer are publicly owned game animals, ranchers can charge hunters for access to their lands. The sale of hunting leases can be a significant part of a ranch owner's income.

In addition to whatever mule deer the mountain lions have not killed, wild turkey (also highly sought game) wander in the rugged canyons of the Davis Mountains. Antelope range the flatlands between the rocky mountains. Bear, once common in the mountains but for generations virtually extinct, seem to be making a comeback along with the mountain lions. The popular theory is that the bears, like the mountain lions, are propagating in the vast Big Bend National Park, where they are protected. Some of the bears, and a lot of the cats, eventually move on to new country outside the park. Bear tracks have been sighted on the Wofford Ranch, but no bears have been seen on the place. The summer before, however, someone had shot and killed a bear that made the mistake of wandering onto Alpine's golf course.

Bobcats also are as common on the ranch as their big cousins, the mountain lion. One of the Troopers told me he'd heard from Wofford's son that their family cat had been cornered by an amorous bobcat. The assault produced a litter of pointy-eared kittens with mean dispositions. After the incident, the mama cat didn't venture outside for two years.

Rattlesnakes, lizards, and hairy-legged tarantulas added to the excitement during the siege. I saw a big rattler crossing the road during one of my trips between the forward command post at the fire hall and the Wofford Ranch. I would not have been surprised to learn an officer had been bitten by a snake during the siege, but none were.

One Trooper did take a large tarantula into custody. He put the Texas-size spider in a box he labeled "Live Animal," saying, "I'm going to take it home for my kids."

While the capture of the tarantula offered a welcome break in the tedium, I had my own live animals to worry about. As I had promised the day before, I arranged for a pool of reporters and still and video photographers to get a little closer to the scene of action. I tried not to be too dogmatic and kept my rules simple: Don't bother the officers or try for any audio.

As I drove with a carful of reporters and cameramen toward the command post, followed by SES Troopers with two other media groups, I chatted amicably—until I happened to look into the rearview mirror. When I did, I saw that despite what I'd just requested, a cameraman from ABC News was rolling as I talked. I stopped the car and said I was ending the pool immediately if he didn't stop. This wasn't an interview situation, I said, since that would not be fair to the other reporters, even though they were supposed to pool their footage. One of the other TV reporters in the group came to my defense.

"Come on, man," he told the cameraman. "Don't act like that."

The ABC man apologized, and I resumed the tour.

The photographers got some good shots: A DPS helicopter landed nearby, officers in camouflage carrying mean-looking weapons strode around, the National Guard had set up tents and generators. The video they got illustrated very well that this was becoming a large-scale operation.

Indeed, the stand-off story had made page one of that morning's *New York Times* and most other newspapers. *Times* reporter Sam Howe Verhovek wrote that "Mike Cox, a spokesman for the Texas Department of Public Safety, defended the decision by a state negotiator to return . . . Scheidt. . . . He said the safety of the couple [the Rowes] had been paramount." I was even more pleased with a sidebar to that story: "Swap to Free 2 Hostages Was Right, Experts Say." After reading the two stories, I felt as if I'd succeeded in getting my point across about the exchange the Ranger captain had engineered.

Though pleased, the little victory reminded me of something that had happened more than twenty-five years earlier. I was police reporter for the afternoon newspaper in Austin, working for the late Jim Berry, an old-style, hard-drinking, tough-guy city editor. A University of Texas co-ed had committed suicide spectacularly by jumping from the twenty-eight-story UT Tower, a city landmark. I rushed to the scene, got the details, and wrote the banner story on the incident for that day's afternoon newspaper. When I came to work the next morning, I found a terse, typewritten note on my typewriter: "Nice job on the jumper. But that was yesterday."

In an ongoing situation like the Republic of Texas stand-off, there is little opportunity to rest on laurels. I had an afternoon briefing to do.

Despite the buildup of personnel and equipment, I was hopeful that the situation would not drag on much longer. As I approached the stand of microphones, I heard a low but distinct "*mooooooooooo*" coming from somewhere in the crowd. At least one journalist had a sense of humor, poking a little fun at pack journalism. Like a rancher about to toss a bale of hay from the bed of his pickup, I had come to "feed" the herd.

"We're optimistic that there's going to be a peaceful outcome to all this," I said, adding that the discussions so far had been reasonable, with no "wild or outlandish threats made."

One of the most frequently asked questions was how many officers were on the scene. "We have ample manpower out here and we have augmented that some, as you've seen today," I said. "And McLaren is aware of that. He is aware that we have slowly moved in his direction."

Despite my refusal to talk numbers, savvy reporters who went to local businesses had no trouble getting information. One grocer said he had been requested to furnish enough meat to feed 300. Someone at a nearby guest ranch said 200 officers were staying there.

Laureen got in late that afternoon. She'd flown to Midland and driven down from there in Caver's state car. The captain's wife had dropped off a bag with fresh clothes and overnight gear at the DPS regional headquarters in Midland for Laureen to bring with her for Caver. I kidded Laureen about getting to drive a real Ranger car, something I had never done.

"Yeah, I had a lot of fun with the lights and sirens on the way down," she joked.

At the evening briefing, I assured the reporters nothing would be happening overnight. The lid was on.

"If I were you," I offered, "I'd go see the Marfa Lights tonight."

I could have done a brief talk on the history of the lights for the benefit of the out-of-state reporters, but I didn't feel like doing anything for their benefit, especially after the ABC cameraman flagrantly disregarded our gentleperson's agreement at the beginning of the pool tour. But the Marfa Lights do make for an interesting story.

I'd first written about the mystery lights as a young reporter, and had been to Marfa many times, but I never saw them until August 1996. On a visit to Alpine with my friend Mark Warren, the assistant commander of the DPS Training Academy, and Larry Wright, an old friend from my early newspaper days who had recently moved from Florida back to Texas, we'd ridden in Larry's Mustang convertible to the viewing area, a roadside park on U.S. 90, nine miles east of Marfa.

When we got there, it looked like a crowd waiting for a drive-in movie to start—people in open convertibles like us, on the roofs of cars, in lawn chairs, on top of picnic tables. But there was no screen and no Everly Brothers music playing over tinny-sounding car speakers; only the lonely Chinati Mountains sixty miles to the southwest. And the stars of the show, the ghost lights.

The Marfa Lights are to Texas what the Loch Ness Monster is to Scotland, except that no one has ever demonstrated that the Marfa Lights are the work of a prankster. In fact, in the more than a century since the first documented sighting, no one has proven anything about the Marfa Lights other than this: Something out there glows in the night.

Larry, Mark, and I certainly saw something that summer night: A tiny speck of white hovered at the crest of the distant mountain range, then seemed to burst into a burning ball as bright as the thin rind of moon hanging over the purple silhouette of the mountains. Then it was gone. But two other lights appeared in tandem, looking like headlights on a huge oncoming car wider than a train is long. They burned intensely and then disappeared. A giant waving flashlights as bright as lighthouse beacons? Radiation-mutated fireflies? Powerful lasers secretly played against the mountains by the Marfa Chamber of Commerce?

"Aw, I think they're just car headlights off there," someone in the crowd said. Others *oohed* and *aahed*. Several dozen people were seeing something—they just didn't know what.

A smaller array of lights appeared, some with a pinkish hue. They looked as if they were bubbling up from the base of the mountain. Binoculars made the lights look brighter and bigger, but magnification offered no clue to their source.

Veteran watchers say sometimes the lights race around, vertically and horizontally. Some claim the balls of light have followed them. There is a story of a small airplane being enveloped by one of the lights and other stories of pilots chasing the lights only to see them disappear like a fading rainbow.

When a Big Bend pioneer and his wife saw the lights in 1883, the first recorded sighting, they thought they were the distant campfires of hostile Apaches. But as they watched the lights move around and change in intensity, they realized Indians were not the cause.

More than a century later, answers to questions about the lights are as scarce as water in West Texas, but there are plenty of legends floating around. Most of the stories are as ethereal as the lights themselves. The folktales include lost Indian spirits, buried gold, witches, and the ghosts of bomber pilots and crews killed in World War II training flight crashes in the Big Bend. More serious theories on the source of the lights range from swamp gas (of course, the Big Bend doesn't have any swamps) to radioactive minerals to magnetic forces. Someone once suggested glowworms clinging to the fur of jackrabbits. If that's right, there are some mighty big insects and hares in those mountains.

I told Laureen about the lights as we rode back to Alpine.

We agreed to meet in the lobby after she checked into her room and changed out of the dress she'd worn on the plane and go for a quick look at the lights.

Back in my room, I pulled off my boots. Taking boots off after a long day may be the best part of wearing them. That particular pair had never fit very well, even though when I bought them they were labeled size 10. I'd had to leave my best pair of boots back in Austin because the heel had come off one of them and I hadn't had time yet to get it fixed. Then, confident I wouldn't be seeing any more Rangers that night, I slipped my feet into my cork-soled European-style felt clogs, the most comfortable pair of shoes I've ever owned.

I met Laureen in the lobby.

"You know what the Rangers would think if they saw you in those?" she laughed, looking down at my decidedly non-West Texas footwear.

But I knew my secret would be safe with her. I could always retaliate with the story of how she used to complain of hearing trains in the night during our stay in Waco—trains I never heard. Maybe my room was better insulated than hers.

After a stop for iced tea, we headed to the roadside ghost light viewing area. Thanks to one of the DPS mountaintop repeater towers, we were able to monitor the two-way for any developments at the resort. If anything happened we were ready to rush back to the command post, but the radio stayed quiet.

Laureen and I climbed on top of one of the concrete picnic tables to get a better view. Even though it was a weeknight, the roadside park was crowded. Despite the darkness, I could make out several TV station vehicles. Some of the reporters had actually taken my advice! I just hoped they didn't notice I had joined them.

The lights put on a good show that night. Even Laureen, who grew up in a small town in South Texas but shed that image for a big city sophistication, was impressed.

The Marfa Lights are one of the reasons I like this part of Texas as much as I do. Despite all of our technological development, no one yet has been able to solve the mystery of those lights.

McLaren had his own theory about the lights. Among the many documents he had filed over the years at the Jeff Davis County Courthouse was a resolution creating the Foundation for the Advancement of Space Laws and Sciences. This filing set forth his belief that the McDonald Observatory had been located in the Davis Mountains because of a mysterious underground energy source in some way connected to UFOs, the Ronald Reagan-era Star Wars program, and the Marfa Lights. The lights, McLaren confided to locals who would listen, served as something of a space lighthouse for extraterrestrial navigators who sometimes landed their ships in the mountains. Of course, the observatory had been on Mount Locke since 1936, long before the term UFO had even entered the American idiom. It was built there because the nights are very dark in the Davis Mountains, not because of power grids.

Late that Tuesday night, as the ghost lights continued their eerie dance against the dark mountains, McLaren called WFAA-TV in Dallas, one of the state's most influential television stations as an ABC affiliate in one of the nation's top ten largest markets.

"We are under self-governance," McLaren said. "We are in a state of war."

"This is not the Alamo"

Wednesday, April 30: Day Four

The motel's complimentary continental breakfast was not even provincial, and I'm not a fussy eater. As my wife likes to point out, I even enjoy airplane food. The blueberry and bran muffins had disappeared earlier in the week. I strongly suspected federal involvement, since the FBI was staying at the same hotel. All that was left by Wednesday morning was dry cereal, instant oatmeal, aging grapefruit, and English muffins. Luckily, I like English muffins. With some butter and grape jelly, they're pretty good. But the muffin I picked this morning was wet. Well, somewhere between moist and soggy. At least the coffee was good.

The television set in the small breakfast room was tuned to CNN. Laureen and I and the FBI agents watched as reporter Charles Zewe did a live shot from the scene. Nothing had happened overnight, he assured the world. The stand-off continued. They rolled some tape from my last press conference the day before.

Actually, something had happened. The CNN correspondent just didn't know it yet. Unfortunately, neither did we.

On our way out of town toward Fort Davis, after stopping for newspapers and gasoline, we were listening to the local radio station. Few people in America had as picturesque a commute to work as we did that morning, but what we were hearing on the radio cut into our enjoyment of the scenery.

The Arlington-based Texas State News Network was reporting the arrest of seven heavily armed Republic of Texas sympathizers at a truck stop on Interstate 20 in Pecos, seventy-two miles north of Fort Davis. I called Sherri at our Austin office on the cellular phone to see what she knew about it. She'd already gotten some media calls asking about the arrests, and had been able to get some information from the DPS communications center at Pecos.

Those arrests were the first sign that people with guns might be heeding McLaren's call for help, a plea similar to the famous appeal William Barret Travis had made from within the walls of the Alamo. We knew there was no way help actually could reach McLaren. The DPS and other law enforcement agencies had the area around the ROT enclave sealed off. The concern was that some militia group might come to one of the DPS roadblocks and try to shoot their way in.

As we approached "Mount Media," we could see someone on the side of the road holding up a sign further underscoring the growing seriousness of the situation:

DPS: To Serve
& Protect—Not
Kill & Destroy
Waco/Ruby Ridge/Here?

We got the details when we reached the command post.

At 1:11 A.M., the assistant chief of the DPS' Traffic Law Enforcement Division, Charles Graham, the department's second-highest-ranking uniformed officer, had sent a teletype to the DPS communications centers in Abilene, Midland, Pecos, and Ozona. The message described a vehicle occupied by heavily armed men believed to be headed toward Balmorhea in Reeves County, only forty-nine miles north of Fort Davis. Extreme caution was urged if any law enforcement officer encountered the vehicle.

The information was so sensitive it could not be broadcast over the DPS radio. Officers were given the warning via word-of-mouth or by secure telephone.

The teletype paid off. At 5:30 A.M., Pecos police officer

Cosme Ortega spotted the vehicle described in the message, a faded yellow 1979 Chevrolet Suburban, at mile marker 43 on I-20. Ortega followed it and another vehicle, a blue 1981 Oldsmobile, to the Flying J Truck Stop on I-20 in Pecos. In all, Ortega counted seven men. As he watched, five of them walked inside the truck stop. Two others stayed behind, one in each vehicle. Soon both men were asleep. They must have been driving all night.

Inside the truck stop, the men ordered breakfast. They told a waitress they were going hunting.

Outside, Ortega got close enough to one of the vehicles to see weapons inside—assault rifles. The officer radioed for help.

By coincidence, Ranger Captain Carl Weathers of Lubbock-based Company C and four of his Rangers, on their way to augment the Ranger contingent already at Fort Davis, had spent the night in Pecos. When he was notified of the situation at the truck stop, Weathers and his men went there immediately.

As truck drivers, waitresses, and other early risers looked on, Pecos police officers, Rangers, and Reeves County sheriff's deputies quickly rounded up the seven men. Soon they were all lying face down on the pavement.

"I'm a born-again Christian," one of the men said, "and I wouldn't kill nobody unless Jesus told me to."

Inside the vehicles the officers found two loaded Chinese-built SKS 7.62mm semi-automatic assault rifles, three other assault rifles, one 12-gauge shotgun, one .45-caliber pistol, several hunting knives, three 30-round clips, two 40-round drum clips, and a quart jar of blasting powder. A metal box labeled "Republic of Texas Defense Forces" contained several thousands rounds of ammunition.

Also found were two military-style helmets with ROT insignias, a bulletproof vest and a SWAT-style ammunition vest, camouflage fatigues, backpacks, medical supplies, military MREs (Meals Ready to Eat), bags of rice, a giant-sized jar of peanut butter, two pounds of marijuana, and thirteen cassette tapes marked "Republic of Texas," including a speech labeled "Come out from there and be ye separate."

The inventory of the reading material found in the vehicles was revealing: In addition to printed ROT literature, there was a booklet titled "Operation Vampire Killer 2000— American Police—Military Action Plan for Stopping World Government Rule," a training booklet, "Disabling a Bridge," prepared by the U.S. Army, and a book explaining how to produce false identification.

The men told the officers, as they had told the waitress, that they were in West Texas to go hunting. They were a little less sure exactly what it was that they were hunting. One time they said their quarry was "pigs," which later changed to hawks. As Ranger Sergeant Steve Foster told a reporter, one thing was certain: "They weren't going duck hunting."

While the arrests in Pecos were good news in the sense that the men with the guns weren't going to be helping McLaren, concern still was high that more sympathizers might be moving toward West Texas. I thought of Captain Benningfield again and his confidential faxes. When news of the arrests hit the wires, Reeves County Sheriff Arnulfo Gomez' office began getting telephone calls from others claiming to be ROT members.

"I know they're headed this way," the sheriff said. "I'm hoping there's no confrontation."

At the command post, contingency planning went into high gear. The DPS had requested help from the Texas Department of Criminal Justice. Caver wanted some of the prison system's mounted teams and their tracking dogs. In addition to the request for horses, DPS had asked for assistance of a more modern nature from the Texas Army Guard: two Blackhawk helicopters. The Alpine hospital was asked to clear a parking lot as a landing site. Hospital personnel went on alert for a possible mass casualty situation.

All of these developments were picked up on by the media and duly reported, adding to the intensity of the crisis.

Further complicating the situation, McLaren had stopped talking—never a good sign when it comes to barricaded suspects. No one understood that better than the FBI's behavioral sciences experts, including one special agent I was about to meet.

With several hundred officers and support personnel on

the scene, I certainly didn't know everyone by name, especially the officers from the FBI and the numerous other agencies. But my mug was beginning to be fairly familiar to them, particularly for any of them who had a chance to see the news media's version of what was going on in Jeff Davis County. Officers and FBI agents occasionally came up to me, shook my hand, and said they liked the way I was handling myself on TV.

"I don't see how you can be so patient with those [expletive deleted]," one officer said. "You're doing good. Keep it up. Don't let 'em get to you."

My wife would debate whether I'm really all that easygoing, but my self-perception has me as a Type B. I don't go berserk when stuck in traffic or get crazy when waiting in long lines. But I am not totally laid back or without character flaws. Actually, people annoy me more than events. Things happen, but people ought to know better. People who are slow studies, to put it kindly, quickly get on my nerves and, as I just demonstrated, I can easily move off into being too judgmental. But I have a lot of friends and an even greater number of more casual acquaintances I get along with well. I like to be liked, and it really bothers me when I realize there are actually some people who don't like me—or at least don't like the way I do things.

One of the FBI agents who introduced himself to me was Gary Noesner, the agency's chief negotiator, a veteran of many high-profile stand-offs across the nation, including Waco. A friendly, easygoing sort, clearly good at his job of understanding and relating to people, he came up to me as I discussed with Ranger Sergeant Jess Malone what I would say at my afternoon briefing. The thirty-eight-year-old Malone had taken over as the primary negotiator with McLaren so that Caver, as incident commander, would have more time to oversee the big picture. Commissioner Holt and Laureen also were in on the strategy session. The arrests in Pecos, and McLaren's sudden recalcitrance, had everyone worried.

Noesner suggested, if Sergeant Malone and Caver concurred, that I do everything I could at the next briefing to de-escalate the situation. The agent recommended a non-threatening, good-ol'-boy approach on my part. Get the point across that this was a law enforcement matter, not the beginning of a revolution. Convey to all the would-be patriots out there with assault rifles that this was merely a little family problem between Rick McLaren and Texas cops. No big deal. He said, in essence, to lay it on thick.

My friends say I tell a joke pretty well. Of course, it's hard to miss with a funny story that begins "This guy walks into a bar. . . ." But my drama resumé is not very long. In the ninth grade I spray-painted my dark hair gray and played the role of Papa in Thornton Wilder's one-act play "The Happy Journey." There were very few props. If you're familiar with the play you'll remember that the family sits on stools (make-believe car seats) as Papa pretends that his hands are on the steering wheel. Our play won an award in Interscholastic League competition, but as the old saying goes—in this case literally true—all I did was drive the car.

My school days long behind me, in the early 1980s I played a bank robber in a televised police "Crime Stoppers" re-enactment and a U.S. senator in a Society of Professional Journalists "Gridiron Show." In 1992 I spent a day costumed and made up to look like an early 1960s gubernatorial aide for a seven- to ten-second appearance as an extra in Clint Eastwood's movie *A Perfect World*, about a Texas Ranger and an escaped convict. Eastwood filmed it in and around Austin with some technical assistance from the DPS.

That was about the extent of my acting career.

But all that had been extracurricular activity. Now I was getting ready to play a role that might really count for some-thing—sort of a chubby Will Rogers without a lariat to spin. Only this appearance wasn't for laughs.

With Commissioner Holt, Laureen, and two Troopers standing behind me ("If anybody asks who I am, just tell 'em I'm your body guard," the commissioner had said), I began the show. CNN was carrying it live.

"For those of you who are not from Texas," I began, "we have a little expression here: 'Sometimes a wheel falls off.' Unfortunately, we've lost a wheel."

As long as I was into wagon metaphor, I decided to keep rolling.

"We thought we had an open dialogue with him [McLaren] and then, kerplunk, a wheel fell off." The DPS had "simply stopped hearing from him," I explained. The department had faxed McLaren a "hey-let's-talk" letter, I said, but he had not responded.

"We're not contemplating any assaults," I said. "Storm troopers are not massed to kick in his doors like the door was kicked in at the Rowes'. We're all anxious to go home, but we want to do this right. We want to give them an opportunity to come out on their own. We're not trying to start a revolution. We're not trying to fight a war."

I continued my theme that the DPS was merely trying to serve some felony arrest warrants. Armed militia members should stay home. In hindsight, I wish I had worked in another of my favorite Texas expressions: "They don't have a dog in this fight."

I decided to invoke imagery of the Texas Revolution. Forty-two years earlier, fifteen miles or so from where I stood now in front of all these cameras, I had been a little boy exploring the ruins of old Fort Davis in my Davy Crockett hat. Now I was about to call on Davy for help in my effort to prevent a modern-day Alamo from getting out of hand.

"We don't want these people [militia members] to feel like they need to come here," I said. "This is not the Alamo. This is not San Jacinto. And I'm not Davy Crockett. We're just a law enforcement agency trying to enforce some felony warrants."

Well, I screwed up the Davy Crockett part. What I meant to say—and I hope it's obvious—is, "*He's* not Davy Crockett." It was obvious to all that I wasn't my childhood hero. Unfortunately, no one in the media questioned what I said or was thoughtful enough to alter the quote to reflect "what Mr. Cox meant to say," as some Washington spin doctor might have done.

Though most of my remarks were intended for McLaren and any would-be rescuers, I had another audience to think about: the people of Jeff Davis County, particularly those who lived in the resort. A few of them, we knew, were sympathetic to the ROT cause, though not actively involved in the movement.

Most of the families who lived in the resort had voluntarily left their homes, as the DPS had recommended, but some of them were not particularly happy about it. Understandably, they wanted to know when they could get back to their houses.

"We know it's a hardship and our hearts go out to them," I said in answer to one reporter's question about residents of the resort. "But we're still not able to allow them back in."

I returned to my main message: "There's still a possibility of resolving this if Mr. McLaren will talk to us. We still have three wheels left."

Flanked by Laureen, Commissioner Holt, and the two Troopers, I left the microphones after promising another briefing later in the day. By using metaphor and the affected good-ol'-boy attitude, I hoped I had helped to defuse the situation.

Back at the command post, I got some handshakes and learned that my performance had not been lost on McLaren and his colleagues. The Alpine radio station had carried the press conference live, and the folks at the "embassy" had listened. How did we know that? Their two-way radio traffic was being monitored by local ham radio operators. One of the hams told me that at one point during my press conference, someone at the "embassy" had said into his radio: "What bullshit!" Could a good ol' boy in cowboy boots ask for higher praise than, as we say in Texas, to have someone "call B.S. on him"?

Now that Laureen was available to assist, I asked the reporters and photographers if they would like us to move the briefings to a meeting hall at one of the churches in Fort Davis. It would be a much more comfortable place for all of us, I said. My proposal, made in consideration for them—and for my sunburned nose—was unanimously voted down.

"Okay," I said, "if you want to stay out here, that's fine with me."

I couldn't blame them, really. Other than my briefings, about the only way for the media to keep up with developments at the scene was to see the traffic that came and went from the resort, talk to anyone who wandered up to the media camp with something to say, listen to their scanners, and follow up on tips or assignments from their editors and producers. Waco had been the same way.

Though the media made much of the arrival in Jeff Davis County of the martial-looking tracked vehicles the day before, they totally missed the significance of the Texas Forest Service vehicles that went by them on their way to the command post. Forest Service personnel work closely with the DPS in major incidents because of their expertise in on-scene coordination. Throughout the siege, Forest Service incident management personnel kept track of who was on hand from where. They charted the organizational structure of those involved and worked closely with the DPS' Emergency Management Service on logistical matters.

But there was another, much more serious reason for the Forest Service presence, one I thought best not to mention to the media until the situation was resolved: Our worst case scenario featured McLaren and his followers starting a wildfire.

I stood in on a briefing from two Forest Service firefighting experts. The situation did not look good. The area was very dry, and the weather conditions—low humidity combined with strong north winds—were just right for a fire to sweep out of control down the canyon straight toward our command post. In between were scores of officers who would be at peril, and hundreds of thousands of dollars of public and private property. The only way to stop the fire, they said, would be by scraping a wide firebreak between the upper canyon and the fire hall-command post. If he wanted to, McLaren could go out in a blaze of glory, just like David Koresh. Because of the distances involved, the world would not see it happen in real time as had been the case at Mount Carmel, but the smoke would have been visible from the media area soon enough.

About an hour after my "This isn't the Alamo" afternoon press briefing, two men with guns were arrested at the checkpoint at Highway 166 and 188. Apparently, they had not had a chance to hear my message that no ROT volunteers were needed at Fort Davis. They certainly hadn't been trying to slip in. Their vehicle bore ROT license plates, not legitimate Texas plates. That would have caused them to be stopped by an officer sooner or later, but with the stand-off going on and officers all over Texas alert for gun-packing crazies answering McLaren's call for help, the ROT plates stood out in Jeff Davis

County like a hooker in church. Found in the car was some ROT literature, and, of much more concern, a Ruger Mini-14—the same type of rifle DPS Troopers carry. The semi-automatic shoulder arm is a legal weapon, but when a Trooper routinely checked the serial number through NCIC (National Crime Information Center), he learned the weapon had been reported stolen. A sixty-year-old man and his thirty-seven-year-old son were taken to the Presidio County Jail in Marfa.

Perhaps thinking some militia group might actually make it to his "embassy," McLaren seemed to be digging in for the long haul. And, at the Wofford Ranch, so were we. By now the DPS had its own hardline phones installed. One of the lines went into a one-room cabin with a table and chairs, one bed and two bunk beds, a kitchen sink and, most important, a bathroom with a shower. Parked in front of the cabin was a DPS mobile command post, normally assigned to our License and Weight Service. The converted RV had two phone lines and a DPS radio manned around-the-clock by one of our communication operators.

The van was being used as the Traffic Law Enforcement Division's command post. The Safety Education Troopers and Laureen and I took over the cabin as the PIO command post. During one of the occasional lulls in the action, I found an old piece of plywood on the ground outside. I broke it in two and made a couple of signs with a pink marker—the only color I could find. On one I wrote "DPS PIO/Ft. Davis/April 27, 1997/PIO West of the Pecos" and on the other simply, "DPS PIO." I leaned the signs up in two of the cabin's three windows.

Having a bathroom nearby was convenient, but its real value to us was as a people-attractor. We became the unofficial potty monitors, informing new arrivals whether the facility was occupied or available and jokingly apprising guests of our user fees. We could have cleaned up as nicely as the dusty, sweaty officers and Guardsmen who came to use it if we could have charged for the shower. While we never actually collected a potty toll, we did exact another kind of charge for the use of "our" facilities: news. Some arrivals seemed compelled to offer us information, as if to repay us for guarding the door to the john. Others we politely queried. Then, too, we picked up news as various players came by to use "our" phone.

We provided another valuable service: answering the telephone. Of course, many times the calls were for one of us, but we took messages or went looking for people. We also found our makeshift office was becoming something of a "USO" for our Troopers, many of whom had reported to the scene suddenly without having a chance to check in with their families. A steady stream of Troopers came in to use our phone to call home.

David Baker, the Highway Patrol captain out of Midland who flew to Jeff Davis County with Caver the first day of the stand-off, graciously let us use his handheld radio to monitor the goings-on, which was a lot of help.

The cabin was not air-conditioned, but with the altitude and lack of humidity, the temperature inside was never uncomfortable. We ate our meals on the round maple table, our fare ranging from fajitas and hamburgers prepared under the supervision of ranch owner Rusty Wofford to sandwiches, candy bars, and coffee from the Salvation Army. You don't know how fine a baloney and cheese sandwich on white bread with no mayonnaise can taste until you're really hungry and it's either the sandwich or nothing. Safety Education Trooper John "Bubba" Barton and I even managed to cop a couple of catnaps in our media relations command post. All in all, it was a snug but comfortable PIO headquarters, certainly better than standing around outside or sardining into the narrow communications vans. Of course, you had to keep an eye out for snakes, scorpions, and tarantulas. And Laureen quickly learned never to set her soft-drink can down—tobacco-chewing officers use them for small, portable spittoons.

We never got around to naming the place, except for my "PIO West of the Pecos" sign, but it was our office until Friday, May 2, when all the communications operations moved up the road to the fire hall. After that, we used our pool car for an office, talked to people under the shade of a covered concrete slab adjoining the fire hall, or stood around outside the communications van the Rangers were using for their command post.

As the DPS endeavored to improve its communication

capabilities by adding more hard telephone lines and bringing in computers and fax machines, work was under way to hinder McLaren's communication flow. For the first several days of the siege, McLaren had been calling out at will. Like Koresh in Waco, McLaren had reached out to the media. He talked with the Associated Press in Dallas, WOAI Radio in San Antonio, a San Antonio newspaper reporter, and perhaps others. "White Eagle" Otto also was doing some interviews.

Though outgoing phone service had been cut from his trailer, it soon was apparent that McLaren and Paulson were calling from other phones. The Rangers believed he or some of his followers had broken into other residences in the general area of his trailer and was using phones in those houses. *San Antonio Express-News* reporter Tom Edwards, the first journalist to write about the ROT movement, later told me that McLaren had called him on a satellite telephone.

McLaren also was continuing to communicate via electronic mail and by posting messages on the ROT Webpage. The media and a crime analyst for the DPS Special Crimes Service were monitoring all the ROT Websites. So were many others around the world. Since the stand-off began, McLaren's Website had been receiving 100 to 200 hits (visits) an hour. As far as I know, the stand-off with McLaren was the first where cyberspace played a role. Certainly, it was the first such incident involving the DPS.

"All [Republic of Texas] Home pages in this Website will have black backgrounds until Texas is a Captive Nation No Longer!!" McLaren's page proclaimed.

A couple of weeks prior to the stand-off, as part of its evidence collection for the civil suit against the ROT, the Attorney General's Office had subpoenaed McLaren's Internet service provider, Fort Davis-based Overland Network, for E-mail names, passwords, log-ins, E-mail, E-mail account records, addresses, and billing and payment information.

Though Overland owner Todd Jagger filed suit to contest that subpoena, he voluntarily shut down McLaren's Web access on Wednesday at the request of Assistant District Attorney James Jepson, who said it was an action necessary to "protect life and property." The closure made history. Austin attorney

Peter D. Kennedy, a practitioner in the pioneer field of Internet law, told the *Fort Worth Star-Telegram* that this was the first time in the United States that the plug had been pulled on a political Website at the request of law enforcement.

The First Amendment implications aside, the shutdown would prevent McLaren from further fanning the flames by calling for help from militia groups around the country. If severing his electronic connection to the world prevented some group of kooks with assault rifles from trying to blast their way through one of our roadblocks, at least on the short term the best interests of society had been served.

By Wednesday evening, McLaren's only communication with the outside world was by short-wave radio and a telephone (blocked except for incoming calls from the DPS). McLaren knew his ability to get his message across was fading, but he did not yet know what else was happening.

Before the "embassy's" telephone service was cut, one of the occupants got through a long distance call to Colorado. Forty-eight-year-old Mike Matson, who had not been charged with any crimes, left a message on his brother Ralph's answering machine. In the recording, Matson, a Chicago-born former Marine who had hitchhiked from California to Jeff Davis County three months earlier, explained the attack on the Rowes' residence as merely an effort to get a comrade in arms out of jail. The Rowes had not been harmed, Matson told his brother, and the ROT personnel who had conducted the operation left behind cash and an IOU to cover Mrs. Rowe's lasagna and the damage to their property.

Ralph Matson later said his brother had become disenchanted with government seven years earlier. When an elderly woman Mike Matson had been taking care of died in March 1990, his brother said, the woman's two estranged stepdaughters won a court fight and Matson lost $110,000 that had been willed to him. An attorney for the woman's family told a reporter that they saw the matter differently—they believed Matson had manipulated the woman into writing him into her will.

Matson, his brother continued, wrote "thousands" of letters requesting an investigation into the circumstances of the woman's death and the court system in Alameda County, California, where the estate went through the probate process. In 1995 his crusade led to his arrest for contempt of court. He spent eight months in jail, then pleaded no contest to eleven counts of contempt, receiving five years' probation. But when he left the state, a warrant was issued for his arrest. Matson's anti-government sentiment grew into paranoia.

"My brother is convinced that if he surrenders, he would end up dead hanging in a jail somewhere," the Colorado man later told a reporter. "It would not surprise me if McLaren decided to negotiate his way out of this. But I do not believe there is any way my brother would come out. This is his Alamo and he believes he's Davy Crockett."

Back on the scene after spending all day Tuesday giving a deposition, Casteel wanted to take another look from the air at the area around McLaren's trailer. But the Ranger commander was worried that if the helicopter came in too low, it might start drawing fire. On the other hand, Casteel wanted to fly over as low as the pilot felt was safe.

The Rangers were particularly interested in a long ridge that ended right behind the "embassy." Casteel knew if McLaren and his "defense forces" were on the ball, they'd have someone on that ridge, which looked right down on the ROT trailer. It was Military Strategy 101: Take the high ground.

"Do you think you can land on that ridge?" Casteel asked Midland-based pilot John Brannon. The pilot said he'd give it a try. If McLaren did have a guard up there, the Rangers were about to find out.

After a few passes over the area, Brannon deftly settled the chopper on the rocky ridge and Casteel and Caver, armed with only their pistols, got out to look around. Their landing went unchallenged. No one with the ROT had been posted on the high ground. The Rangers moved cautiously along the ridge to a point where they could have tossed rocks down on the roof of McLaren's trailer.

Back at the command post, Caver rounded up some officers to set up an observation point on the ridge. Another lookout post was established at a location where officers could observe the ROT trailer from the front side.

When the DPS helicopter returned to the ridge, three camouflage-clad Troopers—members of the department's elite Dive Recovery Team—scrambled out with their weapons and equipment. They had radios, binoculars, cameras, sleeping bags, food, and water.

Quickly they set up a tripod-mounted infrared video camera and trained the lens on McLaren's trailer. Thirty feet of cord trailed back to a monitor they set up at what would be their base camp, a spot at 6,000 feet elevation on about a forty-degree slope.

It was spring, but at that desert altitude, when the sun goes down, so does the temperature. The relentless wind did not help. Also at night the rattlesnakes came out, using their built-in, heat-sensing abilities to search for food. As two of the officers shivered in their sleeping bags and tried to get a little rest, a third watched the monitor for any signs of movement at McLaren's enclave and kept alert for snakes. Slithering around looking for a late night snack, the snakes did not make a lot of noise, but in the absence of any other sound except the wind, they made enough.

Throughout the rest of the siege, officers with assault rifles, rotated in and out by helicopter, were at McLaren's front and back doors. They were not close enough to hear what McLaren and his followers were saying, but whenever any of the ROT were outside, the lookouts had a fairly clear view of what they were doing. One evening the surveillance team watched McLaren and his colleagues cooking steaks outside their "embassy," far better fare than they had at their behind-the-lines posts.

And the ROT members knew the officers were there, within rifle range. At one point, one of them offered the Troopers a friendly wave.

The Terry and Mike show

Thursday, May 1: Day Five

Through their binoculars, officers watched as the ROT "soldiers" busied themselves preparing for the "embassy's" defense. All of the known occupants of the ROT enclave spent the night in camouflaged bunkers arrayed around the approach to McLaren's trailer. Now they appeared to be rigging wire and detonators to fuel barrels. Their plan was obvious: The barrels were positioned so that if the detonators were fired, burning fuel would run downhill from the enclave toward any advancing law enforcement officers.

There wasn't much to say at the 10:00 A.M. briefing. Safety Education Trooper Barton, who had come in from Midland to relieve San Angelo-based SES Trooper Richard Treece, explained that contrary to some media reports, McLaren's power had not yet been cut off. In Austin, Sherri was telling the media that, contrary to rumor, no Davis Mountains Resort residents were missing. She also was prepared to put down a rumor being checked out by the media that another armed militia group, in a vehicle with Arkansas plates, had been confronted somewhere.

McLaren still was refusing to talk to the Rangers, despite my command performance the afternoon before. Knowing that he listened to the Alpine radio station, I suggested to Caver that O'Rourke and I make a plea to him over the commercial airwaves.

Caver thought that was a good idea, so I called Ray Hendrix, son of the station's founder and also the daytime DJ and news director, to see if he would put us on the air. Hendrix readily agreed, since it would be a good story for his station as well as a useful public service, particularly if it resulted in McLaren resuming contact with Ranger Sergeant Malone.

I arranged with Sheriff Bailey to use his office at the courthouse. There weren't enough phones at the command center for O'Rourke and me to be on the same line when we called the station. Besides that, O'Rourke had not been heard from yet that morning.

I drove into Fort Davis to see if I could find him. I checked his motel room, but he was not there. I cruised the rest of the town, checking the handful of stores and places where he might be drinking coffee or having a late breakfast.

I'd left a message at his motel for him to contact me at the sheriff's office if he came in, so, not having found him anywhere, I headed to the courthouse to see if he might be there. On the way I spotted Mike Williams, a writer for *Soldier of Fortune Magazine*, walking into one of the local cafes. I'd seen O'Rourke with him the day before.

Williams told me O'Rourke was at the courthouse. If we had been in Austin, as busy as the Travis County Courthouse complex is, that information would not have done me much good. But in Fort Davis, that intelligence narrowed my search significantly. The notion of Big Government looms as a dark specter in the minds of many in West Texas, even among those not affiliated with the ROT, but in Jeff Davis County it is an imaginary fear, not reality. It took only a minute or two before I found O'Rourke in a small office off the district courtroom, studying a law book. He and I were almost the only people in the building.

We grabbed some coffee and went downstairs to the sheriff's department. Bailey's secretary pointed us toward his office, where each of us got on the phone.

I called the radio station and at 11:30 A.M. Hendrix came out of a station break with an announcement that the station was about to air a special program, live from Fort Davis. For the next thirty minutes, O'Rourke and I answered questions from Hendrix and presented our brief that McLaren needed to get back in communication with the Rangers. I tried to make the point that the Texas Rangers were a law enforcement agency whose roots traced back to the original Republic of Texas, hoping McLaren would like the sound of that.

We ended the broadcast just before noon. O'Rourke went back upstairs to the office he was using, and I stayed behind to check in with Sherri in Austin. Meanwhile, Sheriff Bailey's secretary had gone to lunch, leaving me the sole occupant of the sheriff's office. In fact, the whole courthouse was deserted. No one had locked any doors; everyone had just gone to lunch. In Fort Davis, I realized, it is not a good idea to plan on conducting any business with the county between noon and 1:00 in the afternoon. McLaren's plan to raid the courthouse, especially if he had struck during a weekday noon hour, did not seem as far-fetched as it had the first time I'd heard about it.

As I talked with Sherri, one and sometimes two phone lines in the sheriff's office rang continuously, but I didn't think it was my place to answer some other agency's phone. I hoped no one was calling for help. I envisioned some little old lady, bound and gagged in her home by a burglar, desperately calling for help by dialing the phone with a knitting needle held between her toes. Actually, 911 calls in Jeff Davis County are routed to a twenty-four-hour dispatcher in Presidio County.

(As far as I know, no significant crime occurred in the county during the stand-off, though one night Sheriff Bailey did have to rush away from the command post to break up a fight back in town. He told me he also handled a predawn barking dog case one day during the siege. Routine patrol in Fort Davis was being provided by the Permian Basin Drug Task Force. Those officers had been moved in after someone called in a bomb threat at the Red Cross shelter on Tuesday afternoon. The shelter had been thoroughly searched, but nothing was found.)

When I walked out of the courthouse after talking with Sherri, I saw Laureen and Safety Education Trooper Torres outside, looking for me. We had talked about setting up shop in Sheriff Bailey's office and they were coming to look it over, but over lunch we decided to stay out at the command post, at least for the time being. If the siege went on and on, maybe we'd reconsider.

Back at the command post after lunch, I learned that about a half hour after O'Rourke and I went off the air, McLaren finally picked up his telephone and started talking to the Rangers again. McLaren said they had left a package down the road from their trailer, and Sergeant Malone said they would send someone to pick it up.

Caver told me that so far the conversation with McLaren had only amounted to "chit-chat," but that he was pleased McLaren had at least started talking again. Maybe the "Terry and Mike Show" had helped.

When the packet from the "embassy" was retrieved, it was found to contain a letter from McLaren in which he proposed a novel solution to our problem: Instead of him surrendering to the DPS, our officers should lay down their guns and surrender to him "for invading their sovereign nation."

At the afternoon briefing, I started off with the upbeat news that McLaren had finally begun talking to us again. I explained the effort O'Rourke and I had made over the local radio station and did not get as much heat over it as I had expected. I had imagined the media would complain that they had been left out, but they seemed to take the news in stride. Maybe they actually understood it had only been one more effort to resolve the situation by reopening dialogue with McLaren, not an act of favoritism to the local station.

Someone asked me whether McLaren's electricity had been cut off. His electric power would be kept on as long as he kept talking, I said.

I also reported that ten ROT members had gathered outside the county courthouse in Midland and announced the issuance of a Republic of Texas arrest "warrant" for McLaren. The document cited ten offenses ("common law crimes") including "fraud" and "treason." Laureen helped pass out five pool copies of the document.

When someone asked if the DPS would be serving that "warrant" on behalf of the Republic of Texas faction that had issued it, I said we would be happy to pass it along to

McLaren as soon as he was in custody on the state warrants we held for him and his colleagues.

Not having much else of substance to offer, I tossed out a little color: Our mountain observers had witnessed a military-style memorial ceremony staged outside McLaren's trailer earlier that afternoon.

"They lowered their flag to half-staff, played Taps ["White Eagle" Otto using his bugle], and fired several rounds in salute," I said.

This was in recognition of an ROT sympathizer who had been killed by police at a roadblock in New Mexico while on his way to throw in his lot with the defenders of McLaren's Alamo. At least that's what the ROT members apparently believed. When McLaren offered an explanation for the ceremony during one of his telephone conversations with Sergeant Malone, someone at the command post quickly checked to see if such a shooting had occurred near Albuquerque, as McLaren claimed. Nothing of the sort had been reported.

"No one knows of any such incident [involving a shooting]," I told the media after describing the ceremony.

McLaren may have gotten the idea after hearing over his police scanner that someone had been arrested at 2:00 that afternoon at one of the DPS roadblocks in the area. (The timing was right, at least. The observers reported the ceremony at 2:50 P.M.) The man had gone to jail for having a pistol in his vehicle, but no shots had been fired. He told Troopers he was on vacation, and had come to the area just to see what was going on after hearing news accounts of the stand-off. The charge against him later was dropped.

That arrest, which brought the two-day total to ten, was a perfect example of why the DPS was blocking access to the area. Still, some of the local residents were beginning to get irritated.

Another would-be gate crasher had almost gone to jail two days earlier, but he was unarmed and was only coming to McLaren's defense with words.

"He [McLaren] was just trying to protect what he believes in," resort resident Ron Beames had said Tuesday. Beames, who raises horses, created a scene at the media checkpoint when he tried to get past the Troopers and return to his residence. When told he could not reenter the subdivision, Beames started shouting at the officers.

Seeing the trouble, Ranger Lieutenant Joe Sanders of Midland stepped forward to try to calm the man down. As dozens of reporters looked on and photographers snapped away, Beames pushed the burly Ranger.

"You strike me again and you're going to the jailhouse," Sanders said, shaking his finger at the man.

Wednesday morning the photograph was on page one of the *Dallas Morning News.*

At my evening press conference, a half-dozen or so relatives of people who had chosen not to leave the resort complained noisily—and with the obvious intention of generating media pressure—about phone service to the resort having been cut. One or two locals, clearly happy with the DPS presence, came to the agency's defense—and mine, since I was the one taking the heat.

I said the DPS realized the stand-off was causing hardships for a lot of people, including many of our own employees. I told them that if anyone wanted to leave the resort, the DPS would help them get out. I reiterated that these people were staying of their own free will, even though we had recommended that they leave.

Fielding the complaints of that handful of people was not fun, but I understood it was based on their frustration and I didn't take it personally. A lot of folks were getting frustrated.

"They're trying to negotiate with someone who is out of his mind," one local resident told a reporter.

The only other news I had to offer was that electrical power to McLaren's trailer had been cut off "to show that the Department of Public Safety is serious about bringing this situation to a resolution."

I had said earlier that as long as McLaren kept talking, his lights would stay on. But his talking had resulted in nothing of substance so far, which is what led to the decision to pull the plug, I said. This was standard procedure in these kinds of situations: a non-violent escalation to apply pressure.

District Attorney Valadez had obtained a court order to

cut McLaren's power, and at the time I made the announcement that it had been turned off, we honestly thought it had been done. But I later learned that the electric cutoff was right at McLaren's trailer, and there had been no way for anyone to reach it. Even Caver thought it had been cut.

Between my radio appearance with O'Rourke, the issuance of a Republic of Texas arrest "warrant" for McLaren, his demand that the DPS surrender, and the flag-lowering ceremony outside the trailer, it would seem there had been plenty enough theater for the day. But more was coming.

One person who had been following the sometimes serious, sometimes comic opera-like developments in Fort Davis with intense interest was twenty-nine-year-old Julie Hopkins of Fort Worth—Evelyn McLaren's daughter by a previous marriage. In desperation, she called attorney Dick DeGuerin in Houston.

Julie Hopkins said that her sister, thirty-three-year-old Lisa Rutledge, had offered to come to Fort Davis to try to help convince their mother to give up. Lisa Rutledge had talked to Caver, who told her he couldn't recommend that.

"There's nothing you can do," the Ranger told Lisa. "Just let us do our jobs."

DeGuerin got O'Rourke on the phone and put Julie Hopkins on the line. O'Rourke suggested that she write her mother a letter. Realizing she was too distraught to compose anything, O'Rourke dictated a letter on her behalf. His office faxed him back a hard copy. One copy went in a packet to be delivered to McLaren. Along with that letter was one from O'Rourke, urging his client to surrender. O'Rourke later gave copies of both letters to the media.

"It is essential that you pick up the phone and say you are coming out because they've made it clear that they're going to execute the warrants," the letter to McLaren concluded. "Know that there are people out here that love you and don't want you to die."

Also included in the packet was what O'Rourke called "the best deal I can make under the circumstances." That included an assurance that McLaren and his wife would "be treated with dignity" and that "they will be able to go to the [Presidio] county jail together."

As the sun went down that evening, the curtain went up on the final act in a day full of performances. O'Rourke went to "Mount Media" and did a dramatic reading of the letter he'd written for Evelyn McLaren's daughter: "Mom, I sincerely would rather have you all in prison and not in the line of fire. . . . I miss you and can't bear the thought of anything happening to you," O'Rourke read. "Please, please, please come out."

O'Rourke clearly was doing all he could to see that his client surrendered peacefully, but equally as apparent to Laureen and me, he was relishing the media spotlight. No question, being the center of attention is seductive. But when you're up there like Humpty-Dumpty on that wall of public attention, there's always someone who would be happy to give you a not-so-gentle nudge and turn you into an uncooked omelette.

The line in the sand

Friday, May 2: Day Six

> *"I have to tell you we have no more hope of reinforcements. . . . No doubt at this moment Santa Anna is mounting an assault in force. The outcome of that assault, you can easily guess. . . . I've drawn a line in the dirt. Any of you who care to stay with us, please step over that line."*
> —Richard Carlson as William B. Travis in *The Last Command*, Republic Pictures, 1955

As soon as I saw the headlines in the El Paso and Odessa newspapers that morning, I realized I'd made a big mistake: I'd let O'Rourke be the last one at the microphone Thursday night.

"Leader's lawyer pleads for surrender: Authorities give final ultimatum," read the page-one headline in the *El Paso Times*.

The only problem with that headline, and the story beneath it, was that the DPS had NOT given McLaren an ultimatum. I had never used the word during any of my briefings. In fact, I had continued to stress that the negotiators weren't following any set timetable.

"We have said all along that we want a peaceful outcome and not a Wild West outcome," I'd said the night before.

The DPS was determined that the felony arrest warrants would be served, one way or another, but no one had told McLaren that the DPS was about to charge his personal Alamo.

O'Rourke's strategy was obvious, of course. By implying that the DPS was about to assault the "embassy," he was using the media to put more pressure on McLaren. To that extent, O'Rourke's modus operandi was positive—unless it had a reverse effect and sent McLaren off the deep end—but I didn't like that it appeared O'Rourke was privy to inside information from the DPS. To the contrary, we were being very circumspect about what we said in front of him. While no one doubted that he wanted a peaceful solution to the situation, he was still the attorney for a defendant in a criminal case. Also, it had become increasingly evident that O'Rourke was chummy with one of the television reporters from Houston, as well as the writer for *Soldier of Fortune Magazine*. Particularly apparent to Laureen and me was that O'Rourke was providing information to the TV reporter.

Back in Austin headquarters, Sherri also was worried about the "ultimatum" coverage. She'd seen the TV take on the situation the night before, based on O'Rourke's remarks. It concerned her so much that she had trouble sleeping. By the time I talked to her the first time early Friday morning, she had already written an "if-asked" response to any further questions about an ultimatum: "The DPS Public Information Office gets its information directly from DPS officials at the scene. . . . No one we have talked with at the scene has used the word 'ultimatum.'"

I intended to be less diplomatic than that at the 10:00 A.M. briefing, stressing that O'Rourke was not a spokesman for the DPS. But fresher news pushed my planned comments about O'Rourke off the top of my handwritten outline for the morning press conference.

Shortly after 9:00 A.M., Robert Scheidt—the man whose arrest the previous Sunday had triggered this whole crisis—left the ROT trailer with another "diplomatic" packet. McLaren had called the Rangers earlier that morning to say that he would be sending out another packet, but he had not said when or how. Scheidt could have walked some distance away from the trailer, left the packet in the road, and returned. Instead, he kept walking.

About a mile from the trailer, Scheidt saw two Highway

Patrol cars blocking the road. From fifty yards away, Scheidt yelled out, "Hello!"

When the startled Troopers trained their weapons on him, he called out, "I'm unarmed. I'm a diplomatic courier."

Just the same, the officers frisked him. Satisfied that he was indeed unarmed, a Trooper cuffed him and put him in the back of one of the cars for the short ride to the volunteer fire station.

"I had to get out of there. I couldn't stand it any longer," Scheidt told one of the officers.

I made this news the lead item at my morning briefing. I didn't learn until much later that Scheidt's arrival had come as a surprise, albeit a pleasant one.

"We're encouraged by Mr. Scheidt's decision to let this play out in the state judicial system," I said. "It looks like this situation is winding down."

Scheidt's departure left only seven people in the "embassy."

After relaying all I knew about this latest development, I tried to kill the ultimatum issue, pointing out that O'Rourke did not work for the DPS. As a matter of fact, the way McLaren saw it, O'Rourke did not work for him, either. At least not anymore.

Captain Caver had told me that McLaren had written O'Rourke informing him that he had been "relived [sic] of services in representing both me and the People of The Republic of Texas and its Government."

Local resident Ron Beames, whom Ranger Lieutenant Sanders had threatened with arrest earlier in the week, confronted me at the end of the briefing. "In the name of God," Beames pleaded, getting down on his knees in front of me as the cameras rolled and clicked, "let me go in there and end this peacefully. I'll risk the bullets."

As I headed toward a Highway Patrol black-and-white, shielded by a couple of Troopers, Beames shouted: "They're setting up to murder this guy, and they don't want any witnesses."

Though I had said at the briefing that the DPS was encouraged by Scheidt having walked out, nothing else was looking good that day. (McLaren later said his captain volunteered to carry out the pouch; the Rangers said it seemed clear that Scheidt had simply had enough and just wanted out.)

That afternoon McLaren faxed out a five-paragraph, 174-word letter reminiscent of Travis' last missive from the Alamo, but not as eloquent nor as well-spelled. Addressed to ROT member Carolyn Carney of San Antonio "and the 10th [ROT] Congress," it read:

> This will probably be the last Transmission to you and the Congress if you receive it.
>
> First Ex President Archie Lowe has convinced the Enemy the [*sic*] we do not have any legal or diplomatic standings. You can thank him if we die, it will be of his direct results and god save his soul for what he has done. Tell Tim I expect him to try him and Johnson and those with them for treason and murder.
>
> Terry has been relived [*sic*], their [*sic*] has been conflicting offers and no one can ever be trusted on their side, never use a bar attorney any more even if you no [*sic*] them, they will sell you out.
>
> Everyone has chosen to stay and hold the Sovereign Soil of the Republic and its Foreign Mission, it appears to us that Morales and Bush are the ones pulling the strings you no [*sic*] Daddy Bush.
>
> I pray reinforcements arrive before they overrun the Embassy. Long live The Republic of Texas and the American People and Death to the New World Order.

Ominously, along with the letter came handwritten wills from Mike Matson, Robert "White Eagle" Otto, Gregg and Karen Paulson and McLaren. No wills were sent by Evelyn McLaren or Richard Keyes.

If the letter from McLaren had a mid-nineteenth-century ring to it, the negotiations to get him and his followers out of his imaginary Alamo were being facilitated with late twentieth-century technology. During the siege of the Alamo, messages were carried out by someone riding low in the saddle of a fast horse. Travis defiantly answered Santa Anna's demand of surrender with a single cannon blast. At Fort Davis, much of the communication was via fax machine and, until McLaren's Website provider terminated his connection, over the Internet. The fax machine in the command post trailer spat paper all afternoon.

Shortly before 2:00 that afternoon, the command post received a fax from Boyce Eugene Halbison, another ROT faction "president." Elected to office on April 19, Halbison now ordered McLaren "to surrender the Embassy to the de facto forces surrounding the building. The surrender is to take place immediately." Should McLaren choose not to surrender, the presidential order continued, "I temporarily suspend him from office, pending permanent action by the General Council."

Halbison also faxed the text of an order to ROT "Major General" Melvin Louis Kriewald, instructing him "to order all Republic of Texas military personnel in the Fort Davis Embassy to lay down their arms and surrender." He further ordered Kriewald to tell any other ROT "military personnel" to "stand down and to refrain from any interference with the de facto forces" and to instruct "all militia groups with which you are in contact that the Republic of Texas is in no need of their assistance, and that the Republic would prefer to resolve this problem internally."

These orders were passed on to McLaren, who at 3:44 P.M. announced he would not comply with them.

McLaren's refusal to surrender was the biggest problem we faced that afternoon, but not the only one. Evelyn McLaren's brother, her two daughters, and her young grandson had arrived at the Marfa airport by private plane from Fort Worth. The night before, they had been urged not to come. Their presence would not really help. In fact, it could have hurt.

FBI Agent Noesner, again offering me some welcome advice, explained that contrary to fictional portrayals of hostage situations seen on TV shows and in the movies, an emotional plea from a member of a barricaded individual's family potentially can have an opposite effect.

"Having a talk with a close family member can help a person reach closure," he said. "Sometimes, after talking to a loved one, they go ahead and kill themselves or start shooting at officers and force the issue."

Reporters, of course, are generalists. They don't usually

spend their time reading psychology textbooks. To them, it seemed like a good idea for family members to talk with a person refusing to surrender—in this case, Evelyn McLaren. The only thing better than that, in their opinion, would be a chance to join in the negotiations themselves.

I know. By the flip of a coin, I once lost an opportunity to do that myself.

During the prison siege at Huntsville in 1974, Fred Carrasco for some reason became miffed with the two San Antonio newspapers. He asked to talk to a reporter from the *Austin American-Statesman*, since it was published in the capital and read by state officials. That would be either me or fellow reporter Wayne Jackson. Jackson won the toss and got to talk to Carrasco over the phone. Amazingly, Carrasco did not surrender after talking to the twenty-six-year-old journalist, now a spokesman for AT&T in Washington. But it made a good story for the next day's *American-Statesman*.

At Fort Davis, no one in the media had asked us for a chance to talk to McLaren. Until Wednesday, that had been easy enough for them to do on their own.

When Evelyn McLaren's daughter Julie Hopkins called the command post in desperation that afternoon, I tried to explain to her (without repeating my conversation with the FBI agent) that the DPS did not feel family help was needed. She wanted someone with the DPS to come pick them up at the airport. If she and her sister were not allowed to talk to their mother, she told me, she would talk to the media.

I checked with Captain Caver, and he explained that no one had requested the women to come to Fort Davis. I knew the DPS would not look good if that got out, but I did not see anything we could do about it without making things even worse.

Julie Hopkins, understandably desperate to help her mother, followed through on the threat she had made to me and turned to the media. After getting a ride to "Mount Media," she and her sister, Lisa, were quickly surrounded by microphones and cameras. With O'Rourke by their side, the women made a tearful appeal for their mother to give up.

"Please don't make us bring your two-and-a-half-year-old

grandson to your funeral," Julie Hopkins said, addressing her mother through the media.

At 4:30 that afternoon, I went back to the media area and stressed again that the DPS was making every effort possible to resolve the situation peacefully. I read McLaren's "Travis" letter, reported that he and four of his followers had faxed out wills, and released copies of the orders from the ROT president.

What I could not tell the media was that—based on McLaren's refusal to surrender even after ordered to do so by one of two men claiming to be the Republic's commander-in-chief—Captain Caver that afternoon had ordered officers to move up the road to within a quarter mile of the ROT "embassy." While I was taking questions, black-clad SWAT team members and Rangers, protected by body armor and the two armored personnel carriers, were carefully working their way up the canyon toward McLaren's trailer.

At the end of the briefing, *Austin American-Statesman* reporter Denise Gamino asked me why the DPS had not picked up Evelyn McLaren's daughters at the airport.

"We're not a transportation agency," I responded. "We told them last night we thought they didn't need to come and they came anyway."

I wanted to explain the "why" behind the DPS' seemingly cold-hearted attitude, but I could not.

After the briefing, we drove back to the fire station, where dinner was being furnished by a Texas prison system mobile canteen. The hot dogs tasted like hot dogs always taste, which is good when you're tired and hungry, but the peanut butter cookies were exceptional, chewy and sweet. If the cookies were made by an inmate, and I presume they were, I hope the pastry cook at the Fort Stockton (Texas) prison unit goes into the bakery business when he gets back in the free world.

Earlier in the week, Jeff Davis County Judge Peggy Robertson had called me at the command post and suggested that the DPS participate in a town meeting in the hope of allaying some of the concerns of the local residents. I told her I thought that was a good idea. I ran it by Colonel Thomas, who agreed.

Since Laureen, who had worked in Emergency

Management before she was promoted to PIO, had experience in facilitating public meetings as part of the state and federal disaster mitigation process, I asked her to work with the judge in setting up the town meeting. Laureen was a good smoother of ruffled feathers.

Laureen arranged for the DPS regional commander, Major Lee Smith, and Highway Patrol Captain Baker to be on hand at the meeting to answer questions and explain a credentialing system the agency had developed. A portable machine used to produce photo IDs had been set up at the county courthouse. Davis Mountains Resort residents could come by, get a photo ID, and, by presenting that and their driver license at the DPS checkpoint, be readmitted to most areas of the resort.

With the two officers and a couple of Troopers, Laureen left for the courthouse to handle the town meeting while I held down the fort at the command post.

As the tightening-up operation proceeded, I sat with Colonel Thomas and Lieutenant Colonel Davis and others on the covered concrete slab at the volunteer fire station, listening to the radio traffic as the officers reported their progress. Ranger Lieutenant Sanders was in charge of the operation.

Though the ROT had a scanner capable of picking up some law enforcement frequencies, they could not hear the digitalized, voice-privacy communication of the heavily armed officers moving in their direction. But we were listening to what the ROT members were saying on their radios, and it did not sound good.

Local ham radio operators had been monitoring the ROT's shortwave broadcasts for us for several days. As the SWAT officers and Rangers moved up the road toward the embassy, the radio traffic from the ROT camp became frantic and threatening.

"Mayday! Mayday! Mayday! Hostiles are invading the Republic of Texas embassy," McLaren yelled into a radio. "We have hostiles in the woods. This is a Mayday call for any nation in the world. . . .We are being invaded!"

Then his tone became taunting: "I guess you boys didn't learn anything from Waco or Ruby Ridge . . . and you fools are going to come here and kill me, huh, and overrun this mission. Well, be prepared to take the fall . . . You're dead meat!"

Though that transmission was clearly intended for the law enforcement officers encircling his "embassy," McLaren keyed his microphone with orders for his defense forces: "There's going to be an ambush," he radioed. "Go to Code Black, do not hesitate."

Not all the broadcasts were coming from McLaren. At one point I heard a woman saying, "Fire at will," and "God save the Republic of Texas!"

"Put the laser on him and pluck him," came another transmission from up the canyon.

Despite the ominous-sounding threats, no shots were fired. By dark, the teams were in position within 440 yards of the enclave and settled in for the night. It had not been easy. The officers had found more structures than expected along the way—aerial reconnaissance had missed some residences because of the heavy foliage. Each structure—outbuildings, trailers, houses—had to be checked before the officers could advance farther.

But now that the officers were in position, if McLaren and the others did not come out, the DPS was close enough to go in and get him if Captain Caver gave the order.

All week I had declined to discuss any tactical movements on our part, but with Caver's blessing, I announced the successful completion of the closing-in operation at my final briefing for the day. The captain wanted McLaren and anyone sympathetic to his cause to know that the "embassy" was surrounded. Unlike the defenders of the Alamo, McLaren still had a back door, but getting out would require a rough hike through desolate mountain country. The nearest pavement was fifteen miles behind the "embassy," and there were no roads leading to it. But between McLaren and that open country were DPS officers and Texas Parks and Wildlife Department game wardens with rifles.

Unless McLaren tried to do something stupid, the show was over for the night. I told the media I'd have no more information for them unless a significant development occurred.

After Laureen returned from the town meeting—which

she said had gone fairly well, pro-DPS sentiment far out-weighing any negative comments—she and I left for Alpine. It had been a very long day, and it didn't look like Saturday was going to be any easier.

That morning, the DPS plane had brought in some more equipment from Austin, and, of more importance to me, a suit-case from home with more clothes. Back at my motel room that night, I found a couple of nice surprises. Linda had got-ten the heel repaired on my good boots. And packed among my clean shirts were a card from Linda and a story from three-year-old Hallie, "The Blue Bear," with a notation in Linda's hand: "Dictated to Nana, 5/1/97." This is what Hallie wrote:

> One day a big, blue bear came to my house.
> He ate *all* my other bears.
> I gave the blue bear some Milk Bones to eat but
> Rosie [our Golden Retriever] ate them up.
> I gave the blue bear some fish to eat but Max
> [our black-and-white cat] ate them all up.
> Then the bear ate all of Rosie's food and
> all of Max's food. He ate my Cheerios.
> Then he ate all of my books.
> And that was just TERRIBLE!
> -30-

Reading my daughter's short story, complete with the tra-ditional journalistic "30" to signify the end of a piece of copy, reminded me there were a lot of things more important than what was going on in Fort Davis. Maybe if we sent Hallie's blue bear in after him, McLaren would come out peacefully and I could go home.

At any rate, the day was certainly ending better than the day before.

Thursday night I had walked into my motel room feeling pretty beat up. It seemed that I just couldn't satisfy some of the reporters, no matter how hard I worked at it. Also, early that afternoon I had been taken to the proverbial woodshed for a mild managerial "redirection" by Colonel Thomas, who thought I'd hammed it up too much at my Wednesday press

conference. My explanation that it was a deliberate bit of the-
atrics suggested by the FBI had not seemed to make a difference. Finally, I'd noticed a high-ranking uniformed officer
deliberately walk away from me when he was obviously trying
to have a confidential conversation with another officer. That
bothered me because it said that even after my twelve years
with the agency, at least one person in upper management
didn't trust me to keep my mouth shut. I hadn't even heard
what they were talking about. I was only on my way to get a
cup of coffee.

During one of the times the soft-spoken Sergeant Malone,
who had plans to be married on May 31, was between phone
calls with McLaren, I told him about the heat I was getting
from the media and maybe I whined a little about a few of my
other problems.

"As long as you know you're doing the best you can do,
that's all that counts," the Ranger said, his empathic manner
showing me why he was doing such a good job of negotiating
with McLaren. He was a good listener and said the right things.

Laureen was equally supportive.

Even so, I had not completely drifted out of my funk until
I started shaving early Saturday morning and, like the department's two-way radios do when they are first switched on,
went through a programming "self check." I reminded myself
that only three years earlier, almost to the day, I had been
lying in the recovery room after cancer surgery, just awake
enough to realize that for some reason my right arm was paralyzed. The use of the arm had come back and I had endured
chemotherapy. Nothing that had happened in Fort Davis—
including criticism—compared with what Linda and I had
gone through. Nothing matters more than your health and
your family.

Nothing.

The Republic's flag comes down

Saturday, May 3: Day Seven

As soon as we got to the fire station command post Saturday, I found Captain Caver and asked him if anything of interest had happened overnight.

"We started talking to Evelyn," he said. "We talked until about eleven o'clock last night. She wants to come out this morning at eleven." Caver's low key delivery made the news sound routine.

Maybe her daughters' pleading had made a difference after all. Or maybe it had finally sunk in on all of them that no one from outside the "embassy" was charging to their rescue. However it happened, Evelyn apparently had come to the realization that there was no percentage in carrying an Alamo analogy any farther.

Evelyn and Ranger Sergeant Malone talked again that morning. She was still planning to come out, she said, but needed some time to pack.

Laureen took care of the 10:00 media briefing, announcing the upbeat news that Evelyn McLaren had said she would be giving herself up in an hour. Despite the fact that her husband had fired O'Rourke, she had requested that the lawyer be present when she came out. Reporters asked Laureen what made Evelyn McLaren decide to give up. She replied that she had no information on the woman's state of mind, but said the DPS was delighted with the turn of events.

One of the mountain-based spotters radioed that Evelyn was indeed packing her white Blazer, which was parked in front of the trailer.

At 11:16 A.M., a Ranger radioed that he had stopped a Blazer driven by a white female and had her and the vehicle secured. He asked for a female officer to come search the woman, as a routine precaution to make sure she was not armed.

Voice communication by radio is virtually instantaneous, but driving the rocky, two-rut road winding down the canyon takes time. At noon, an unmarked Ranger car pulled up outside the fire station. Another officer drove the Blazer in.

Wearing a red blouse and denim skirt, Evelyn McLaren emerged from the Ranger's car with a brown file folder in her hands. Since there were no state charges pending against her, she was not cuffed. On the concrete slab at the fire station, she and O'Rourke embraced. Caver and Malone came up and shook hands. It was all very cordial. She was smiling.

After a moment or two, they walked inside the volunteer fire department office and someone shut the door. From there, after a brief interview with the Rangers, they went to the FBI trailer, where Sergeant Malone had been manning the phone connection to McLaren. With several FBI agents and Malone listening in with earphones, Evelyn picked up the phone to talk to her husband.

"How are you?" he asked.

"They're treating me well," she replied.

"What's the code?"

"Code 99."

The couple had arranged the code before she left him that morning. Depending on what numbers she used, McLaren would know whether she was being candid with him.

"That's great!" McLaren said.

With the small talk and code-checking over, the tone became serious. Evelyn explained that the Rangers had a four-paragraph "cease-fire" document for him to sign. The agreement, written by O'Rourke, was styled, "International Agreement and Terms of Cease Fire Between The Republic of

Texas and its Body Politic . . . and . . . The State of Texas and its citizens. . . ." (See Appendix)

"Rick," she pleaded, "there is no other way. You must approve this thing as it is."

Sergeant Malone sat next to Evelyn, listening to both sides of the conversation and writing suggested comments to her on a notepad.

"This is it," she said. "The tanks are rolling."

Malone wrote some more.

"I love you," Evelyn said. "I really want you out of there."

McLaren read the document as each page came out of his fax machine.

"That looks good to me," he said. "It looks good."

McLaren asked for fifteen minutes to talk to his colleagues about the proposal. Sergeant Malone agreed and hung up the phone. At that instant, the phone system crashed—an unexplained equipment failure that threatened the whole deal.

If McLaren tried to call back and found the line dead, he might think Evelyn's assurance of "Code 99" was only a setup. He might panic and do something stupid. Fatally stupid.

FBI and DPS techies scrambled to get the connection back up again. Their desperate efforts worked: The system came back, and soon McLaren was on the line again. He and his colleagues would sign, he said, but he needed a little more time.

Worried he might change his mind if he had too much time to think about it, the Ranger told McLaren to make it quick.

Not wanting to contribute to the crowded conditions in the command post van, I sat in the state car and listened to reports from the observation posts over my handheld radio. Using the car as an office kept me out of the sun and offered a bonus not available either in the command post or the covered patio of the fire hall: a soft seat.

At 2:28 P.M., the DPS observers watched as McLaren and the other three ROT members began stacking weapons around their flagpole. Two minutes later, all officers in the vicinity of the trailer were notified that McLaren was giving up and were told to stand by. McLaren then got on a tractor that had been blocking the road to the trailer and moved it, something he'd said over the phone that he would do.

At 2:34 P.M., the Ranger command post radioed that four persons would be coming out one at a time and would walk toward the M-88, the Army Guard's tank retriever.

Two minutes later, an observer reported that McLaren appeared to have called everyone to the flagpole for a surrender ceremony. Their weaponry, ten long arms ranging from conventional hunting rifles to assault-style weapons, was arrayed in a circle around their flagpole.

At 3:05 P.M., an observer reported that one person, wearing camouflage and a full backpack, had walked off from the trailer, headed northwest up the canyon. This was the second person the officers had seen leaving the "embassy." During the noon hour, another person, also in camouflage, had left the ROT property.

The observers, following orders, kept radio traffic to a minimum. At 3:26 P.M., an officer reported that three ROT members were outside hugging each other and that a fourth person, presumably McLaren, had gone back inside the trailer. When he came back out, the ROT members at the flagpole saluted him.

McLaren and Otto began walking down the road toward the M-88 at 3:28 P.M. McLaren, wearing jeans, boots, a tweed sport coat and a white straw cowboy hat, was carrying a briefcase. Otto had on farmer-style overalls.

At 3:42 P.M., Caver ordered the SWAT team members to move farther up the road in the Smith County armored personnel carriers. The DPS team was in the lead APC, followed by the Midland County Sheriff's SWAT team in the second track.

Ranger Sergeant Johnny Allen of Del Rio radioed that he was "10-95" with McLaren at 4:04 P.M. That meant the self-styled ambassador was in custody. Two minutes later, Ranger Sergeant Coy Smith of Uvalde reported that he had Otto handcuffed.

The Paulsons were arrested near the flagpole at the trailer about the same time by SWAT team members. One of the officers struck the Republic's colors—a blue flag with a single yellow star in the center—folded it, and presented it to Lieutenant Vance. Other team members quickly moved the Paulsons to the back of the lead armored vehicle, patted them down for weapons, and placed them inside the APC. With two ROT members, now known to be Matson and Keyes, still missing, and being prudent about the possibility of booby traps, the two APCs moved back down the road with the Paulsons.

The Republic of Texas stand-off was over and no one had been hurt. The only downside was that two ROT members were still unaccounted for. At the time, I thought only Keyes was wanted for a crime. I was unaware of the California arrest warrant for Matson.

Now I needed to get the word out to the media.

Before I did a briefing, Commissioner Holt wanted to run what I planned to say by Governor Bush's office. I told him I would simply outline what had happened and then say something to the effect that patience, perseverance, and professionalism had paid off. I'd make up the rest as I went along, I said. There wasn't time to write down many notes.

As the commissioner talked to someone in Austin from the pay phone at the fire hall, I heard a CNN report on the satellite television set nearby that McLaren had walked out of the embassy. I called Sherri and she told me that the Associated Press had already called wanting to confirm a report that McLaren had given up.

We were losing the edge on our own good news.

I don't make a habit of telling my boss' boss what to do, but I thought it was imperative that I go make the announcement immediately. Part of the unwritten DPS philosophy is reliance on individual judgment. I decided to push now and try for forgiveness later, if necessary.

"Commissioner, I *really* think I need to go tell them what's happened right now," I said, hoping my tone of voice helped communicate the sense of urgency.

"Okay, let's go," he said. "Get a Trooper to get us down there in a hurry."

I saw a Highway Patrol corporal and told him that the commissioner, Laureen, and I needed to get to the media area as fast as we could.

We got in his black-and-white, and the corporal did a great job of rapid transport. Maybe it was just my imagination, but at times, on the bumps, it seemed that we were airborne for a moment or two. I snuck a quick glance at the speedometer at one point and decided, as I had done five years earlier on the way to the Luby's in Killeen, not to look again. Just to make it a bit more exciting, I couldn't get my safety belt fastened, though I continued struggling with it until we got to "Mount Media."

We screeched up in a cloud of dust just before 5:00, with a few seconds to spare before the next cycle of CNN's "Headline News" and the beginning of the early Texas television newscasts. Just to make sure the media knew the department had something to tell them, one of the Troopers at the checkpoint tapped his siren.

I detailed the sequence of events regarding the surrender and explained that Keyes and Matson were missing, though I stressed that Matson had not been charged with any crime.

"As you can imagine, there is a lot of handshaking going on up there," I said. "We said all along that we wanted a peaceful solution. I hope the Department of Public Safety has shown the world how it's done right."

Among the viewers of the press conference was Colonel Thomas, who had flown back to Austin late Friday night. He called a short time after I got back to the command post.

"Well, not bad," he said. "Just remember to keep stressing the whole agency, not just the Rangers. And thank the community and other agencies for all their support any time you get a chance."

The colonel was right. Throughout the siege, I had been too prone to use the word "Ranger" as a synonym for "DPS officer." Everyone—from one of the commissioners and both colonels to the Troopers manning the roadblocks and the communications personnel working the radios—had been involved in this operation, not to mention all the other city, county, state, and federal officers.

The atmosphere around the fire hall after the surrender was somewhere between what it's like when your football team runs off the field toward the showers after winning a big game and the last day of finals when you don't have your grades yet, but you know you did pretty good on all the tests. SWAT and DPS Dive Team members, Rangers, and other officers who had been on the ground for twenty-four hours or more started coming in for food, pulling off their heavy ballistic body armor, and stowing their unused assault rifles in their car trunks. The officers were dusty, sweaty, and dead tired, but they were smiling and clearly relieved that no one had had to do any shooting.

I saw the Rowes walking around shaking hands and even hugging some of the officers. Joe Rowe came up and shook my hand. "We've been watching you on TV," he said, putting his arm around my shoulder. "You and the whole DPS have done a great job."

A short while before we talked, Rowe had presented the DPS with the Texas flag that had been flying from a staff at his house when the three Republic of Texas members attacked the week before. After making the couple prisoners in their own home, one of the men in camouflage had disdainfully ripped down the state flag.

Not long after Rowe handed the flag to one of the Rangers that afternoon, it was raised from a metal cross found on the ridge behind McLaren's trailer. As a group of Rangers and DPS Special Crimes investigators did the honors, a DPS pilot flying overhead snapped a picture of the moment. Not exactly a replay of Iwo Jima—when WWII Marines raised the Stars and Stripes over that newly recaptured rocky Pacific Island in a scene preserved forever by a *Life* magazine photographer—but for some of the officers who had slept on the ground at the observation post when it got down to 37 degrees at night, it was a personally satisfying moment.

From the pay phone at the fire hall, I called my mother in Austin. After talking with her, I called my dad in Amarillo. I had not had time to talk to them during the week. In fact, I had hardly had time—or energy—to call Linda every day. By the time I dragged into my room each night, I had talked about as much as I could stand. To try to explain to Linda, or anyone else, what I had been up to that day would take more energy than I had left. And in the mornings when I got up, she and Hallie would still be asleep.

Major John Standifer, a public affairs officer with the Texas Army Guard, had told me earlier that he could arrange a ride if I wanted to go up in one of the Blackhawks. When I saw that Captains Caver and Baker and several others were going up to take a look at McLaren's trailer and the area around it, I asked the major if Laureen and I could go as well.

The major got the necessary approval, and Laureen and I soon were strapping ourselves in the big helicopter. I sat next to the door so I could take pictures.

After we lifted off and began moving toward McLaren's now unoccupied "embassy," the wind hitting my face felt like one constant slap. I held my hat with one hand and my glasses with the other. My camera hung from my neck. If I had been a contact lens wearer, I would have been in a lot of trouble. Even with my glasses, the prop wash and airspeed stung my eyes.

Despite that, it was a great ride.

As we circled over the area, I wished the media had been able to see what I was seeing. I think the reporters would have had a greater appreciation of the difficult situation our officers and others in law enforcement had been facing. Even from a thousand or so feet above these mountains, the country still looked big. True, we had several hundred officers on the scene, but it would have taken an army to thoroughly cover all of that area by foot.

The media, of course, would have loved to see the same thing. Unfortunately for them, in a move they didn't like but one that was absolutely necessary from the law-enforcement perspective, the Federal Aviation Administration still had a no-fly zone in effect. TV station helicopters and planes chartered by the media would not be allowed over this area for several more days, I was sure.

Before the ride was over, though, I had had enough. The shadows were growing long and the temperature was beginning to drop. With only a T-shirt and long-sleeved cotton shirt on, I was beginning to get cold. I'm glad that I was able to see the area I'd been talking about all week, but when the Blackhawk set down at the fire hall in a cloud of dust and flying grass, I was equally as happy to be back on the ground.

Burros and booby traps

Sunday, May 4: Day Eight

The T-shirt one of the Explosive Ordnance Disposal team members wore that Sunday morning captured both the upbeat mood of the officers on the scene and the dangerous job that remained to be done:

> **I'm a Bomb Technician**
> **If you see me running**
> **try to catch up**

Twenty-four hours earlier, the stand-off could have gone either way. The atmosphere around the command post had been tense. Now, the morning after the surrender, the edge was off, even though two ROT members remained at large. People had had a chance to get a hot meal and catch up on their sleep. Some had even been able to shower.

About 9:00 that morning, Colonel Thomas and Lieutenant Colonel Davis arrived from the Marfa airport. They'd flown in from Austin to get a briefing on the situation and to congratulate the officers and support personnel for their role in the peaceful resolution of the stand-off.

Laureen and I rode with the two colonels, Caver, and several others from the fire hall to the farthest point the officers had reached on their advance Friday night. Beyond that, because of the pipe bombs and fuel containers around the property, it still wasn't safe.

Caver said it would probably take all day for the EOD personnel to sweep the area. Only then could the Rangers and crime lab technicians move in to start collecting evidence.

Not until we moved out from the fire hall did I fully appreciate the difference only two miles made. The road leading up the canyon got rougher and the timber thicker as we continued to gain elevation. A wild burro, descended from strayed frontier-era pack animals, stared at our vehicle as we bounced along the road. Those feral creatures used to be common even in Fort Davis, but now are found only in the mountains.

When we pulled up at the final staging area, a trailer house about a quarter mile from the ROT property, it looked like a scene from a war movie. Rangers and other officers were gathered around in clumps—some sitting, others lying down—their assault rifles nearby. They were talking and resting. There wasn't much for them to do but wait until the area around the "embassy" was safe to enter.

Paulson had agreed to walk officers through the ROT area and show them where explosives were located. The work was done by EOD teams from the Ector County Sheriff's Office and the Midland Police Department.

We had been warned to expect occasional explosions as the EOD experts blew some of the explosive devices they were finding. The first blast rolled down the canyon at 12:35 P.M. More followed throughout the afternoon.

Around 1:30 P.M., Laureen and I got a ride back down to the fire hall. We'd promised a 2:00 P.M. briefing and as slow as travel on the road was, we'd be cutting it close.

At the briefing, I announced that Keyes and Matson were still missing. Still not knowing about the California warrant for Matson, I said that though Keyes was the only one wanted on a criminal charge, the DPS did want to talk with Matson. (When arrested, he'd probably be charged with engaging in organized criminal activity like the others, but I didn't make that point publicly.)

A reporter asked how the two men managed to escape with so many officers on hand.

"We watched them leave," I bristled. "We didn't let them slip through anything. . . It was an absolute and deliberate decision of the commanders not to stop those two individuals. There was a tremendous amount of concern that if they tried to intercept those two people we would endanger an officer's life."

Another reporter wanted to know if the residents of the Davis Mountains Resort were safe with these two men still out there somewhere.

"There is no indication whatsoever that there are any people back there," I said. "There is literally nothing but open country. I promise you . . . there is nothing but mountains, wild burros, mountain lions and deer."

When some of the reporters continued to press for details as to why officers had allowed the pair to walk off the day before, I had some ammunition.

First of all, Caver had not wanted to jeopardize the surrender of McLaren, Otto, and the Paulsons by moving in to arrest Keyes and Matson as they left. Second, as I had already explained, it would not have been safe.

"We didn't want an officer killed or maimed by a booby trap. The more we learn, the more we realize just how volatile the situation was and the happier we are we resolved it peacefully," I said. Then I listed what had been found so far in the vicinity of McLaren's trailer:

- Twelve gasoline containers rigged so that the fuel in them could be ignited and flow downhill. This could have sparked the wildfire the Forest Service had been worried about.
- Thirty to forty crude pipe bombs scattered along the two dry creeks around the ROT property. (The final count came to sixty.)
- A five-pound propane tank filled with explosives.
- Myriad trip wires possibly connected to booby traps.

In addition, officers found that the ROT members had constructed at least eight bunkers at various points around the property. Most of them were made of stacked rocks with tents or camouflage netting over them. They had not yet been thoroughly checked because of the danger of booby traps.

Then I announced the bad news. I had asked if Laureen and I could take in a pool, but no one felt it was safe yet to allow the media into the area. I ticked off the reasons: the possibility of explosions, two armed men still on the loose, the fact that the area was now a crime scene needing to be processed for evidence, and finally, the area was private property, as was the road leading to it.

Even local residents were not going to be allowed back in to the upper end of the canyon, I said. Only people who lived south or east of Tomahawk Trail were going to be able to return to their residences on that day. And they would first have to go to the courthouse in Fort Davis to get an ID badge.

Laureen and I had not been back at the command post very long when we heard that a couple of Highway Patrol Troopers had been hurt when the patrol car they were driving went off a road. In the vernacular of the agency, they had been involved "in a fleet [accident]."

A rancher had reported seeing two men in camouflage on his property and the two Troopers, Billy Horton and Sylvia Cardona, were en route to the area on an unpaved ranch road when their car slid out of control and crashed into an iron cattle guard. Neither Trooper suffered life-threatening injuries, but they had to be flown to the hospital in Alpine for treatment.

I did a short evening briefing, but there wasn't anything significant to report.

If someone ever decides to write *A Guide to Fort Davis Restaurants and Nightspots*, it will be a very short book. I can count off the really good eating places on one hand and have two fingers left over, though we did not have time to patronize those places very often. In fact, Laureen and I ate at restaurants only twice during our ROT tour of duty. The most enjoyable meal was that Sunday evening.

After the final briefing, we drove back to Fort Davis and had supper at the Limpia Hotel Restaurant, the best traditional restaurant in town. The Limpia, built in 1913, is Fort Davis' oldest hotel. The food was great, but we were not able to eat entirely in peace. The place also was popular with the news media, and several reporters came up with questions. As nicely as I could, though it took some energy, I made the point that we were trying to have dinner and would appreciate the chance to eat in peace without having to field more questions. Another reporter came up and complimented us on the job we'd been doing. That made the earlier intrusion a little easier to swallow.

After we paid our checks, I gave Laureen a short tour of the town before we drove back to Alpine. That was the first evening we'd returned to our rooms during daylight. I even managed a little recreational reading before I drifted off to one of the better night's sleep I'd had. We figured tomorrow we'd catch a plane for Austin.

True, Keyes and Matson were still at large, but unless something unusual happened, we could handle the search for them and the mop-up operations by phone from headquarters.

"We're shutting it down," I had told the reporters. "This has become a routine manhunt now."

Shots fired!

Monday, May 5: Day Nine

After what we assumed would be our final continental breakfast in Alpine, we checked out of our rooms, loaded our luggage into the state car and headed for the Davis Mountains Resort. We'd stop at the command post, do a final media briefing, and then leave for Midland, where we'd turn in the pool car and catch a commercial flight home.

At least, that was the plan. But that's not the way things worked out.

As we checked out of the motel, we ran into Caver in the lobby.

"I just got a call," he said. "They've shot at some dogs. I don't know any more than that."

When we got to the command post, we learned that about 5:00 the afternoon before, a campsite had been discovered. Officers found a tent, a bedroll, and some MREs (Meals Ready to Eat).

At daybreak Monday a team of seventeen men—including mounted Texas Department of Criminal Justice dog handlers, their tracking dogs, and Rangers on foot and horseback—began moving into the area in search of whoever had abandoned their camp. The horse and dog teams had come from the prison unit at Fort Stockton. Ten minutes after they reached the deserted campsite, the dogs picked up a hot trail.

Their noses to the ground and their tails in the air, they raced ahead of the mounted men.

About 8:00 A.M., the officers heard loud pops echoing off the rocks. Someone was shooting at the dogs with a .22. Dog handlers and Rangers rushed in the direction of the sound, their weapons at the ready.

Five shots had been fired, wounding two of the hounds. After being hit, both dogs turned and ran back to their handlers. At the time, it was unclear whether the dogs had cornered both of the missing ROT members or just one. Somehow, the shooter or shooters managed to disappear.

As two helicopters, one from the DPS and one operated by the Border Patrol, criss-crossed the area, more officers moved in to take up the trail. Rangers teamed up with the prison dog handlers, who are not commissioned officers.

By 9:21 A.M., Rangers with assault rifles were moving along a ridge above the McLaren trailer and up a nearby ravine. At 9:49 A.M., the command post called the warden at the Department of Criminal Justice's Wallace Unit at Colorado City, more than 200 miles to the northeast, and asked for as many horses and dogs as they could bring to augment the horse and dog teams already on the scene.

An hour later, the high altitude and rising temperature were beginning to be a problem for some of the Rangers and other officers, who were radioing for water. They were running a manhunt in some of the prettiest but harshest country in Texas, not a particularly forgiving environment.

Trooper David Nesbitt, the only Highway Patrol Trooper assigned to Fort Davis full-time, rushed into town to collect all the bottled water he could find for the thirsty officers. By 11:30 A.M., a DPS helicopter was dropping water bottles and fresh radio batteries to Rangers and other officers working their way up the canyon from the ROT trailer.

The two wounded dogs, Jane and Susie, were taken to Janet Greathouse, a vet in Fort Davis. Susie was the more seriously wounded, shot in her chest. Jane had been hit in a leg. Though it was still not known who had fired the shots, that person had committed a felony by shooting a law enforcement dog.

As DPS officers and the prison dog handlers continued

their search in the rugged canyon, a federal prosecutor in Dallas was holding a press conference to announce the unsealing of the bank and mail fraud indictment that Marshal Dean had told us was likely to be returned.

McLaren, his wife, and five others had been named in an indictment on April 29 (two days into the siege) accusing them of printing more than $1.8 billion in official-looking but worthless Republic of Texas checks and attempting to pass them to various merchants, banks, and credit unions from December 1995 to January 1997.

The indictment also accused McLaren and the others of depositing $5 million in worthless Republic of Texas checks into a Puerto Rican bank account.

"This indictment sends a clear message to those who try to rip off residents and then ride off into the sunset by wrapping themselves in militia doublespeak," said Paul Coggins, U.S. attorney for the Northern District of Texas. "Our message to bullies is: Don't mess with Texas."

Indeed, the prosecutor said, if McLaren were convicted on all twenty-five counts in the indictment, he could face up to 725 years in prison and $24.25 million in fines. Evelyn McLaren's maximum possible sentence for conviction on the six counts in her indictment would be 155 years and $5.2 million.

"These defendants were not proud Texans," Coggins continued, "but paper terrorists. They're not revolutionaries, but ripoff artists. They're not patriots, but parasites."

The federal case, however, had nothing to do with Keyes and Matson, who were still messing with Texas. Laureen and I stood around in the Highway Patrol command post vehicle, listening to the radio traffic and taking notes as officers continued to search for the pair.

At 1:15 P.M., someone reported that the dogs seemed to be on a trail. After that, the radio was quiet except for occasional routine transmissions.

But at 1:52 P.M., one of the Rangers radioed that he had found a cave and some blood on the ground nearby, indicating that was the spot where the dogs had been wounded that morning.

A minute later, a Ranger radioed that a shot had been fired.

Caver picked up his microphone: "Unit 95 . . . return fire if fired on."

Three minutes later, I heard over the radio that more shots were being fired. No one had time to be specific.

Not wanting to tie up one of the two phone lines used for incoming and outgoing calls, I scribbled "Sherri—1:53 P.M. shot fired MLC" on one of the pages in my legal pad, ripped it out, and faxed it to her in Austin.

From the air, DPS helicopter pilot Reggie Rhea of Lubbock said he could see some of the prison dog handlers in the dry creek bed looking uphill, as if that were where the shots were coming from. This was happening nine-tenths of a nautical mile southwest of McLaren's "embassy."

At 2:03 P.M., the pilot radioed that one hostile, wearing fatigue pants and a black T-shirt, was down and not moving. On the same piece of paper that contained my first note, I wrote: "1 hostile down lots shots 2:03 p" and faxed it to the office.

Two minutes later, I sent another note: "Advise Col. 1 bad guy shot—not moving gen. gunfire continuing—MLC"

The only mistake in my message was by that time, all the shooting had stopped. But the radio traffic had been so fast and confusing I didn't know that yet.

Finally, I got it sorted out. The man in camouflage had shot and killed another one of the prison dogs. A second dog was missing and presumed wounded or dead. The prison dog handler, thirty-one-year-old Field Lieutenant Joe E. Pechacek— the only person who had had a clear view of the shooter— raised his rifle, a .270 loaned by his grandfather. The lieutenant had only four shells. Seeing that the man was now shooting at the DPS helicopter, Pechacek aimed for the man's gun arm and fired.

At that point, Ranger Coy Smith opened fire with his AR-15 in the general direction he believed the hostile to be, expending twelve rounds. To cover Smith and the dog handler, Ranger Gene Key fired eighteen rounds from the helicopter with a Mini-14. Still, the dog handler was the only one who could see the man who had killed one of his dogs, Sugar Ray. The shooter had been moving downhill, firing up at the DPS helicopter as he walked. From 150 feet away, Pechacek could see the muzzle blast and faint smoke with each shot.

The lieutenant's first round knocked the man down, but now he was back up. His right arm hanging limp from the wound, he grabbed the pistol with his good left arm and raised it again, aiming at the helicopter. When the man started firing again, the lieutenant laid the cross hairs of his scope over the gunman's torso and squeezed the trigger. The man went down, and this time he did not get back up.

Ten minutes after the shooting, Rhea reported that all the dog handlers were safe and accounted for. The Rangers were doing a head count to make sure none of them had been wounded in the brief but intense firefight. Soon all of them were accounted for. No one had been hit.

At any moment, I expected to hear of more shooting. One ROT member, presumably armed, was still missing. But as the afternoon wore on, no further sightings were reported. The dogs did not pick up a new trail.

Another task lay ahead now: The Rangers would have to collect any evidence and do an investigation into the circumstances of the shooting. Their findings would be routinely passed on to the district attorney for presentation to a grand jury.

More Rangers and crime lab personnel, already on hand to process McLaren's trailer and the area around it, moved to the location of the body. Measurements would have to be taken, photographs and a video made.

The next step would be removing the body of the man and the dog he had shot. The Rangers had trouble reaching the scene, which was in a rocky area above a dry creek bed. A horse could not get to the spot, much less a vehicle. The only way to get the body out would be by helicopter, a job that would be handled by a Medical Assistance Surgical Team (MAST) helicopter out of Fort Bliss at El Paso.

As darkness neared, dusty, tired officers began showing up at the volunteer fire hall for something to eat and drink. Justice of the Peace George Vickers arrived. Under Texas law, it was his job to formally pronounce the man dead and then to determine the cause of death.

"I hope they have the decency to take the dog off first," he said when he learned the two bodies would be coming in by helicopter.

When the Blackhawk roared overhead, I grabbed my camera to get a few shots of the chopper being unloaded. As the rotors began to slow, one of the crew members, still wearing his helmet, emerged from the ship with something in his arms. Looking closer, I could see it was the dead dog. The Guardsman carried the body firefighter style. I snapped a couple of frames, wishing I had a camera with a longer lens. The redboned hound had died a hero's death. I noticed a few people dabbing their eyes as they watched.

Sheriff Bailey and Wofford moved out to take the dog from the crewman in the flightsuit. It would be taken for necropsy to the same veterinary office in Fort Davis where the two wounded dogs were being treated.

As the sheriff and Trooper Nesbitt looked on, four volunteer firefighters carried the body of the gunshot victim from the helicopter in a foldable orange plastic basket. I moved closer to take a picture. As they walked past me, I noticed a black combat boot sticking out from one corner of the basket. They took the body to the metal building where the ambulance and fire trucks were parked. There Judge Vickers could go through the legally required formality of pronouncing him dead. After that, the body was taken to a funeral home in Marfa. The next stop would be the Bexar County Medical Examiner's Office in San Antonio, where an autopsy would be performed.

Though no identification was found on the body, we knew the dead man was probably Matson. In deference to his family and friends, however, I told the media that he had not yet been positively identified—which, of course, was true. I did say that he appeared to have been middle-aged, which for all practical purposes revealed who he was.

That night Matson's brother, Ralph Matson, told an Associated Press reporter that he believed his brother was dead. "I knew he wasn't going to surrender," the brother said. "He went down there to be McLaren's bodyguard to the end. He told me, 'I'll never surrender.'"

Indeed, Matson had faxed out a will. The still-missing Keyes had not.

The nearly weeklong stand-off had not lessened McLaren's enthusiasm for talking to the press. In a telephone interview from the Presidio County Jail that night, McLaren called on Keyes to surrender peacefully.

"This is Ambassador McLaren with the Republic of Texas," he said. "We're down here in the Marfa jail, and they're taking excellent care of us. I respect the Texas Rangers for what they have done, and they will live up to the deal."

Though McLaren knew Keyes would not be reading the next morning's newspaper, he told the reporter who interviewed him that he hoped someone else would relay his statement to Keyes via shortwave radio. If Keyes got the message, he did not come walking out of the canyon with his hands up.

That evening we went back to the motel for one more night. This time, they even had a regular room I could rent.

Before dawn on Tuesday, May 6, the aircraft with its heat-detecting equipment made one more search over the area. The pilots did not pick up any promising signatures.

Caver decided to call off the search. One fugitive wandering around in a wilderness area, the captain believed, was not worth risking lives over. Getting a dead man and a dead dog out of that canyon had been hard enough. Evacuating injured or wounded would have been a nightmare. Unless something significant happened that morning, he said, the command post would be shut down at 3:00 that afternoon.

With no concerted search planned for Keyes, Laureen and I didn't need to stay around in West Texas. I held a final briefing late that morning, informing the media that we were leaving and that the Texas Department of Transportation was pulling the chemical toilets from the rest area. One of the reporters made a crack about a possible connection.

"We no longer have any indication at all that [finding Keyes] would merit an extensive search," I said. "Eventually, somewhere, he'll show up."

Even before the final briefing the number of reporters had begun to drop off. Those still hanging around hoping for some startling last minute developments were as tired as Laureen and I. The questions were tame. The confrontational attitude was gone. A few reporters actually thanked us for our help.

We were all eager to get home. The show was over.

We headed to Fort Davis for only our third sit-down meal (not counting motel breakfasts) since the stand-off began. After Mexican food and several glasses of iced tea, we left to return our pool car to the DPS regional headquarters in Midland and then catch a flight back to Austin.

But first I drove to the Overland Trail Museum near the federally maintained ruins of the old cavalry fort. I presented the curator one of my handmade DPS PIO signs for the museum's collection. The museum is located in the house once lived in by Nick Mersfelder, Fort Davis' first eccentric. The stand-off involving his successor in eccentricity, Richard McLaren, was now a part of Jeff Davis County history. Maybe not as colorful as the so-called Camel Experiment—when in the 1850s U.S. Secretary of War Jefferson Davis ordered the Army to try camels as a possible mode of transportation in the arid Southwest—but no less bizarre.

Preventing a second disaster

Even without Doppler radar and all the other high-tech gizmos that television stations use to tell us about the weather, anyone who has spent much time in Texas could do their own forecasting that afternoon by simply looking to the north.

What no one could have predicted was just how bad it was going to be.

The printer in our office was spitting out weather advisories from the National Weather Service continuously. A tornado watch was in effect, and now we were getting reports of tornado warnings. Laureen was on the phone with one of our lieutenants in Waco on another matter when he told her a tornado was reported on the ground south of the city. But so far, it merely seemed like an average stormy spring afternoon.

The impending weather did not deter me from leaving the office early. It was Tuesday, May 27, 1997—our seventh wedding anniversary. A babysitter was coming over to watch Hallie so Linda and I could go out for dinner and a movie, something we had not been able to do all that often since Hallie joined the family.

Typical husband that I am, I went straight from the office to the closest shopping mall to get Linda a last-minute present. By the time I emerged from the mall, the sky to the north was noticeably darker than it had been only a few minutes before.

Listening to the radio on the way home, I began to understand that we were in for more than a typical spring thunderstorm. Other people in their cars were calling the radio station on their cellular phones to report tornado sightings.

As soon as I got home, I turned on the television and switched to the National Weather Service cable channel. The radar showed a huge red mass that looked as big as the spot on Jupiter bearing down on Austin. I clicked over to the local station that usually does the best job on reporting weather. The meteorologist looked worried. The station's newsroom was beginning to report storm damage.

At the office, Sherri got a call from the radio operator at the DPS district office on the far north side of Austin. The Highway Patrol captain wanted her to contact local news media outlets and tell them to urge workers in the Austin metropolitan area to stay in their offices and not try to go home until the storm passed.

"Call Robin [our babysitter] and tell her not to get out in this," I told Linda. "I hate to leave you on our anniversary, but I need to get back to the office and I want to get there before this hits. Keep the TV on and if it looks really bad, you and Hallie get in the closet."

At the DPS, our customer service employees were ushering citizens out of the glass-lined lobby into safer interior offices. Fortunately for Austin, the storm was beginning to play out. But other parts of Central Texas were not as lucky.

At 3:45 P.M., a giant tornado had lumbered into the Double Creek Estates Subdivision on the north side of the small Williamson County community of Jarrell, north of Austin. With telephone lines down and law enforcement officers frantically busy, it was a while before we began to realize at headquarters how bad the situation was in Jarrell. I was in Colonel Thomas' office when Chief David McEathron, the agency's highest-ranking uniformed officer, called and said Troopers on the scene in Jarrell were reporting mass casualties.

A short time later we learned that the roof of a large grocery store in Cedar Park, also in Williamson County, had collapsed when a tornado cut through that area. Numerous people were reported trapped inside.

Colonel Thomas told Chief Frankie Waller, head of the Department's Administration Division, to tell the Training

Academy staff to put the khaki-clad cadets on standby for emergency duty. Out-of-town DPS Troopers at the Academy for in-service training were ordered to put on their uniforms and report for duty. Half would be sent to Jarrell, half to the grocery store at Cedar Park.

By 4:30 P.M., the storm had moved into Travis County, headed toward Austin.

Near hurricane force winds were blowing sheets of rain outside the Headquarters building by shortly after 5:00 P.M. The storm, which was spreading out and losing some of its punch, moved through the capital fairly quickly. Damage in North Austin seemed minimal, but the electricity was off.

I called the Associated Press bureau in Dallas to pass on the report of multiple injuries and possible fatalities at Jarrell, told secretary Laura Luckie I'd need her to stay after 5:00, and told Sherri to get ready to go to Jarrell. A few DPS offices in the Headquarters complex have emergency lighting, but not PIO. We did our work by flashlight for the next couple of hours.

When Laureen and I had returned from Fort Davis, I had promised Sherri that she would be the first PIO sent to the next major situation. I just hadn't expected it to be so soon.

"I know traffic's going to be horrible, but get the staff car and head for Jarrell," I said. "Just go north on I-35. You can't miss it."

I got Laura to page Laureen, who also had left early to take care of an appointment.

"I need you to go to the Albertson's grocery store on Highway 183," I said when she called in on her cell phone. "It was hit and there's a rescue operation under way. We've got Troopers split between there and Jarrell, and Sherri's on her way there."

Laureen had ridden out the storm at her fitness center. She'd been in an exercise class and had to go home and change. I tried to talk her into going straight to the scene of the roof collapse, but she insisted she had to change. Besides that, she had her husband Wally with her and needed to drop him off. On top of everything else, she was stuck in a horrendous traffic jam.

The way this afternoon imploded is a perfect illustration

of the one great truth about emergencies: They never happen when you're ready for them. I had planned a rare night out with Linda for our anniversary celebration. Laureen and Wally were at their fitness center. Sherri and Laura had plans with their families. But for everyone in the DPS Public Information Office, the stormy afternoon turned into a long night.

Still, for us it was merely inconvenient and tiring. For the people of Jarrell, it was a night of tragedy. At one point, we thought as many as thirty-one people had been killed by the tornado. The final count was slightly less—twenty-seven dead.

When Sherri reached the devastated community, traffic was so bad she had to park the DPS car and set off on foot down a dirt road toward the hard-hit subdivision. Only later did she learn that the road was not really unpaved. The tornado had sucked up the asphalt. The destruction was so complete that the scene of the disaster didn't even look all that bad—just a big open field. But that was deceiving. Almost everything had been ripped apart and blown away.

One Austin television crew had rushed north on I-35 with the initial storm warning and captured incredible video of the giant storm. Now the news media blew into Jarrell like a second squall line. By the time Sherri reached the scene, numerous media vehicles clogged the only roadway leading to the subdivision. Reporters and camera crews were roaming the area freely.

Though they came home late each night to get what sleep they could, for most of the rest of the week, Sherri and Laureen helped Williamson County officials cope with the media. They conducted press conferences, assisted the local justices of the peace in releasing the names of the dead, and listened to complaints about access from the media.

Three days after the storm, Williamson County Sheriff Ed Richards called me to say how much he had appreciated our help. Since Laureen and Sherri happened to be sitting in my office (this Friday was their first day back at Headquarters), I put the sheriff on my speaker phone. His tone of voice told the story.

"I've got one more favor to ask," he said. "Could I have my communications people refer the media calls to your office for a while? I've got to get a little rest." And then, almost as if it had just occurred to him, he added: "You know, the media's really been part of our problem here."

Richards had learned the hard way that week what anyone in government must keep in mind: The news media, just like the F5 level tornado that devastated part of Jarrell, is an extremely powerful force in our society, one capable of producing considerable chaos. Unlike a tornado, however, the media can be a positive force. Austin television and radio stations did an excellent job of warning Central Texans of the approaching storm. In a disaster, the media also plays an important role in alerting authorities, assessing damage, collecting information useful in decision-making, stimulating and coordinating rescue and relief activities, accounting for missing people, and motivating for disaster preparedness efforts.

But the media also can create a whirling cyclone of rumor, misinformation, lies, panic, and confusion, not to mention the exaggeration and distortion of reality. When a half-mile-wide tornado bears down on your community, about the only options are fleeing the area or, if there is not time for that, taking cover. But there are steps that can be taken to prevent the arrival of the news media from amounting to a second disaster.

It is hard to plan for the unexpected, other than to realize that sooner or later it will happen. In other words, expect the unexpected. Between 1988 and 1992, according to a 1994 report by the Annenberg Washington Program, sixty-six disasters which killed more than 100 people occurred worldwide. During the same period, an additional 205 disasters resulted in damages exceeding one percent of the Gross National Product of the country or countries affected. Obviously, an incident does not have to be above these benchmarks to be considered a disaster.

Fortunately, of the three types of crises—sudden, developing, and ongoing—emergencies are the least common.

A mid-1990s study of 50,000 news stories by the Institute for Crisis Management at Louisville, Kentucky, revealed that only fourteen percent of business crises were unexpected. The remaining eighty-six percent were what the

Institute called "smoldering crises," known situations building to a flashpoint.

The Waco incident and the Fort Davis stand-off were smoldering crises. The Killeen mass murder was a sudden crisis. For the Clinton administration, the Whitewater affair has been an ongoing crisis. The 1998 sex scandal arrived a little more suddenly.

In situations where the unexpected is not all that unexpected, a spokesperson needs to be alert to possibilities. The spokesperson should also be able to depend on advance word of possible trouble. Agency and department heads need to have enough trust in their spokespersons to give them a heads-up when something major is in the offing. If the person whose job it is to speak for your organization cannot be trusted with sensitive information, that person should not be on the payroll.

The strategy from the spokesperson's perspective is to work to earn the confidence of those in charge by showing them on a day-to-day basis that he or she knows when to keep quiet. A spokesperson with a media background should cultivate sources inside his own agency with the same energy he or she once devoted as a reporter to the care and feeding of contacts. Build trust.

Though no crisis situation is ever exactly the same, it is possible to have a generalized disaster plan. Here are some steps to insure readiness:

• **Have a written public information policy**. Most large organizations have such a policy in place. If yours does not, get some samples and develop one for incorporation into your agency's operating procedures. The central thesis of this policy should be that your agency, to the extent it lawfully and ethically can, will cooperate with the news media in the release of public information.

• **Prepare a checklist of basic steps which should be taken in the advent of possible scenarios, from airplane crashes to a stand-off situation**. Keep these standard operating procedures in your computer system but also distribute paper copies to those likely to be involved if the situation arises.

• **Maintain ready-to-go equipment and supplies for emergency situations**. Make sure you have the equipment you need before you need it. Since each situation is different, you'll need something one time that you won't need the next, but some items are indispensable. Each of the DPS public information officers keeps a packed go-bag of essential items in his or her vehicle.

• **Have a media credentialing system in place**. The DPS issues press identification cards to the mainstream, working media—journalists who are likely to cover major crimes, accidents, or disasters. The only intent of these cards is to enable DPS officers to be able to identify media representatives at such scenes. They are not free passes to athletic events and rock concerts or get-out-of-jail-free cards.

Here's a crisis communications strategy for law enforcement emergencies and disaster situations:

1. **Assess the situation**. After the initial notification, make sure something's truly significant before you go into full-bore crisis mode. An overreaction can give a situation inflated significance. Make this assessment as quickly as possible, of course. If an event is a major crisis, the sooner you move into action, the better.

2. **Designate a spokesperson**. If your organization is large enough, a spokesperson should already be on the payroll. Actually, if the organization is of some size, it should have several spokespersons on staff.

A trained, experienced spokesperson who already has good credibility with the news media is indespensible in crisis situations. And credibility is not something developed overnight. It is earned through accumulated experience and a solid understanding of the media and its needs. It is continually strengthened by day-to-day contact with the media and ongoing professional development. In short, your PIO should be a pro, someone the media—and the public in general—will know they can trust.

But if you do not have someone functioning as the media lightning rod, the first step in a crisis is to give someone that authority—and responsibility. The person selected to work with the media should not be the same person who has overall command. That person will have enough problems without having to take time to talk to the media. Generally, it helps if the emergency spokesperson has media experience or at least experience in dealing with the media. The spokesperson should be someone who can think on his or her feet, be cool under pressure, and high enough in the organizational chart to be as autonomous as possible.

3. **Cover the telephones**. While at least one spokesperson is en route to the scene, others should be handling the phones at the office, releasing whatever solid information is available. Get help. The phones need to be answered. If the people answering the calls cannot do interviews, they need to take messages and assure the caller someone with information will get back to them as soon as possible.

4. **Get the spokesperson to the scene**. Some crises, of course, can be handled from the office. Not all emergencies have a physical location. But when something big has happened at a particular place—a disaster or major incident—it is vital to get someone to the scene as quickly as possible. The media will be rushing to the scene too. In all likelihood, they will get there first. And if no one is around to take control, they will add to the chaos.

At the scene, the spokesperson should immediately approach the media and establish that he or she will be the contact person. Set up any necessary ground rules. The cameras probably will be rolling, but keep your comments to a minimum unless you have some useful information. Since you will have just arrived on the scene, you probably won't have anything of substance to report. The important point is to establish that you are in control of the situation as far as media relations are concerned. That control needs to be maintained throughout the duration of the incident.

5. **Set up a media staging area**. While the incident commander is establishing a command post, the spokesperson needs to be gathering the media at an appropriate location. Consider these points in selecting a site:

• Safety for media personnel, agency personnel, and the general public.

Mike Cox addresses media at a daily briefing, Fort Davis stand-off.
— Photo by Bob Daemmrich Photography, Inc.

Texas Department of Criminal Justice dog team and horses outside DPS command post.

— Courtesy Texas National Guard.

DPS command post at Davis Mountains Resort.
— Courtesy Texas National Guard.

Laureen Chernow and armored personnel at Fort Davis.
— Courtesy Texas Department of Public Safety.

From left: DPS Public Safety Commissioner Robert Holt, Capt. Barry Caver, Mike Cox, and Laureen Chernow.
— Courtesy Texas National Guard.

Gregg Paulson in custody.
— Courtesy Texas
National Guard.

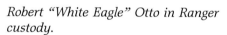

Robert "White Eagle" Otto in Ranger custody.
— Courtesy Texas
National Guard.

Karen Paulson after her arrest outside the ROT embassy.
— Courtesy Texas
National Guard.

Evelyn McLaren and Terrence O'Rourke talk as Captain Caver (left), Ranger Sergeant Malone, and FBI agent look on.
— Courtesy Texas National Guard.

"White Eagle" in custody.
— Courtesy Texas Department of Public Safety.

McLaren and Captain Barry Caver.
— Courtesy Texas Department
of Public Safety.

Richard McLaren in custody.
— Photo by Bob Daemmrich
Photography.

Mike Matson's body removed.
— Courtesy Texas
Department of
Public Safety.

Joe and M. A. Lowe with author.
—Courtesy Texas
Department of
Public Safety.

From left: Captain Barry Caver, D.A. Albert Valadez, and Mike Cox.
—Courtesy Texas
Department of
Public Safety.

The author with (future spokesperson?) Hallie Cox.
— Author's photo.

• Legal issues: Is the location a public place? Can the media legally be invited to a particular area?

• A location separate from the law enforcement and disaster relief command posts, yet close enough to allow for convenient coverage without interfering with law enforcement or relief operations. (Warning: The media seldom will be satisfied with the place you select as a staging area. If most reporters had their way, they'd be walking shoulder-to-shoulder with rescue workers picking up body parts at the aircraft crash site, or rolling their cameras as your SWAT team members take their positions.)

Despite the First Amendment, the news media does not enjoy an absolute right to gather news. The U.S. Supreme Court held in a 1972 opinion, *Branzburg v. Hayes*, that while news gathering clearly has First Amendment protection and journalists have the right to get information "from any source by means within the law," the First Amendment "does not guarantee the press a constitutional right of special access to information not available to the public generally. . . .Newsmen have no constitutional right of access to the scenes of crime or disaster when the general public is excluded. . . ."

Once the media know where they can set up their equipment, it should be their responsibility to see to their own logistical needs. The conventional wisdom used to be that the government agency in charge should provide the media with tents, phones, electric power, and other necessities. But as a general rule, most of those needs should be provided by the media. At Fort Davis, a utility company set up power lines for the media and the telephone company installed seventy phone lines at a reported cost of $10,000. The Texas Department of Transportation had nine portable toilets brought in to the staging area.

As for food and drink, when word spreads that a media encampment has sprung up, private enterprise, sensing a quick buck, will undoubtedly enter the picture. At Fort Davis, local restaurants came to the media encampment and sold burritos, pizzas, and box lunches. The Salvation Army may have a canteen truck nearby as well.

6. **Establish flight restrictions if necessary**. If television station helicopters swirling above a scene like so many metal dragonflies is a problem (and it usually is) the incident commander should contact the Federal Aviation Administration to request emergency flight restrictions over the area. At Fort Davis, the restriction was 5,000 feet and five miles. A flight restriction is never popular with the media, but it is a safety issue. TV helicopters could interfere with law enforcement or medical evacuation helicopters and create a dangerous level of noise and distraction.

7. **Gather and verify information**. As soon as the media knows where it can come for information, the spokesperson needs to start getting a handle on what happened. In effect, a spokesperson becomes a reporter, seeking out accurate information from the incident commander and others with knowledge of what has happened. Beyond information-gathering, the information must be evaluated and verified before it can be released.

8. **Call a briefing**. Once the spokesperson has enough accurate information to brief the media, make sure the appropriate co-workers and supervisors have it first. It is critical that the spokesperson in the field and whoever is handling calls at the central office or headquarters exchange information frequently to insure that the same story is coming from both places. They may know something you don't know or have a good reason for you to withhold some aspect of what you have learned. Then have someone notify the wire services and other major news organizations when and where the briefing will be. A briefing should be held as soon as possible after the event. If you don't start talking, someone else will. And you might not like what they have to say.

9. **Release information**. I would have been lost at Killeen, Waco, and Fort Davis without a yellow legal pad. It became my alternate brain, and was considerably more reliable than the original 1948-model hard drive I have between my ears. Write information down as it comes to you, but before the briefing, go somewhere quiet and private—your vehicle will do if you don't have someplace better—and prepare an outline for your briefing.

I used a simplified variation of the I, II, III / A, B, C / 1, 2, 3 outlining system we all learned in school. In journalism school, budding journalists are taught to arrange their stories in order of importance, starting with the most important development and moving toward the least important. But since some reporters invariably still will be setting up their equipment when you start talking, I usually try to start off with softer information before moving to the big news. Knowing that the media has a short attention span, I try to sandwich the important information in the middle, then taper off to conclude the briefing with housekeeping matters: when the next briefing will be, how soon they can expect a pool, who to contact, and other routine points.

Since it is vital to have a consistent message, don't be shy about writing that down and referring to it as you talk. Repeat it often.

Five considerations are paramount in anything you say:

• Public safety: Warn of any ongoing hazards and pass on what steps to take to protect life and property in a continuing situation.
• Accurate information: Erroneous information must be corrected quickly and rumors dispelled.
• A caring attitude: Not only does it sound and look good to express concern for the public, it is the right thing to do.
• Legal issues: What you say could result in lawsuits against you personally and your organization. In criminal cases, remember a defendant's right to a fair trial and the right of all citizens to a certain level of privacy. In hostage situations and stand-offs, don't reveal tactical information. Don't say anything that would hinder an ongoing investigation.
• Your organization's good name: When the world is watching you and your agency, you want it to like what it sees.

Don't do a media briefing off the top of your head. You will invariably forget something important or say something you should not have. Remember: Off the top of your head = off with your head.

Once you have gone through your outline, take questions, but don't stay in front of the cameras too long. Set up some ground rules, such as no shouting and only one follow-up question. If you've done a good enough job with your initial statement, most answerable questions should have been answered. Don't waste a lot of time with the unanswerable questions. You can better serve the media by getting back to the command post and getting the latest information. Fifteen minutes is about right for a briefing. Anything above thirty minutes is too long.

Depending on the circumstances, you may want to have uniformed law enforcement officers present at your briefing for security.

10. **Establish a public information center**. In a protracted on-location situation, the lead agency's public information staff should have its own office, staffed with at least one spokesperson along with clerical help. This office should be open to the media, but it is important to have an area where confidential discussions can be held. The office becomes the center for information collection, rumor control, and administrative matters—from credentialing to arranging pools. Ideally, another spokesperson needs to spend most of his or her time at the command post, keeping abreast of the latest developments.

11. **Organize a media pool**. No matter how detailed your information and colorful your descriptions are, the media will rightfully want to reach their own conclusions. They will want access—both to talk with the people involved and to get still photographs and video.

In the early stages of a crisis, the best way to deal with this pressure is to offer a limited number of journalists the opportunity to go inside your perimeter with the understanding that they will share their information and images with their competitors.

12. **Coordinate with other agencies or organizations**. The response to a major incident may involve many different agencies. Often one entity, usually a law enforcement agency, takes the lead. But not always. Some of the other agencies involved may not have trained spokespersons, and there is a

potential that someone could say the wrong thing or release inappropriate or incorrect information. During the early stages of the July 1996 TWA crash off Long Island, for example, too many different people were talking to the media. The best strategy is to have one person do the talking. If that is not possible, try to work with each other so that you all stay on the same sheet of music.

13. **Evaluate**. Once the situation is over and the number of media calls have returned to normal, evaluate how you and your staff handled everything. Arrange newspaper and magazine clippings chronologically (your staff can do the clipping or you can hire a clipping service if you don't already use one) and then read them that way. As you read the coverage, note which of your remarks were quoted and which were not, how accurate the stories were, who else the media talked to, and whether the story was positive, neutral, or negative. If you want an impartial analysis of media coverage, there are consultants who will do this for a fee.

Also, encourage those who were involved to prepare written evaluations of how the situation was handled with suggestions for improvements. Make lists of the things you learned— the things you did right and what you did wrong. Capture any innovative solutions you came up with.

14. **Get ready for the next time**. Get some rest. Seek critical incident stress debriefing if necessary. Take any necessary remedial steps. Purchase the equipment you didn't have when you needed it.

Silver bullets

Try this trivia question the next time you want to show how clever you are: Who was Captain Daniel Reid?

Every Baby Boomer and almost everyone else knows about Captain Reid, but not by that name. The captain and his younger brother were Texas Rangers, so the story goes. The notorious Cavendish gang ambushed the brothers and four other Rangers, killing everyone. Or so they thought. Badly wounded, Reid passed out and was taken for dead. The outlaws rode on.

When the Ranger came to, he found himself in a cave. A silhouetted figure moved toward him from the cave's mouth. The Ranger saw the man was an Indian.

"Me . . . Tonto . . ."

"What of the other Rangers?" Reid gasped. "They were all my friends. One was my brother."

"Other Rangers all dead. You only Ranger left. You lone Ranger now."

Tonto and the Lone Ranger, created in 1933 by writer Fran Striker for radio station WXYZ in Detroit, rode off to help tame the fictional Wild West and become American icons.

Fortunately for those facing a ride through the media Wild West, there is a set of learnable survival techniques. The Lone Ranger, in addition to a good horse and a faithful friend, relied on silver bullets for his survival. He used the silver slugs as the ultimately ironic calling cards in the timeless struggle between good and evil, but also, as one writer later put it, as "a constant reminder . . . to shoot sparingly and always to remember the high cost of human life."

For the media relations classes I teach, I developed a set of silver bullets for dealing with the question-askers. Silver bullets worked for the Lone Ranger, and they will work for spokespersons, from routine media contacts to their own Killeens, Wacos, Fort Davises, and Jarrells.

But before we dig into the ammunition box, some general thoughts about the news media:

The first step in successful news media relations is understanding the mass media. We all know there are newspapers and magazines along with radio and television stations, but there are some things about the media that most people don't know.

Newspapers

I first learned of the *Challenger* disaster and the Oklahoma City bombing, not from the traditional news media, but by word-of-mouth. Other than informal oral communication, which remains one of the primary ways we get our news, newspapers are the oldest form of what we have come to call mass media.

In America, newspapers were society's primary news source from pre-Revolutionary War times until the advent of commercial radio in the early 1920s. Afternoon newspapers published several editions a day, from the early "bulldog" for street sales to a home delivery edition and then a final edition for late sports and stocks. People didn't have to wait for the next morning's paper to read about a major event. Really big stories prompted EXTRA editions, day or night. Large cities used to have two or more competing newspapers, often with opposing viewpoints on local issues and national politics. These days, most cities have only one newspaper.

Radio superseded newspapers in terms of immediacy, but newspapers remained the dominant medium until the electronic industry came up with a way to transmit pictures along with words via radio waves.

But what newspapers lost in speed of delivery, they kept in their ability to cover more topics in greater depth than can broadcast news. A radio newscast is over in two to five minutes. The total amount of time devoted to news during the local half-hour television news slot is twelve minutes. Even that twelve minutes is diluted with household hints, consumer education, tips on entertainment and dining out, and medical information usually too brief to be helpful. The rest of the time is taken by weather, sports, and commercials. The networks offer twenty-four minutes of news during a half-hour show.

Several years before his retirement in 1981 as anchor of "The CBS Evening News," Walter Cronkite pointed out that the entire script for one of his broadcasts would barely fill two-thirds of the front page of the *New York Times*.

In fact, Cronkite's take on TV news, offered in his highly readable memoir, *A Reporter's Life*, is the best I've ever read:

> The major problem is simply that television news is an inadequate substitute for a good newspaper. It is not too far a stretch to say that the public's dependence on tele-vision for the bulk of its news endangers our democratic system. . . . Hypercompression of facts, foreshortened arguments, the elimination of extenuating explanation— all are dictated by television's restrictive time frame and all distort to some degree the news.

Here are four important things anyone who deals with the media should keep in mind about newspapers:

• Print reporters, for the most part, have been educated and trained to think in terms of the written—not spo-ken—word.

• Print reporters have more space for news. They will need more information than broadcast journalists. They will ask more detailed questions. They may also want copies of statistical reports, documents and memoranda, or access to electronic databases and information that can be used in the preparation of graphics.

• Print reporters have more time to prepare their stories. On breaking news, they may have a deadline of midnight or later. For an in-depth story or a series of two or more articles, they may have several days or even weeks to gather their information.

• Print reporters tend to be more experienced and better paid than broadcast reporters, though television news readers who anchor shows often command high salaries, generally because of their "star" appeal. Print reporters are more likely to file requests for governmental information under federal or state open records laws.

No thinking person can deny that newspapers generally produce a product of greater quality than a television newscast, but the print end of the industry is changing.

These are the realities: Despite increasing population, circulation is declining in all but the wildest boomtowns, and young people are not acquiring the habit of reading newspapers.

Today only a handful of American cities have competing daily newspapers, and afternoon newspapers are a thing of the past in all but the smaller markets, where some Monday-through-Friday afternoon newspapers still publish. Nationally distributed newspapers have come into their own in the last two decades. Transmission of data by satellite and remote printing plants have enabled the *New York Times*, *Wall Street Journal,* and *USA Today* to be available anywhere in the nation on the same day of publication—something impossible when newspapers were shipped by train, truck, or even airplane.

The World Wide Web is allowing these national newspapers, and others, to "publish" with a timeliness that may put them back on an even playing field with radio and television in terms of immediacy. Also, the Web gives even local or regional periodicals international reach. So far, newspaper Websites only offer a portion of their paper product, but the likelihood is that as more consumers buy personal computers and get on the Internet, the electronic versions will become more comprehensive.

Newspapers are using their Websites as extra "space," as well. During the Fort Davis stand-off, several Texas newspapers published some of Richard McLaren's letters and documents on their Websites. In the spring of 1997, in a significant first in publishing history, the *Dallas Morning News* chose to "scoop" itself by publishing an exclusive story on its Website before it ran in the paper the next morning. *The San Angelo Standard-Times* and *Midland Reporter-Telegram* have their Republic of Texas stand-off coverage archived on their Websites. The San Angelo newspaper's site also offers "sound bites" of the players in the drama, a gallery of photographs, and the text of McLaren's siege-related Website offerings.

In addition to the newspapers with national and international circulation, America still has its Big Three traditional news magazines, *Newsweek, Time,* and *U.S. News and World Report.* These magazines used to be more of a weekly summary of the news than they are today. They have lost readers along with the newspapers. Now, trying to survive in a world of virtually instant publication, these magazines tend toward trendy stories and a focus on the American Zeitgeist.

My favorite line from news magazine writers: "My deadline's Saturday and the magazine won't be out until Monday, so you can go ahead and tell me since the newspapers will have it anyway by the time we're on the stands."

Broadcast news

The four major television broadcast networks—ABC, CBS, Fox, and NBC—are hardly in a position to laugh at the problems of newspapers and news magazines. Viewership of network news also is declining.

From 1993 to the spring of 1996, the number of people who said they regularly watch television network news declined from 60 percent to 42 percent. More viewers watch their local newscasts, but even that percentage is down, from 72 percent in 1995 to 65 percent in 1996. The number of people watching television purely for pleasure also has dropped. The networks' prime time audience in the first half of 1997 was 62.1 percent, down from 65.2 percent in 1996. Cable channels had 32.4 percent of the prime time viewing audience, up from 29.5 percent the year before.

However, research also shows that television news viewership dramatically rises during major events, such as the Gulf War, the Oklahoma City bombing, and the death of Princess

Diana. In other words, we don't pay a whole lot of attention to what's happening in the world on a day-to-day basis, but as soon as we hear about something really big (and the way we find out may well be by word of mouth), we turn on the television.

To cope with this overall decline, albeit one punctuated by occasional spikes when the big stories break, TV news is becomingly increasingly soft, the distinction between news and entertainment increasingly blurred. That's why a development like the O.J. Simpson murder case was an ideal story for television. It offered the best of both worlds: lurid crime and celebrity involvement.

So where are the newspaper readers and TV viewers going?

In the case of newspapers, faithful readers are getting old and dying, while young people are watching MTV or surfing the Internet. Network viewers are moving to the cable and its multiple choices and to the Internet. Or they eschew immediacy altogether and go to the store and rent a video of a movie they missed on the big screen.

The key points to know about broadcast media news:

• Though they generally use "sound bites" captured by tape recorders and edited video, both TV and radio can easily operate in real time, showing events—or providing audio—as they happen.

• No matter if you are being interviewed live or on tape, the time devoted to your message is limited. The average radio story is only seconds long. The average television story is ninety seconds. A two-and-a-half-minute TV news story (excluding TV news-magazine pieces, which run longer) is the broadcast equivalent of a full-length book. The time devoted to what you and others have to say in these stories is even shorter. In 1992 the average "sound bite" afforded presidential candidates was slightly more than eight seconds.

• The broadcast media, by offering information that print media can't—such as tone of voice, body language, and dramatic action—is more powerful in shaping public opinion.

There are three major points to keep in mind about the news media in general:

• Perception is reality. It does not make any difference whether what someone perceives is actually correct—that perception, once reached, is what a person believes. Changing that perception is extremely difficult.

A perfect example of this is the general public's perception of the crime rate. The homicide rate in the United States dropped 20 percent from 1993 to 1996. But during the same three-year period, the number of crime stories on network television increased by 721 percent. An average viewer's perception is that the incidence of crime, particularly murder, is out of control and getting worse, that it is not safe to walk into your own front yard. Yet the reality is that virtually all categories of major crime are down. America is actually safer than it used to be. But perception is reality. Watch "America's Most Wanted" more than a few times and, if you didn't know better, you'd be thinking the nation was on the verge of anarchy.
• Information is available so fast, and from so many different sources, that it can be overwhelming. Technology continues to improve, but we're stuck with the same old brain to process it all. Nancy Woodhull, executive director of the Media Studies Center, put it this way: "We don't have an information explosion because people want more information. We have an information explosion because of . . . technology."
• Competition, though different than it used to be, is still strong. In fact, the traditional sort of competition to get the news first is now accompanied by a near desperate effort to be interesting enough not only to attract consumers, and thus lure advertising dollars, but to hold readers and keep viewers from hitting the mute button on their remote control or clicking over to watch an R-rated movie on Home Box Office or over to the Discovery Channel to watch a lion eat a gazelle.

For anyone who has information the media may need,

from the corporate world to government, the result of all this is harder questions and more pressure coupled with a very real risk of distortion. It's back to the Wild West.

"Hi-Yo, Silver, awa-a-ay!"

The silver bullets come in two "calibers": ethical principles and considerations of good judgment.

Silver Bullets of Ethics:

1. **Abide by the law and applicable rules**. These include recognizing a defendant's rights in criminal cases, protecting any individual's right of privacy, and observing the requirements of your state's open records law and the federal Freedom of Information (FOI) Act.

Most government offices and large corporations have their own internal policies which must also be followed.

2. **Be fair**. Don't play favorites. Sure, you may have a friend, perhaps even a former colleague, with station WXYZ and really dislike the coverage station KXWZ gave you or didn't give you. But it's a very bad idea to favor one broadcast outlet, or one publication, over another. Playing footsie with one station might get you a favorable story one time, but it will not win you any friends with the other guys and will likely cause problems over the long term.

After the Luby's massacre, the Killeen Police Department granted CBS anchor Dan Rather and the show "48 Hours" virtual *carte blanche* in doing a story on the tragedy. A CBS camera crew was present even while one of the witnesses gave a statement to one of the Texas Rangers assisting in the investigation of the case. The result was a great episode for "48 Hours" and a lot of animosity from ABC and NBC.

But there is more to it than that. During the stand-off in Fort Davis, my office was besieged with requests from the television networks for separate interviews or appearances on their morning shows. We said no thanks to "The Today Show" repeatedly (despite persistent efforts on the part of their producers) as well as to "Good Morning America" and CNN.

Our decision to say no to separate interviews was built on two major points:

First, if you do one interview, as a matter of fairness you are obliged to agree to all other requests for separate interviews. This is time consuming. When someone really pressured us for appearances, I explained that my time was better spent at the command post trying to learn what was going on than in going from camera crew to camera crew repeating the same information that I had already given in my briefings.

Second, declining separate interviews also keeps you out of trouble by reducing the possibility you will tell one interviewer something new or different, thus opening the door to conflicting statements. Doing multiple interviews is like subjecting yourself to a deposition process. The difference is, you probably won't have a lawyer with you to make sure you keep your story straight.

More sinister than granting an interview to one media outlet and not another is the deliberate, clandestine release of information. Journalists call this a leak. In Washington, this is the way many news stories are born. Someone with something to gain secretly releases information—which may or may not be accurate or complete.

Leaks that get out of control can sink ships and scuttle careers. They ruin lives. The best example of the damage a leak can do is the Richard Jewell case. On July 27, 1996, someone planted a pipe bomb in Atlanta's Centennial Olympic Park. Jewell, working as a security guard, saw a suspicious backpack under a bench, told police about it, and then helped move people away before the bomb exploded. The explosion killed one woman and injured 111 other people. At first, Jewell was hailed as a good old boy hero. Three days later, however, the FBI began questioning the thirty-three-year-old Jewell in connection with the case.

Unfortunately for Jewell, someone leaked that information to the *Atlanta Journal*. The newspaper's editors thought so highly of the FBI's interest in Jewell that they ran a rare EXTRA to report it. From there, the rest of the media picked up the story. The only problem was, though it was correct that Jewell was a suspect, he never was charged. In fact, the FBI later said Jewell had nothing to do with the case. Jewell filed big-time lawsuits. His suits against the National Broadcasting Corporation, CNN, and an Atlanta radio station were settled out of court for undisclosed but presumably substantial amounts. More than a year later, other lawsuits were pending, including one against the *Atlanta Journal*. As Jewell told the *New York Times*, "My life's path was forever changed, and it wasn't my choosing."

3. **Be honest**. Never lie to the media. Pick your favorite cliché. "Honesty is the best policy," "The truth will out," or "Liar, liar, pants on fire." Morality aside, you may get away with one untruth, or even several. But the odds are that eventually you will be proven a liar. This is bad for you as a person, bad for your career in communications, and bad for your agency or company.

Don't engage in cover-ups. A cover-up is a series of lies as part of an orchestrated effort to keep something quiet. As we learned after Watergate, cover-ups usually don't work. They may hold for a while, but partisan leaks and special prosecutors have a way of uncovering cover-ups.

If you have bad news, the best thing to do is announce it before someone else does. It may be painful, but it's the best bet in the long-run, and it gives you the control.

4. **Be courteous**. Don't try to avoid the media. Journalists don't take stonewalling lightly. If you duck into a car or into the sanctuary of your office to avoid a journalist, that makes great video. Even if a camera crew does not get a shot of you disappearing, the story will usually note that so-and-so avoided an interview or "failed to respond to our request to appear on the program." Trying to cover the camera lens is a particular no-no. A hand-over-the-lens shot is sensational footage on the evening news, making you look like some freshly indicted mobster trying to keep his mug off the TV screen.

Answer telephone calls and don't hang up on reporters.

Return a journalist's phone calls, even if it is to say that you are sorry, but you cannot discuss the matter they are asking about.

Hanging up on anyone is rude, no matter how tempting it may sometimes be. If you slam down a phone on someone while in your capacity as a government employee, it is inexcusable. Even in the private sector, where you have no absolute obligation to be accountable to the public (even though you have a common-sense or organizational obligation), it is not a good thing to do.

Silver Bullets of Good Judgment:

These, while not ethical considerations, are common-sense points to keep in mind for successful media relations. (My definition of successful is that your plane arrives at its intended destination without crashing and burning.)

1. **Avoid "off-the-record" talk**. When I teach media relations techniques to law enforcement officers, I tell them to view "off-the-record" discussions with the media with the same caution they would a gun. A gun, even if you believe it is unloaded, should always be treated as if it were loaded. Same thing with this issue.

"Off-the-record" is journalistic parlance for "King's X," or "We're not playing for keeps." Some journalists call it "deep background." It means that if you or the journalist invokes the off-the-record privilege, in theory anything you say during this off-the-record period cannot be attributed to you. You both have to agree to it, however.

If you have been disingenuous enough to say something stupid, then realize what you've done and try to fix it by saying "That was off the record," you are most likely out of luck unless the journalist agreed in advance not to quote you.

I would only go off-the-record if I had an overwhelming tactical reason to do so (say, if lives or a criminal case depended on it) or if I knew the reporter well enough to know he or she would abide by the agreement. Unfortunately, there are some journalists—an ethically challenged minority, thank goodness—who will ignore an off-the-record accord in the interest of a big story.

2. **Avoid flippant, glib, opinionated, racist or sexist remarks**. You might get away with saying something flip, funny, or opinionated, if you do it carefully and are lucky. But racist, sexist, or blatantly politically incorrect remarks are career-killers.

The story of Captain Ernie Blanchard is a worst-case example. On January 10, 1995, in his official capacity as the spokesman for the U.S. Coast Guard, Blanchard gave a speech to Coast Guard Academy cadets and their guests. Telling his audience he intended to "dispense with the political correctness," he launched off into a series of risqué jokes. By about his third joke, the laughter had ended.

Academy officials and some of the cadets, including several of the women who had been in the audience, complained about the jokes. Though Blanchard quickly apologized for the remarks, complaints continued. Coast Guard officials ordered an investigation into the incident.

Blanchard, forty-six, had been in the Coast Guard nearly thirty years. Married and the father of two children, he worried about the loss of his pension if he were court-martialed. Finally, he offered to resign if the investigation were dropped. Four days after his request was denied, on March 14, 1996, the Coast Guard's chief of public affairs put a pistol in his mouth and pulled the trigger. Incredibly, the first round misfired. But he squeezed the trigger again.

No note was found, but a military psychological autopsy concluded: "The emotional pain and shame that Captain Blanchard felt he had brought upon himself and the Coast Guard led him to choose suicide as a solution."

If you do say something stupid, don't expect that a reporter will overlook the remark out of courtesy to you. Especially in situations where the official information available to the media is tightly controlled, such as during a stand-off or in the aftermath of a major crime or disaster, the difference between a ho-hum, just-like-everyone-else-is-filing story and a piece, either in print or broadcast, that's considered superior can be as little as one colorful quote: yours.

On its "Perspectives" page each week, *Newsweek* singles out the best quotes of the previous week or so, from the editor's perspective. The quotes selected are not always the best quotes from the viewpoint of the person who uttered them. Similarly, other magazines and newspapers often print these notable quotes twice, once in the main body of the story, and again, in larger type, as an illustration. These are called pull-out quotes.

Readers like snappy quotes, utterances that make them want to laugh, cry, say, "Boy, I wish I'd said that" or "Wow, I can't believe she actually said that!" Good and bad one-liners and their electronic counterpart, "sound bites," tend to get taped to refrigerators and show up in quotation books.

3. **Never say anything you wouldn't want to see printed or broadcast**. Even if it's not flippant, glib, opinionated, racist, or sexist. And never say anything your boss wouldn't want to see printed or hear broadcast.

As the mother whale told her youngster, "Remember dear, when spouting, you're apt to be harpooned."

4. **But don't rely on "No comment."** Always try to say something. To answer a reporter's question by saying, "No comment," you may as well be saying, "There's something important here I don't want you to know about." Those two words, short of the all-too-common prime two-word derogatory comment, are the worst two words a person can say to a reporter. Even if you aren't trying to hide something bad, those words make it seem that way.

Sometimes a government spokesperson simply can't comment on a particular issue, such as pending litigation, a personnel matter, or an ongoing criminal investigation. But with practice, you can learn how to say something without saying anything at all. Certainly most politicians are masters of the technique—but don't quote me on that.

When I was a newspaper reporter covering Austin's city government in the mid-1970s, Austin had a fine city manager, Dan Davidson. I don't know how many times I interviewed him, took copious notes, and then went back to the newspaper office to write my story only to find, in flipping back through my notebook, that the city manager hadn't said a thing. He was a master at saying "No comment" in an innovative way.

I don't favor complete smoke-blowing in answering questions from the media, because I believe government has an obligation to be as forthcoming with its citizens as possible. Usually there is at least something to say about any situation. Given their tight time restrictions, radio and television reporters can get by with brief comments. Newspapers need more detail, but you also have more time to think about what you're going to say.

Here's an example of how to make a statement without releasing sensitive or confidential information: Suppose there's been a shooting at the Road House Bar. Someone's on the floor near the pool table and they won't ever be racking'em up again. What do you tell the TV crews outside?

Try this: "We're investigating the shooting death of an unidentified individual inside the bar. Our crime scene technicians will be gathering evidence and then the body will be released to the Medical Examiner's office for an autopsy. At this time, no arrests have been made. That's all I know at this point."

It's not likely that a TV station would use even that much, which is fifty words. But in saying that, you have not released anything that could possibly harm the investigation or identify the victim, whose family has yet to hear of their beloved's demise. You didn't even give up the person's age or gender.

But if you had gone before the cameras and said, "No comment," the broadcast journalists might have had to go with what some drunk in the parking lot had to say.

5. **Stay away from speculation**. The day after accused killer Andrew P. Cunanan was found dead of a self-inflicted gunshot wound in Miami Beach in the summer of 1997, some official connected to the investigation responded to a media question with: "To answer that, I'd only be speculating." And then he proceeded to do just that.

In a courtroom, with your attorney sitting alertly a few feet away ready to hop up with an objection any second, you can afford to answer a question that begins, "Now, hypothetically . . ." But if a reporter asks a question requiring speculation on your part, don't fall for it. There is no Fifth Amendment protection here, or any other kind.

Some examples of this type of questioning:

- "What caused the plane to crash?"
- "Do you think foreign or domestic terrorists are behind the explosion?"
- "Did the people of (the community) have adequate warning before the storm hit?"

These are all sensible questions, but it is not sensible for you to try to answer them, especially early in any of these particular scenarios. Most speculative questions are far less reasonable than these, often to the point of bizarreness or tastelessness.

6. **Make sure your information is accurate—stay general until information is firm**. In a major situation, reporters will want as much detail as possible as quickly as possible. But it pays to make sure your information is solid before you release it.

A major media preoccupation in the aftermath of a disaster is the body count. In journalism, the significance of any event is judged on the number of people killed. Unfortunately, disasters are not like football games. There is no computer-operated scoreboard. During the first few hours after a mass casualty situation, fatality and injury counts tend to wax and wane: People initially feared dead because they were missing show up alive and well, names get counted twice, or someone who shouldn't takes a wild guess. In situations involving severe trauma, such as airplane crashes, fires, tornadoes and hurricanes, it may take the work of a team of rescuers and pathologists days or weeks to determine an accurate death toll.

In the first few hours after a major disaster that has left people dead, it is best to say there have been multiple injuries and fatalities and leave it at that until the facts begin to sort out. It looks bad, and can be unnecessarily alarming, to say twenty people have been killed and then come back later and say, "Well, at first we believed twenty people had been killed but now it looks like only fourteen died and six suffered only minor injuries. That's where the twenty came from—someone mistakenly added fourteen and six." Of course, there are endless scenarios here.

In the Watergate era, Richard Nixon's White House spokesman Ron Ziegler would have explained that the previous day's press release containing the incorrect information was "now inoperative."

The strategy to keep in mind in releasing information is to always start with the general and move toward the specific as details become available.

7. **Avoid using jargon**. Each field, from law enforcement to data processing to journalism, has its own language. Using terms particular to your field is fine if the only people you are talking to are colleagues, but when it comes to making comments to the general public, don't use jargon.

In my law enforcement media relations training, I suggest that officers refer to persons under arrest or being sought in criminal cases as suspects. On the East Coast, cops seem to prefer calling bad guys "perps" (as in perpetrators) and on the West Coast, crooks are often called "actors." Of course, in and around Los Angeles, that's sometimes literally the case. But the word "suspect," or after they have been charged with a crime, "defendant," are the best words to use.

8. **Develop a relationship of trust with editors and reporters**. Learn the names of the journalists assigned to cover the activities of your agency and invite them out for a cup of coffee. Or a soft drink. It seems to me that fewer and fewer reporters are using the beverage which used to be considered as fundamental to the practice of journalism as ink itself.

Good reporters cultivate sources, and if you expect to have satisfactory dealings with the news media, you should cultivate them.

When I offer these Silver Bullets to law enforcement officers, I remind them that they have the ultimate weapon in dealing with the press. It is not a .45 or a .357, but the power to cut the water off from any reporter or editor who turns you around.

Sure, government employees must at all times be responsive and courteous to the media and the general public, but beyond that there are subtle degrees of cooperativeness.

Fortunately, most reporters with any sense at all know this truism about news: Nothing is deader than yesterday's newspaper or broadcast. Old newspapers get recycled at best, or used to accommodate puppies or wrap trash at worst. Except for archived video images and tape-recorded broadcasts, electronic transmissions continue on into space for eternity, traveling ever onward toward the end of the universe.

So a smart reporter also knows that there is little percentage in blowing up a useful news source (you) for the sake of today's story. Tomorrow is another story, and they will need your help again. But keep those silver bullets in your gunbelt, Kemo Sabay, just in case.

Remembering the Alamo, Killeen, Waco, and Fort Davis

The siege of the Alamo continues to reign as Texas' bloodiest and most significant stand-off. The battle would have been one of Texas' biggest spot news stories, but no reporters were there to witness what happened and no spokespersons were on hand to brief the media as the victors stacked the bodies of the defenders and collected wood for a funeral pyre.

News of the fall of the Alamo took nearly five days to reach the settlement of Gonzales, less than seventy miles from San Antonio. The first newspaper account of the garrison's fall was not published until March 16, ten days after the battle.

As he pushed east to complete his suppression of the Texian rebellion, Santa Anna eventually seized *The Telegraph and Texas Register*, Texas' only newspaper, and dumped its printing press into Buffalo Bayou.

Imagine how the Alamo might have played out if the news media had been there to report what was going on. In the 1950s, CBS News did just that with its innovative television series, first begun on radio, called "You Are There." Network correspondents played themselves at various major events in American history in that show from the golden era of live TV. I remember being mesmerized by Walter Cronkite's "coverage" of the Alamo in the May 23, 1953, broadcast of "You Are There: The Defense of the Alamo." In 1971 the network briefly resurrected the series and did another take on the Alamo, but the series (intended for young viewers) didn't last long.

While the Alamo fell in a news vacuum—the end signaled

only by the silence of the guns—it could never happen again. When McLaren was playing Alamo in the mountains of West Texas, and I was making cracks about not being David Crockett, the ambient light generated at night by all the live-shot equipment, production vans, and satellite trucks at "Mount Media" could have been seen from the moon, if not Mars.

During sniper Charles Whitman's ninety-minute reign of terror from the top of the University of Texas Tower in Austin in 1966, anyone watching television heard the shots and saw the puffs of dust in real time as high-powered police bullets powdered limestone above Whitman's "fortress." KTBC Radio (now KLBJ Radio) provided live coverage.

As a cub reporter for the *Austin American-Statesman* (reporter Don Vandiver and I got to Whitman's house before the sniper's wife was found murdered inside), I remember thinking that his bloody rampage would be the biggest story of my career, even though I was then only seventeen years old.

After the Luby's massacre in Killeen, I told people I did not expect ever to be involved in another situation more horrible or stressful. Not even two years later, David Koresh made that statement invalid.

Though all of these incidents were big stories, the technology available to the media continued to advance, and the media played more of a role each time.

While the Republic of Texas stand-off was not a horrible event—in fact, if Mike Matson had not died, the whole thing could be viewed as somewhere between a Mel Brooks movie and a Woody Allen film—at times it was stressful.

With Texas the second largest state both in size and population, the DPS and other law enforcement agencies will undoubtedly face future crises. And I know the news media will always be part of the equation. Before starting work each day during the Republic of Texas stand-off, I tried to make notes on things I was learning about dealing with the news media during a crisis. Not only was my learning curve expanding, I was relearning the importance of things I already knew. What I learned in West Texas, and earlier at Killeen, Waco, and all the smaller crises my office has handled, will pay off in the future—for me, and I hope you.

The following observations, divided into major categories, can be chalked up as practical lessons learned or old lessons reinforced by my experiences in Killeen, Waco, and Fort Davis.

Operational/Technological Considerations:
• **Keep a log**. Try to keep track of all media contacts: name, organization, and telephone number. Also log major events as they happen, noting the time they occur.
• **Triage calls**. During the Korean War, the military developed the triage system for handling battlefield casualties. Medics and nurses sorted the wounded into three categories: those who were going to die no matter what, those who could be saved if they received prompt medical attention, and those with non-life threatening injuries who could afford to wait before a doctor saw them. Thanks to the television series "M*A*S*H," the word triage entered the American idiom.

In a crisis, media calls will start coming in as fast as the victims. In a major situation, one that awakens the interest of the nation or the world, calls will come faster than they can be handled. During the first few days after the fire at Mount Carmel, the call volume was so heavy that my office had to resort to triaging.

Here's my personal, unoffical telephone call/e-mail hierarchy:

Priority One, Non-Media: Your family, your office, and the pizza place checking to make sure they have your address right.

Priority One, Red: Your boss.

Priority One, Redder: His boss.

Priority One, Media: The wire services first, particularly local or regional bureaus, since they can spread the word quickly to the largest number of people.

Priority Two, Media: Local and state media. These are the people you work with every day. Getting back to them is always more important than out-of-state; i.e., national media.

Priority Three, Media: The major television and cable networks, nationally circulated dailies and news magazines.

Priority Four, Media: Out-of-state radio and television stations who have picked up the initial report of your big news on the wire and are looking for a quick sound bite.

Priority Five, Media: Free-lance magazine or book writers, Hollywood production companies (unless they are offering you a contract), and other entities out to make money off a particular situation. (I'm all for private enterprise, but the mainstream mass media has to take priority in a crisis.)

Priority Six, Media: International radio and television stations, newspapers, or magazines. I have done live radio interviews for stations in Australia, Canada, Columbia, and other places I've forgotten, but the point is: So what? What real obligation do I have to take time during a crisis to let listeners in Australia get a laugh out of my funny Texas accent? I'm not trying to be an isolationist, merely practical.

Drop Dead Last, Media: Tabloid newspapers published on any continent, tabloid television shows originating on any continent, and "reality" shows originating on any continent or planet.

Drop Dead Last, Non-Media: Drunks (especially those who tell whoever has answered the phone that they are your best friend), sober crazies, zealots, ax-grinders, telephone solicitors, and anyone who begins by saying, "Congratulations, Mr. Cox, you have just won. . . ."

• **Do situation-briefs**. If you don't have time to do it yourself, have someone in your office write a daily situation brief. This is history in the making, and you'll be surprised how fast you'll start forgetting details when the crisis is over. Given that fact, take copious notes; use a tape recorder or a laptop computer to capture as much information as you can while you can.

• **Record press conferences**. Videotape media briefings if at all possible. If you can't do that, at least make an audiotape. This gives you something to fall back on if you are misquoted or if your boss hears only a few of your comments out of context. At the bare minimum, get someone to take notes on what you say during a briefing. If you don't get anything on tape, electronic clipping services will happily sell you video footage of your media appearances.

• **Monitor your news coverage**. When developments occur rapidly, it's hard to have time to keep track of the way a situation is playing in the media, but it's vitally important.

Once we settled into something of a routine at Fort Davis, my office faxed me a representative sample of the major newspaper and wire service coverage each morning. We had a satellite-connected television set at the command post, so I was able to monitor CNN when I had an opportunity. This paid off a couple of times. On the day of McLaren's surrender, I learned that word had leaked out that the ROT members had given up. I quickly went to the microphones so I could tell the full story.

Shortly after the shooting of Matson, CNN reported that Texas Rangers had killed him. While that was a logical enough assumption, it was absolutely incorrect. The second I saw that report I literally ran to the telephone to call CNN and tell them that was not the case. When the smoke clears, which in some situations is not just a figure of speech, analyze the coverage the incident received. Media analysis is a growth industry in the public relations field, and deservedly so.

• **Go as high-tech as possible.** My office uses our voice mail system to record news updates for the media. We give the media a number to call and note at the beginning of each message that what follows can be recorded for broadcast. This is a time saver and keeps everyone on the same page with what we say. Some large corporations, with more sophisticated equipment at their disposal, put an entire news conference on their recorded information line. If your agency can afford it, this is a great idea. Also, statements to the media can be disseminated by fax (now considered relatively low tech), by E-mail, and on your agency's Webpage. Bottom line: In a crisis, go with the best technology you can afford.

• **Cellular telephones.** They are wonderful, but if a crisis occurs in a remote area, they may not work. Ditto for pagers.

Communication Considerations:
• **That's my story and I'm sticking to it.** Keeping to the core message is very important. Communications research has shown that one of the best ways to get a message across—because there always is some form of static—is to send it more than one time, even to the point of repetitiveness. The core message at Fort Davis: The Texas Department of Public Safety

is in charge, we want a peaceful solution, but McLaren's coming out. As the adage goes, Tell 'em what you're going to tell 'em . . . tell 'em . . . then tell 'em what you told 'em.

• **Don't answer a question someone hasn't asked—unless you want to**. Good media relations includes knowing when to keep your mouth shut. Helpfully volunteering some piece of information might backfire on you. The best strategy is to stick to the questions you get. They will be tricky enough. On the other hand, if there is a legitimate need to say something, say it.

• **Sometimes the answer is no answer**. Just because someone asks, you don't have to answer. Some questions simply do not deserve an answer. They are too off-the-wall to be given serious consideration. They are posed by reporters too naive to be covering a big story, by someone with an obvious bias, by someone who's not even a journalist, or by someone who is a couple of enchiladas shy of a full combo plate. I got questions from all four types at Waco and Fort Davis. Ignore these people courteously, of course.

• **Watch the buzz words**. During intense situations, buzz words proliferate faster than weeds after a two-inch rain. After a few days of hearing and reading McLaren's rhetoric, I found myself using words like "embassy," "diplomatic pouch," and "compound." I made a conscious effort to refer to McLaren's property as his trailer or simply as the Republic of Texas property or enclave. While McLaren may have believed the papers the DPS delivered to him from his attorney were in "diplomatic pouches," for me to use those words would appear to give his separatist position credibility. The DPS was attempting to arrest accused felons, not conduct international diplomacy.

• **Keep the rank and file informed**. Law enforcement and military operations usually have a "need to know" attitude. While this is vital when there is truly sensitive information, and has kept many an investigator alive over the years, some of the rank and file folks will begin to feel left in the dark. Keep the officers guarding the perimeters, and other support personnel, as up-to-date on what's going on as possible.

• **The O'Rourke Factor**. Named in honor of Terrence O'Rourke, who beat me at my own game the night he told the media that the DPS had issued McLaren an ultimatum, is this truism: If you want the morning headline, be the last guy at the microphone the night before. The media will go with the freshest and the sexiest development, even if it's not correct. (In defense of the media, reporters may not know something is incorrect, but they'll usually go with it if someone who seems authoritative tells them. This is especially true in fairly tightly controlled situations such as Waco and Fort Davis.)

• **Sorry, right number**. Be careful who you give telephone numbers and pager codes to, and how you relay the information. At one point during the Fort Davis siege, we started getting media calls over one of our supposedly restricted command post lines. When Laureen asked a TV journalist how she had gotten the number, the reporter said one of our own lieutenants—someone 175 miles away in Midland—had given it to her. If that journalist had shared the telephone number with colleagues, the mistake could have killed the effective use of one of our phone lines.

• **Is this line secure?** In fact, be careful with any unsecured mode of communication. It is illegal to do so, but cellular phone conversations can be monitored, even though such eavesdropping is becoming more difficult thanks to digital technology. Obviously, voice transmissions over unscrambled law enforcement radio frequencies can be monitored by anyone with a scanner. Even when an operation is unfolding in the middle of nowhere, the media will have scanners and they will be listening. At the Branch Davidian siege at Mount Carmel, there was some concern that illegal monitoring of cellular telephone conversations was taking place. During the Republic of Texas siege, the media established a radio listening post at McDonald Observatory.

• **Timing is everything**. Unless you have hot breaking news to relate, try to set press briefings so that the media will have enough time to digest the new information before their story deadlines. At Fort Davis, we tried for 10:00 A.M., 2:00 P.M., and 7:00 P.M., though sometimes we were too busy to be there exactly on time. When we'd set a time for a briefing, I'd call the headquarters office and get Sherri Green to notify the Associated Press and the other wires so they could put out an advisory with the time of the briefing.

• **Call your office**. At Fort Davis, Laureen and I tended to get busy with this issue or that and were sometimes slow to call our Austin office with updates. That made Sherri's job tougher. During a crisis, good communication is even more important than it is normally.

• **You're probably talking to the other side**. Remember that in some situations, the opposition may be hearing what you tell the media. This is both good and bad. In stand-offs, if the bad guy or guys listen in, you have an opportunity to reinforce certain points your negotiator might be trying to make.

In Waco and at Fort Davis, the opposition was listening.

Considerations of Mind and Body:

• **Stress**. A crisis is an unstable situation, rife with stress. Anger, disbelief, depression, confusion, lack of information, distrust, blurred lines of authority, intense scrutiny from your boss and the rest of the people of the world, the feeling that no one's on your side, a lack of control. . . . You'd better have some good internal coping mechanisms.

• **Easy on the machismo**. Try not to be too authoritarian in dealing with the press. Sure, your agency may be in charge, but this is still a democracy. Law enforcement agencies have no right to seize cameras, film, videotape, or notes unless those items are legally considered evidence in a criminal case. Arresting journalists is bad form unless it is absolutely necessary. Short of compromising safety or the law, we tried to do everything we could for the media (though several still protested that we were not doing enough). It helps to remind the media frequently that you are trying to assist them as much as possible.

• **If you want to join the circus, get a clown suit**. Don't let all the attention you'll get as a spokesman during a high-profile situation go to your head. You're just someone doing your job. Don't add to the circus atmosphere by show-boating. If Hollywood calls you, fine, but remember the attention you are receiving from the media has probably come at someone's expense, perhaps at the cost of many lives.

• **Get some sleep**. During a crisis, or following a disaster, fatigue and stress quickly come into play. The pressure can take a toll on you and those around you. Get as much rest as you can. In Waco and four years later at Fort Davis, Laureen and I asked our communications center not to call or page us with telephone messages from the media after 10:00 at night unless it was an emergency. To cut down on the chances of hurt feelings, I'd usually call AP in Dallas and report that we were shutting down for the night so we could get some sleep. The AP, like other wires and other major news organizations, is a twenty-four-hour operation. But they accepted my assurance that if they would not bother me, I would call immediately if I were notified of any major development.

• **Kill the messenger syndrome.** In ancient Greece, when a breathless runner brought royalty (read management) distressing news, it was customary to kill the messenger after he delivered his report. Such executions must have helped alleviate some of the stress, with the exception of those employed as messengers. The news media occasionally will invoke this bit of classical history when bemoaning how some readers and viewers don't like journalists or their product. The same principle applies to spokespersons. In times of stress, the most visible people make the best targets. These days, of course, messengers aren't usually killed, but they can be used for verbal target practice.

I particularly noticed this phenomenon after Killeen, when someone from another law enforcement agency complained about some of my comments to the media. Then DPS Director Colonel James Wilson had the DPS regional commander in Waco look at videotape of my press briefings, and he concluded I had not said anything I should not have. The complaint against me was from someone who was taking a considerable amount of heat as well.

• **Attention all units: Be on the lookout for a green-eyed monster.** Aside from the obvious high stress level during and immediately after the event, some tension-building factors continue even longer. You will find that some people, both in and outside your organization, are jealous of the attention that you received, even though you were just doing your job. Some of the most jealous may be your co-workers. The only solution is to take it in stride. Consider it a left-handed compliment that you were doing a good job.

• **Get another job**. Having read these mind and body considerations, if you don't have a hide tougher than a pair of alligator-hide boots, you might want to consider a different career or, when a crisis does occur, delegate the speaking duties to someone else in your agency or on your staff. Being the spokesman in a high-profile situation can be harmful to your health, as I discovered after Waco.

Finally:

• **Turn out the lights, the party's over**. Eventually, having daily news briefings tends to perpetuate a situation. Once news has slowed to a trickle, stopping the briefings is the best way to end, or at least greatly diminish, coverage of an event. In Waco, reporters were grateful when we announced that we would have no further briefings.

Follow-up: ROT

Not all the lessons of Fort Davis have to do with news media relations.

In an address to the Sheriff's Association of Texas at their convention in Fort Worth on July 21, 1997, Ranger Captain Casteel reflected on the Republic of Texas stand-off.

"Any experience like this is a learning experience," he said. "No matter how well you plan, there's always going to be something different. That is the first lesson of Fort Davis: Texas is too big and has too many people for us to reasonably expect that the Republic of Texas situation was the worst situation Texas law enforcement will ever face." Eventually, the captain continued, "Texas law enforcement agencies will . . . find ourselves in another situation where we have to invent some of the rules of the game as we play it."

The Republic of Texas stand-off was a large-scale tactical operation by numerous law enforcement agencies, led by the DPS, with a specific mission. As I had repeated frequently in my media briefings, it was not the beginning of a revolution.

"In the final analysis," the captain concluded, "it was not the DPS versus the Republic of Texas, not the State of Texas versus the Republic of Texas, not the New World Order versus the Republic of Texas—it was law enforcement versus a group of suspected law breakers. Some people broke the law in Jeff Davis County and they got arrested. That's all this was about."

But there are others—people with dark visions of unmarked black helicopters, United Nations troops secretly billeted on American soil, and government plans for concentration camps—who are convinced the future of the United States is in their hands.

On the Sunday after McLaren's surrender, Sheriff Bailey, who had asked me to speak on his behalf during the crisis, met with the media for the first time. He thanked the DPS and all the other agencies that had a hand in the operation and then said something I could not have said: "We've cut the head off the snake."

True enough in the case of McLaren and his closest followers, but there are a lot of rattlesnakes in West Texas—and a lot more metaphorical diamondbacks lurking under rocks all across the country with guns, explosives, and the warped idea that violence in furtherance of their ideas will somehow make the world a better place.

While the Fort Davis stand-off is history, the Republic of Texas movement, though fractured, did not end with the arrest of McLaren and his followers. But is there anything to his argument that Texas should not be part of the United States? Every historian queried on the issue has had the same answer: No.

"It's basically baloney," was the assessment of Rex Ball, executive director of the University of Texas' Institute of Texan Cultures in San Antonio. "They're ignorant of their history, or their history is very selective. . . . Their theory is goofy. People wanted annexation [to the United States]. They expected it."

One of the ROT movement's major arguments is that the United States Congress lacked authority to annex Texas, that only a treaty could have accomplished the admission of Texas into the Union.

"I know of nothing in the Constitution . . . that prevents an annexation by the United States of any political entity that is willing to be annexed," University of Houston law professor Sid Buchanan told the *Houston Chronicle*.

Texas Tech University law lecturer Ralph H. Brock, who wrote a lengthy article on the issue for the school's *Law Review*, said, "Texas could not have been made a state by treaty because the Constitution says Congress shall admit new states." Further, Brock said, under the principle of international law known as acquisition prescription "even if a country acquires territory illegally, if the territory acquiesces long enough . . . it's going to be deemed to be a valid acquisition."

Added University of Texas Associate Professor of Government Janice May: "The U.S. Constitution does not tell specifically how to acquire territory. By international law, you can acquire territory by treaty, discovery or occupation. The admission of Texas to the Union was very valid. The point is, it wasn't forced on Texas. A vote was required by Texas and people approved it."

The vote to approve a state constitution, a prerequisite for annexation, was 4,254 for, 257 against.

Although a citizen army did not rise to McLaren's defense in the spring of 1997, the militia and patriot movements continue.

Klanwatch and the Militia Task Force of the Southern Poverty Law Center in Montgomery, Alabama, identified 858 active patriot groups in 1996—488 patriot support groups and 370 militias who say they are opposed to the "New World Order." Of those groups, forty-eight were said to be active in Texas. Five of those groups called themselves the Republic of Texas or used those words in their name.

The lead editorial of the *New York Times* on June 14, 1997—only a few days after convicted Oklahoma City bomber Timothy McVeigh was sentenced to die by lethal injection—assessed "The Militia Threat."

Despite the outcome of the McVeigh trial, the newspaper said, "the violence of the militias that inspired him has probably not been extinguished. The militias are different from anything that preceded them because they gather not to take out their rage on Communists or minorities, but to wage war against a Government they consider treasonous."

The editorial went on to urge "more laws at the national and state level making it easier to prosecute people who terrorize public officials." Strangely, the editorial writer did not mention those who would terrorize the general public, though the editorial went on to urge "the importance of public condemnation of violence."

Finally, the editorial praised the FBI for its restraint in its handling of the eighty-one-day Freemen stand-off in Montana, though no mention was made of the recent essentially successful conclusion of the Fort Davis situation in Texas.

"The growth of the organized militia movement," the FBI reported in the July 1997 issue of *Law Enforcement Bulletin*, "represents one of the most significant social trends of the 1990s. This significance is due less to the actual size of the movement—by all measures, militia membership remains an almost imperceptible percentage of the population—than it is to the potential for death and destruction emanating from the most radical elements of the movement."

Special Agents James E. Duffy and Alan C. Brantley, the authors of the article, have done extensive research on militias. Brantley was at Fort Davis.

Militia members, the agents wrote, are generally white males ranging in age from their early twenties to mid-fifties. They usually are opposed to gun control, particularly the Brady Law, which requires a background check and five-day waiting period before a handgun can be purchased, and the 1994 Violent Crime Control and Law Enforcement Act, which limits the sale of certain assault-style weapons. Most members profess strong Christian beliefs and say they firmly support the Constitution. They see themselves as modern-day patriots opposed to governmental oppression and excessive, unjust taxation.

Special Agent Brantley and former Special Agent Gregory Cooper developed a four-category "Militia Threat Assessment Typology" for law enforcement agencies to use in evaluating militia groups (see Appendix). The categories range from groups which conduct paramilitary training but engage in no known criminal activity to groups which "plot and engage in serious criminal activity . . . homicide, bombings, and other acts of a terrorist nature."

"Clearly," Duffy and Brantley wrote, "elements of the militia movement represent a threat to law enforcement and to the general public. At the same time, the . . . movement is far from the monolithic terrorist conspiracy that some media accounts have portrayed it to be."

But the threat of violence continues.

Before dawn on July 4, 1997, shortly after the Duffy-

Brantley article was published, FBI agents and DPS officers arrested two heavily armed men: Michael Leonard Dorsett, forty-one, and Bradley Playford Glover, fifty-seven, at Colorado Bend State Park in San Saba County, a remote wilderness area on the Colorado River a little more than a hundred miles northwest of Austin. Officers seized five handguns, a homemade silencer, two rifles, 1,600 rounds of ammunition, chemicals and fuses they believed were intended for bomb making, a cannister labeled "riot smoke," a night vision scope, body armor, a radio scanner and a manual, *Militia Soldiers Operations Handbook.*

Glover, a Vietnam veteran identified as a commander in the First Kansas Mechanized Militia, had recently moved to the Fort Worth, Texas, area from Towanda, Kansas, after his wife filed for divorce and put their home on the market. Dorsett, who carried a bogus driver license featuring his own photograph but a fictitious name, was from Arlington, Texas.

Investigators said the two men, along with three other men and two women, had planned a "hit and run" attack on nearby Fort Hood, the large Army post outside of Killeen. The attack was conceived, according to the Missouri State Highway Patrol, at an April 1997 gathering in Independence, Missouri, "The Third Continental Congress." Undercover Missouri state police officers attending the meeting reported the plot, and an investigation by the FBI and law enforcement agencies in Texas, Colorado, Kansas, and Missouri was begun. The plan had been to attack Fort Hood on July 4, when the installation would be packed with people attending the base's open house and Independence Day celebration.

The FBI said the two men had intended after the attack to flee to Creed, Colorado, an old mining town, and meet up with other militia members. By July 11 all the other members of the group had been arrested.

"We were lucky; we were extremely fortunate," Missouri Highway Patrol Lieutenant Richard Coffey said following the arrests. "They [militia groups] are not to be taken lightly as a bunch of crazies. They feel a responsibility to fight what they believe is a worldwide conspiracy where the United Nations will become a world police force and trample people's rights."

The day that Dorsett and Glover were arrested, thirty-five people met in an abandoned courthouse in the near-ghost town of Sherwood (about thirty miles southwest of San Angelo) to begin drafting a constitution for the Republic of Texas. The convention, timed to coincide with the anniversary of a similar meeting of people bent on governmental reform in Pennsylvania in the summer of 1776, got some newspaper coverage but did not accomplish much.

One thing that didn't happen: No one introduced any resolutions in appreciation of McLaren's stand-off in Fort Davis. In fact, those attending were eager to distance themselves and their movement from any perceived connection to McLaren and his cadre of supporters.

"We may have radical ideas," one delegate told a reporter, "but we are civilized radicals."

McLaren and three of his followers—Otto and the Paulsons—were arraigned in 394th District Court in Fort Davis on July 10, 1997. All refused to enter pleas, and only Otto was represented by an attorney. Judge Kenneth DeHart entered automatic pleas of not guilty on behalf of each defendant.

The charges against Scheidt, the man whose arrest had triggered the stand-off, were dismissed and he left Texas.

At a pretrial hearing in the heavily guarded Jeff Davis County Courthouse on August 22, Judge DeHart set October 27 as the trial date for McLaren and Otto. The Paulsons would be tried separately.

On August 28, 1997, Sheriff Bailey arrested two women at the Davis Mountains Resort for criminal trespass. The women, who said they were ROT members, had just "served" the Rowes with a copy of a lawsuit filed against them in U.S. District Court in Washington, D.C., by McLaren. Bailey, Ranger Captain Caver, District Attorney Valadez, rancher John Wofford, and a long list of others with some involvement in the stand-off also were named as defendants in the civil suit, which sought $10 million in damages.

For more than four months after the siege, Richard Keyes was Jeff Davis County's number-one most wanted person. Rangers and DPS Special Crimes investigators, working closely with the FBI, vigorously sought to locate the young Republic of Texas sympathizer.

The Kansas Bureau of Investigation had him on its ten most wanted list as well. In addition to the state charges, Keyes was wanted on a federal warrant for unlawful flight to avoid prosecution.

At first, many assumed he had died alone in the mountains, succumbing to lack of water or food. Most locals figured his bones would turn up by deer season. A few others believed Keyes still was in hiding somewhere in the rugged canyons above the vacated ROT trailer, faithfully awaiting reinforcements like some fanatic Japanese soldier on a Pacific island after World War II. But on June 25, Keyes showed up—in Cyberspace.

On its Website, *Mother Jones* magazine published a story that purported to be based on an exclusive telephone interview with Keyes, who said members of a New Mexico militia group had helped smuggle him out of the mountains.

"Now I'm in a place that's armed to the teeth," he said. "If we have to make a stand, we can."

Keyes was on the verge of becoming legendary, a young man who somehow had managed to elude a veritable army of law enforcement officers, including the Texas Rangers. The *New York Times* observed that Keyes was "fast becoming a West Texas version of D.B. Cooper," the hijacker who bailed out of a Boeing 727 over the Pacific Northwest in 1971 with $200,000 in ransom money and was never seen again.

At 2:25 P.M. on Friday, September 19, FBI agents and DPS officers arrested a man in the Sam Houston National Forest as he walked along Farm-to-Market Road 1375 near the small community of New Waverly, about fifty-five miles north of Houston and more than 500 miles east of the Davis Mountains.

The man carried no identification, but a photograph faxed to authorities in Kansas, along with fingerprint comparisons, soon confirmed that he was Keyes. The fugitive was booked into the Harris County Jail in Houston.

"It feels great," Joe Rowe told a reporter after learning of Keyes' apprehension in East Texas. "I can't wait for them to get his butt out here to the Presidio County Jail to be with his

Republic of Texas friends. . . .let the criminal justice [system] work on them a bit."

The work of the criminal justice system began in late October 1997, when McLaren and Otto stood trial in Brewster County, where Judge DeHart had moved the trial from Fort Davis.

Testimony began on Monday, October 27, after a half-day jury selection process. The two defendants steadfastly refused to recognize jurisdiction of the court and did not allow their court-appointed attorneys to act in their behalf.

McLaren did cross-examine witnesses, but he and Otto were escorted from the courtroom dozens of times after outbursts that Judge DeHart considered disruptive.

The most startling testimony in the trial came on Wednesday, October 29, when Robert Stewart, who was identified as an FBI informant, said McLaren had negotiated with him to purchase semi-automatic rifles and shoulder-fired Stinger missiles capable of bringing down an airplane. The government informant said McLaren had intended to use the weapons in an attack on Texas Governor George W. Bush and Attorney General Dan Morales.

"One of his constant banters was that the Republic of Texas was going to rise and seize agents of government," Stewart testified.

Stewart said McLaren had begun negotiating with him to buy the weapons before the siege, and continued for several days after the stand-off began.

The jury also heard three telephone conversations between McLaren and Stewart that had been taped by the FBI.

"Things have gone condition red," McLaren said on April 27, the first day of the siege. "If your boys have any extra stuff, we'd appreciate some support."

Midland police bomb disposal expert Sergeant Andy Glasscock testified on Thursday, October 30, that the pipe bombs and other homemade explosive devices found around McLaren's trailer after the stand-off could have "killed or maimed."

"They knew what they were doing," he continued. "This is not something you learn in Boy Scout training."

On Friday—Halloween—the seven-man, five-woman jury took only ninety minutes to find McLaren and Otto guilty of engaging in organized criminal activity.

Four days later, on Tuesday, November 4, Judge DeHart rejected a motion by McLaren and Otto's attorneys that the crime they were convicted of be downgraded to a second-degree felony since the Rowes had been released voluntarily. The judge then went on to sentence McLaren to ninety-nine years in prison and a $10,000 fine— the maximum. Otto was given fifty years and a $10,000 fine.

The next day, escorted by Senior Ranger Captain Casteel and Captain Gene Powell, McLaren and Otto were flown on a DPS airplane from Alpine to the TDCJ's diagnostic facility at Huntsville.

Attorneys for McLaren and Otto said they intended to appeal their clients' convictions. In early 1998, the Paulsons and Keyes still were awaiting trial.

The Republic of Texas, though denouncing any ties to McLaren and his followers, continues an active Website on the Internet, labeling itself as the "True and Lawful government of the Republic of Texas."

Epilogue

On November 7, 1997, after watching her dad take part in a panel discussion on the vagaries of writing during the final session of the second annual Texas Book Festival, Hallie Cox climbed onto a chair and pushed it toward the microphone as the room started emptying.

Seeing she still had a potential audience, she began singing "The Peanut Song." Her little voice echoed across the hearing room in the Capitol.

Hallie's four now, and is not shy about being in front of microphones or cameras. She likes to have stories read to her and has already been in more book stores than many adults. Who knows, maybe she'll be a spokesperson someday. Or a writer, like her father, grandmother (Betty Wilke Cox), grandfather (Bill G. Cox), and great-grandfather (the late L. A. Wilke). Of course, her mother and I would just as soon she go into medicine.

Linda and I are doing fine health-wise, enjoying watching Hallie grow up, and are well aware that despite whatever we might have in mind, she'll do whatever she by gosh wants to do.

Appendices

A. Joint Resolution for Annexing Texas to the United States, March 1, 1845

B. Republic of Texas Documents, 1997

C. Republic of Texas Website Postings from Richard McLaren, April 27-29, 1997

D. FBI Militia Guide

E. Press Conference Guide (DPS Public Information Office)

F. Speak Into the Mic: Tips for Broadcast Interviews (DPS Public Information Office)

G. Channel 24 Rules, Policies (KVUE 24)

H. National Association of Government Communicators Code of Ethics

I. Cox's Media Event Scale: A Guide for Public Relations Professionals

A. Joint Resolution for Annexing Texas to the United States
March 1, 1845

1. Resolved by the Senate and House of Representatives of the United States of America in Congress assembled, That Congress doth consent that the territory properly included within, and rightfully belonging to the Republic of Texas, may be erected into a new State, to be called the State of Texas, with a republican form of government, to be adopted by the people of said republic, by deputies in convention assembled, with the consent of the existing government, in order that the same may be admitted as one of the States of this Union.

2. And be it further resolved, That the foregoing consent of Congress is given upon the following conditions, and with the following guarantee, to wit: First, Said State to be formed subject to the adjustment by this government of all questions of boundary that may arise with other governments; and the constitution thereof, with the proper evidence of its adoption by the people of said Republic of Texas, shall be transmitted to the president of the United States, to be laid before Congress for its final action, on or before the first day of January, one thousand eight hundred and forty-six. Second, Said State, when admitted into the Union, after ceding to the United States, all public edifices, fortifications, barracks, ports and harbors, navy and navyyard, docks, magazines, arms, armaments, and all other property and means pertaining to the public defense belonging to said Republic of Texas, shall retain all the public funds, debts, taxes, and dues of every kind, which may belong to or be due and owing said republic; and shall also retain all the vacant and unappropriated lands lying within its limits, to be applied to the payment of the debts and liabilities of said Republic of Texas, and the residue of said lands, after discharging said debts and liabilities, to be disposed of as said State may direct; but in no event are said debts and liabilities to become a charge upon the Government of the

United States. Third, New States, of convenient size; not exceeding four in number, in addition to said State of Texas, and having sufficient population, may hereafter, by the consent of said State, be formed out of the territory thereof, which shall be entitled to admission under the provisions of the federal constitution. And such States as may be formed out of that portion of said territory lying south of thirty-six degrees thirty minutes north latitude, commonly known as the Missouri compromise line, shall be admitted into the Union with or without slavery, as the people of each State asking admission may desire. And in such State or States as shall be formed out of said territory north of said Missouri compromise line, slavery, or involuntary servitude (except for crime) shall be prohibited.

3. And be it further resolved That if the President of the United States shall in his judgment and discretion deem it most advisable, instead of proceeding to submit the foregoing resolution to the Republic of Texas, as an overture on the part of the United States for admission, to negotiate with that Republic; then,

Be it resolved, That a State, to be formed out of the present Republic of Texas, with suitable extent and boundaries, and with two representatives in Congress, until the next apportionment of representation, shall be admitted into the Union, by virtue of this act, on an equal footing with the existing States, as soon as the terms and conditions of such admission, and the cession of the remaining Texian territory to the United States shall be agreed upon by the Governments of Texas and the United States: And that the sum of one hundred thousands be, and the same hereby, appropriated to defray the expenses of missions and negotiations, to agree upon the terms of said admission and cession, either by treaty to be submitted to the Senate, or by articles to be submitted to the two houses of Congress, as the President may direct.

B. Republic of Texas Documents

[Transcribed as written on original documents]

Embassy of the Republic of Texas
Office of Foreign Affairs
(Fort Davis Diplomatic Mission)

Memo: To Carolyn Carney and the 10th Congress
From: Richard Lance McLaren

May 2, 1997

Dear Carolyn and the 10th Congress:

This will probably be the last Transmission to you and the Congress if you receive it.

First Ex President Archie Lowe has convinced the Enemy the we do not have any legal or diplomatic standings. You can thank him if we die, it will be of his direct results and god save his soul for what he has done. Tell Tim I expect him to try him and Johnson and those with him for treason and murder.

Terry has been relived, their has been conflicting offers and no one can ever be trusted on their side, never ever use a bar attorney any more even if you no them, they will sell you out.

Everyone has chosen to stay and hold the Sovereign Soil of The Republic and its Foreign Mission, it appears to us that Morales and Bush are the ones pulling the strings you no Daddy Bush.

I pray reinforcements arrive before they overrun the Embassy. Long live The Republic of Texas and the American People and Death to the New World Order.

Richard Lance McLaren
Chief Ambassador and Consul General
The Republic of Texas

May 3, 1997

International Agreement and Terms of Cease Fire Between

The Republic of Texas
and its Body Politic known as
"We the People of The Republic of Texas"

Known Hereafter as Party 1

and

The State of Texas and its citizens of the United States operating as a Political Subdivision of the UNITED STATES Inc. its agencies, and departments, and as a member nation and founding principal of the United Nations

Known Hereafter as Party 2

Terms and Conditions

1. The parties to this agreement hereby certify that they have the delegation of authority pursuant to their specific laws and constitutions under the law of nations to enter into and to execute the following international agreement and upon execution of agreement pursuant to the third clause of this agreement both parties shall present documents of authority or delegation to certify their ability to enter into this International Agreement.

2. That all parties hereby agree to a <u>Texas Wide Cease Fire</u> including all those lands as specified in actions pursuant to Acts of the Congress of The United States involving a "Treaty with a Foreign Country", dated April 25, 1838, at US Stat.

511 and filed at the Congressional Record of the 104th Congress, Second Session of The United States, Tuesday April 30, 1996 at H4304 PETITION.ECT., Under clause 1 of rule XXII., 71 at Article Two of this Treaty, (Exhibit "1")

3. The First party hereby agree to a Formal International Cease Fire on the soil of Texas and agrees to immediately cease physical hostilities towards the second party under the law of nations and to commence legal actions in the District Court of The District of Columbia for the rights of the inhabitants on the soil of Texas to by popular vote decide issue of Texas independence.

4. The Second Party agrees that the First Party shall have the right to preserve its flag and embassy at is current location on Texas soil until the Third Section of this agreement may either be denied by the court, or by Popular vote of the People of Texas.

Attached and Incorporated Exhibits
Made Part of this Agreement

1. April 30, 1996, United States Congressional Records, April 30, 1996, with attachments.
2. March 9, 1868, Proceedings of the Fortieth Congress of the United States, Second Session of 1868 at pages 1421, 1632, and 1760
3. April 15, 1997, International Notice to the United Nations of Implementation of Full Self-Governance of The Republic of Texas and Attached April 9, 1997 Final Notice of Fatal Variances
4. April 19, 1997, Implementing Declaration and Certification 10th Congress of The Republic of Texas, with April 12, 1997 Texian Citizens Petition for War.

Signed, sealed, and executed this the 3rd day of May, 1997.

Signatory For Party 1

Richard Lance McLaren
Chief Ambassador and Consul General
The Republic of Texas, Its Body Politic
and The Davis Mountains Land Commission
and Its Body Politic

Signatory for Party 2

Delegated Agent of Authority:
  Barry K. Caver
  Captain, Texas Rangers

Third Party Witness:
  Terrence L. O'Rourke
  Evelyn Ann McLaren

C. Republic of Texas Website Postings from Richard McLaren, April 27-29, 1997

[Transcribed as written on original documents]

Status: RED Alert Now in Affect !!

Update for April 27th, 1997, 11:00

Within the last the Captain of the Embassy Guard was captured by Sheriff Bailey in the last 30 minutes in a trap triggered by the spy Joe Rowe. The Guard has mobilized and we are now at red alert. All warrants are being executed on the foreign agents on the soil of Texas as of now. All citizens are advised to take every precaution for their safety and all militia units are advised to upgrade to the level they are best able to handle. The Guard is moving with our plan for securing the area in full lock down. The AGIS internet pipe for our web access has been under an attack by hacker (?). Therefore your access, as well as ours, may be difficult and sporatic.

Update for April 27th, 1997, 13:30

The first military target has been taken and the perimeter of the Resort has been secured as of this time. The "Javalinas" took their first objective with no causulties on either side. The spy and his wife are being held for a prisoner exchange for our captured Captain and citizen Turner who has been held for $25,000 bond for a civil court contempt and has been moved to a state correctional facility. Moralless and his staff did not appear for a hearing to set the bond.

A prisoner trade is being arranged for one of the spies in custody who has a heart condition. Units from the US Border Patrol and US Marshals have entered the area as reinforcements for the local law dog who set this off. De facto state police have also come in according to the scanners. Shots were fired but it appears there has not been an exchange of gun fire between hostile forces. Local, state and federal officers have withdrawn to the blacktop road, 5 miles from the perimeter. Word on the scanner is they are cordoning off the access to our

264

area. We request all incoming units to coordinate through the Major General of the Republic military at (210) 964-4144.

Update for April 28th, 1997, 00:41

The Captain of the Embassy Guard was released from capture within the last hour. The Tactical Unit has released the captured prisoners and vacated the Rowe's House. The units of the de facto have promised to attack our position here at the Embassy after dawn. The information from the debriefing of our officers will be posted if it can be done in the next 24 hours. There has been a small victory for the people of The Republic as now the de facto know that we will not tolerate this unlawful harrassment of our citizens. We are still under Red Status as are many units across Texas and criminals in government office that have arrest and deportation warrants on them are being captured under the laws of war and are being put over the borders. If this is the last posting to this site, God Bless The Republic of Texas and hold our people in prayer and protection. Do not let our deaths be in vain. Stand up Texians and Americans! Tell your public servants that enough is enough.

Maybe now someone in government will finally come forward and talk.

We lost land lines, C130 landed and unloaded, black tents on the blacktop 166, Time 20:00

Update for April 28th, 1997, 10:00

The sun rose on a beautiful Davis Mountains morning and all is quiet. The Capt. of the Embassy Guard was setup by Joe Rowe who called sheriff Bailey. Bailey was laying wait for him and pulled him over with no "probable cause." He was ordered out of the vehicle at gunpoint as Mr. Bailey had an M16 pointed at him. He was arrested for speeding (false arrest) and taken to the lockup while Bailey and his accomplices ravaged his vehicle and stole his property, his funds and his private papers. He was put in irons and held for the rest of the day in a cell. After his release he was transported back to the area, his head was bagged and he was taken into what was probably the Wofford Ranch for a talk with law enforcement. He was then allowed to drive his van back into the Davis Mountains and the tactical team met up with him after their withdrawal.

The information on the landing of the C130 on a highway somewhere in the county has not been fully confirmed. Most roads cannot handle such aircraft so if one landed it was either in Alpine or Marfa.

It has just been confirmed that the Wofford Ranch is being used as the command post for the foreign forces. The owner of the "Paradise Ranch Bed & Breakfast" said on national news that they would be offering their ranch to the feds for a base of operations. Mr. Wofford is a US Border patrol agent. This ranch was designated as a military target some months ago. All support units should be aware of this designation and the current status as active and hot.

Update for April 28th, 1997, 13:00

The de facto agents have begun to remove any and all witnesses to their planned event. Word from inside military ranks is that the information and the law that we have disclosed is too threatening to the New World Order plans that it and we must be made to go away.

Any and all units that can bring pressure to bear on the forces arrayed against us are hereby requested and all movements need to be coordinated by Major General Kreiwald at (210) 349-8994 or (210) 964-4144.

All civilians in the area are being restricted in their travel and access to mail services etc. We are not within 10 miles of postal facilities nor are we restricting any civilian travel. We have no interest in any civilian comings and goings and only wish to continue on to get the political question to the people of the Nation of Texas. We are concerned that our neighbors are being harassed needlessly as we present no threat. We are a defensive unit.

Update for April 28th, 1997, 15:00

I just got off of the line with a group of negotiators that we were able to get into contact with through a contact of ours in the alternative media circles. The two gentlemen from the Critical Incident Group are going to work on getting our international legal group into contact with the foreign agents in charge of the siege group outside of our area.

There is a report on CNN that there are at least 3 federal teams in the forces arrayed against us. Other reports about our harassment of our neighbors is false and misleading. Even Rush Limbaugh has told folks to support us and get to Texas to keep it from Alamoing.

We witnessed a miracle last night when the agents of a foreign aggressor on our soil released the prisoner of war that they had captured. We have just been informed that the Texas Rangers arranged the release of our Capt. and we have been contacted by the Texas Rangers finally and begun to have talks. Our legal group will be handling the negotiations and the initial dialog has been good and there is a lot of common ground. All parties involved are wishing for a peaceful resolve to this issue. As a retired Texas Ranger said to us a few weeks ago, if this comes down to a confrontation then the people of honor on both sides will spill each others blood on sacred ground and the honorless criminals who occupy the Austin and Washington political machinery will get away with their game intact to pray on more people.

Update for April 29th, 1997, 10:00

Sorry for the slowness in updating, without land liner I have to get this up with covert difficulties from a remote location. Last night the blood of Texians was warmed by the support of our fellow Americans who have joined with us in a bald move to take back America for the People and not the UN or the One World Government. The word on the shortwave was that if these UN, US, INC. and STATE OF TEXAS, INC. agents violate this diplomatic mission's sovereign immunity as granted by the Supreme Court of the District of Columbia, that the People's militias of America will issue a joint declaration of war on all of these foreign agents operating in disguise as the government of the People known as the FED.

Word has reached us that over 5,000 Texian militia and Republic Defense Force units are in the field, hundreds of support units are moving from all areas of the soil of Texas protected by Deed filings and the People's Eminent Domain

Trust and the conveyance of true right to property and title alloidium to the people on the land.

Joe Rowe and Sheriff Bailey may go down in history, as having inadvertently set off the liberation of America from New World Order tyranny for a personal vendetta and ficticous speeding charge.

Update for April 29th, 1997, 11:30

Word just reached us that they are moving APC into our area. National Guard units are now involved so Govenor Bush (or his daddy) has issued the order to wipe us out. More later if possible.

D. FBI Militia Guide

Category I Militia Groups
- Conduct paramilitary training.
- Base their organizational philosophies on antigovernment rhetoric.
- Maintain a primarily defensive philosophical posture. Plans for violent action are contingent upon perceived government provocation.
- Engage in no known criminal activities.

Category II Militia Groups
- Conduct paramilitary training.
- Base their organizational philosophies on antigovernment rhetoric.
- Maintain a primarily defensive philosophical posture. Plans for violent action are contingent upon perceived government provocation.
- Engage in criminal activity to acquire weapons and explosives. Criminal activities may range from minor firearms violations, e.g., illicit weapons sales and transfer, to illegal firearms modifications and property crimes.

Category III Militia Groups
- Conduct paramilitary training.
- Base their organizational philosophies on extreme antigovernment rhetoric, denoting deep suspicion and paranoia. Group may direct threats toward specific individuals or institutional targets.
- Maintain a primarily defensive philosophical posture. Plans for violent action are contingent upon perceived government provocation, but response plans are highly detailed and may include an escalation of overt acts beyond planning, such as testing explosive devices, gathering intelligence, and identifying/conducting surveillance of potential targets.

• Engage in criminal activity, ranging from property crimes to crimes of interpersonal violence, e.g., resisting arrest, armed robberies, burglaries, and attempts to provoke confrontations with government officials.

Category IV Militia Groups

• Demonstrate many of the same traits and characteristics as category III groups but are likely to be smaller, more isolated cells or fringe groups whose members have grown frustrated with their peers' unwillingness to pursue a more aggressive strategy. Unlike militias in the other categories, category IV groups often maintain an openly offensive, rather than defensive, posture.

• May grow out of other less threatening militia groups or may evolve independently from any other group associations.

• Often attract individuals with frank mental disorders. These individuals may either act alone or with a small number of associates who share similar paranoid/disordered beliefs.

• Plot and engage in serious criminal activity, e.g., homicide, bombings, and other acts of a terrorist nature.

FBI Law Enforcement Bulletin, July 1997

E. Press Conference Guide
Prepared by the DPS Public Information Office
Revised 8/97

Press Conferences

A press conference allows you to tell your news to many media representatives at the same time, ensuring that they get the same information. It also allows all reporters to ask questions and hear the same answers about the issue you're addressing, which can save a lot of time compared to responding to many reporters individually.

• Is a press conference necessary? Is your news important to the general public? News that is important only to your company, agency, or organization is not news that warrants a press conference. Consider a press release, if necessary, instead.

• When should the press conference be held? Generally, mornings and early afternoons are best for reporters—between 9:30 a.m. and 1:30 p.m. Monday through Friday as a rule—with Tuesday, Wednesday and Thursday being preferred days. Knowing the schedules of your local media will help you determine the best time for you. Try to avoid conflicting times/places with other scheduled press conferences—don't make the media choose; your information could lose.

• Where should the press conference be? Usually, a conference room or auditorium is the best location. Some situations lend themselves to an off-site location, but before you fall in love with the idea of taking your press conference on the road, make sure your location will accommodate a press conference. This is especially important if the location is outside (one press conference got ruined, as did some expensive equipment, because an outdoor sprinkler system came on during the conference) or in a noisy or difficult to access location. Airport landing patterns, heat, and wild animals have also been known to keep a press conference from flowing smoothly.

• How long should a press conference last? There is rarely a need for a press conference to be longer than 30 minutes, including time for a question and answer session.

• Who should speak at the press conference? Usually the principal of your organization and his/her counterpart from any other organization involved. A technical person (who can speak in easy-to-understand language) or someone who is directly involved in the program/event being discussed might also be important. Whenever possible, limit the number of speakers to no more than three. Five minutes per speaker is generally sufficient, less is better. A press conference is not the time to ramble or get sidetracked. Reporters are busy and have other assignments to cover.

• Arrange a briefing for the speakers and others involved well in advance. Have ready a list of questions that could be asked—include the hard questions you hope not to be asked. Reporters may also take the opportunity to ask questions about other issues as well. Decide in advance what those issues might be and how, or if, they will be responded to at the press conference.

• Be prepared and brief. Unless the speaker is adept at extemporaneous speaking, he/she should read a brief, prepared statement that gives the main points. Even if a prepared statement is not used, main points should be written on note cards to be used as a reminder.

• Plan ahead. Don't surprise the media with your press conference. Give them at least a week's notice by faxing a media advisory to them with basic information – the purpose of the press conference, who will be speaking and when and where it will take place. Getting on the media's calendars early will help ensure coverage.

The Media Pool

When access to a site/event must be or should be limited, a media pool can get reporters the up-close-and-personal look they desperately want while allowing officials to keep some control of the situation by holding disruption of ongoing activities to a minimum. A media pool consists of several reporters who have agreed in advance to share the information they collect with other reporters and news outlets, even direct competitors.

• How many reporters can you/should you accommodate? That depends a lot on whether you will need to supply transportation to a site and how many escorts are available to you. While one escort for a group of five or six reporters usually is adequate, two is even better. At a minimum, a pool should consist of a print reporter, a print photographer, a radio broadcaster and a two-person TV broadcast team (cameraperson and reporter). Make sure the print reporter and photographer have AP connections for ease in sharing information and if possible, designate a local print reporter to be a member of the first pool (don't assume that because national media have shown up to cover your event that you should cater to them—your local media will be with you much longer). If you can accommodate more reporters, consider a magazine reporter and an additional print reporter and/or photographer. Designate "hard news" reporters before those doing special interest reporting, news magazines shows, morning shows, etc.

• Let the media themselves decide who will be represented. Give them twenty minutes or so to work it out and tell them what time and where the selected reporters should meet. At that point, establish ground rules—how long the reporters will be allowed access, where they can and cannot go, etc.

• Announce the next pool time. At the conclusion of that pool, reporters will immediately want to know when the next one will be. Let them know as soon as possible.

F. Speak Into the Mic:
Tips for Broadcast Interviews
Prepared by the DPS Public Information Office
Revised 7/97

Comparing broadcast to print media:
- Broadcast reporters are less interested in detail but more interested in immediacy.
- Generally, broadcast reporters may know less about your community or your agency because they move from station to station more frequently. Also, the smaller your market, the younger and less experienced the reporters are likely to be.
- Print journalists generally have one to three deadlines a day—the most common being fairly late at night. They have more time to develop stories and delve into details.
- TV reporters usually need info by 11:00 A.M. or earlier for noon broadcasts, by 3:30 to 4:00 P.M. for the 5:00 P.M./6:00 P.M. broadcasts and by 8:30 or 9:00 P.M. or so for the 10:00 P.M. broadcasts.
- Deadlines are almost immediate for radio reporters. Some stations have news casts every half hour, and radio reporters can easily go live from the scene.
- The visual aspects of a news event are very important to the television media.

When being interviewed by the broadcast media
- Prepare your message and condense it into concise "sound bites." Broadcast reporters will use only 10 to 20 seconds of your interview. Repeat the same message in different ways so they are more likely to pick the sound bite you want them to use. You can control the interview through preparation.
- Think before you speak. Use complete sentences. Avoid verbal pauses like "um," "uh," "y'know," "well."
- Dress appropriately for TV interviews. You want the reporter to focus on your message and not how you look.

—If you normally wear a uniform, make sure it looks neat.

—If you don't wear a uniform, avoid busy patterns or loud colors.

—Don't wear solid white or black around your face.

—Don't wear flashy jewelry, sunglasses, hats or too much makeup.

—Be conscious of nervous movements.

• Look at the person, not the lens.

• Stand up straight, even when doing radio interviews over the phone. On TV, you will look better, and on radio, you will sound better.

• Don't try to avoid an interview by holding your hand over a camera lens. Doing so shows that you don't feel like you are in charge of the situation. It makes you look like you are hiding something, and they *will* use it on the air.

G. Channel 24 Rules, Policies
KVUE 24 • Television

GUIDELINES FOR COVERING HOSTAGE/STAND-OFF CRISES, PRISON UPRISING

1) Always assume that the hostage taker, gunman is watching your television coverage.
2) Seriously weigh the benefits to the public of what information might be given out versus what potential harm that information might cause.
3) Be extremely cautious not to compromise the officials or the hostages involved.
4) Avoid describing with words or showing any information that could divulge or compromise the tactics or positions of law enforcement officers.
5) Live shots should only be done if there is a strong journalistic reason. Ask if the value of a live, on-the-scene report is really justifiable to the harm that could occur.
6) Be forthright with viewers about why certain information is being withheld, if security reasons are involved.
7) Give no information, factual or speculative, about a hostage taker's mental condition or reasons for actions while a stand-off is in progress. (The value of such information to the audience is limited.)
8) Give no analyses or comments on a hostage taker's or gun person's demands.
9) Exercise care when interviewing family members or friends of those involved. Record sensitive interviews to use after the situation is over. Remember: the hostage taker or gun person may be watching.
10) Do not report information obtained from police scanners. It may compromise communications between officers and negotiators.
11) Never telephone a hostage taker or gunman/woman. We are not trained in negotiation techniques. One wrong thing you say could jeopardize someone's life.

12) If the hostage taker calls us, tell him/her to contact police. Notify authorities immediately.

13) When reporting live or otherwise, limit your information to whatever the public needs to know to avoid the area, such as maps.

KVUE-TV, INC.
5201 Steck Avenue
Austin, Texas 78757-9098
P.O. Box 9927 • 78766-0927
(512) 459-8521

H. National Association of Government Communicators
Code of Ethics

Members of the National Association of Government Communicators pledge and profess dedication to the goals of better communication, understanding and cooperation among all people.

We believe that truth is inviolable and sacred; that providing public information is an essential civil service; and that the public at large and each citizen therein has a right to equal, full, understandable, and timely facts about their government. Members will:

- Conduct themselves professionally, with truth, accuracy, fairness, responsibility, accountability to the public, and adherence to generally accepted standards of good taste.
- Conduct their professional lives in accord with the public interest, in recognition that each of us is a steward of the public's trust.
- Convey the truth to their own agencies' management, engaging in no practice which could corrupt the integrity of channels of communication or the processes of government.
- Intentionally communicate no false or misleading information and will act promptly to correct false or misleading information or rumors.
- Identify publicly the names and titles of individuals involved in making policy decisions, the details of decision-making processes and how interested citizens can participate.
- Represent no conflicting or competing interests and willfully comply with all statutes, executive orders and regulations pertaining to personal disclosure of such interests.
- Avoid the possibility of any improper use of information

by an "insider" or third party and never use inside information for personal gain.

• Guarantee or promise the achievement of no specified result beyond the member's direct control.

• Accept no fees, commissions, gifts, promises of future consideration, or any other material or intangible valuable that is, or could be perceived to be, connected with public service employment or activities.

• Safeguard the confidence of both present and former employees, and of information acquired in meetings and documents, as required by law, regulation, and prudent good sense.

• Not wrongly injure the professional reputation or practice of another person, private organization or government agency.

• Participate in no activity designed to manipulate the price of company's securities.

I. Cox's Media Event Scale
A Guide for Public Relations Professionals

Level 0: "You sure you called all the media?" No one shows up for your press conference. Except your boss.

Level 1: Your hometown daily asks if you'd mind faxing them your news release. No one available to go to your press conference. Local radio station does show up, but news director's tape recorder is not working.

Level 2: The daily's reporter shows up, but no photographer. There's been an accident with injuries on the highway near the truck stop. TV reporter and videographer showed up, but they've got to leave before you start the press conference because of the accident near the truck stop. Radio news director's not there. He was the driver of one of the cars in the truck stop accident.

Level 3: Full turnout: Newspaper, TV, radio. TV crew arrives twenty minutes late, but newspaper guy actually asks a few polite questions.

Level 4: All local media plus a few out-of-town stations.

Level 5: Oh, my God! The networks arrive. Even ESPN and the Comedy Channel. The Capitol Press Corps actually leaves the capital city. Entrepreneurs have started selling T-shirts at the scene.

Level 6: All of the above PLUS foreign TV crews. Your office says a producer for Larry King is on the line. Jay Leno is beginning to joke about your event. Get an agent. The clock's ticking on your fifteen minutes of fame.

Bibliography

Bailey, Brad and Bob Darden. *Mad Man in Waco*. Waco: WRS Publishing, 1993.

Bailey, Ilse D. "Beware Blind Pigs & 'Patriots'." *The Texas Prosecutor*, Vol. 27, No. 3, May/June 1997.

Bailey, Steve. Interview with author, August 22, 1997.

Bark, Ed. "Cult leader's address dominates the rating." *Dallas Morning News*, March 5, 1993.

Brock, Ralph H. "The Republic of Texas Is No More: An Answer to the Claim that Texas was Unconstitutionally Annexed to the United States." *Texas Tech University Law Review*, May 1997.

Campbell, Frank. "Stand-off at Fort Davis." *Texas Highway Patrol Magazine*, Fall 1997.

Casteel, Bruce. Interview with author, July 17, 1997.

_____. Speech to Sheriff's Association of Texas, Fort Worth, Texas, July 21, 1997.

Cooper, Matthew. "Shutting Down a Siege." *Newsweek*, May 12, 1997.

Cronkite, Walter. *A Reporter's Life*. New York: Alfred A. Knopf, 1996.

Dees, Morris with James Corcoran. *Gathering Storm: America's Militia Threat*. New York: Harper Collins, 1996.

Duffy, James E. and Alan C. Brantley. "Militias: Initiating Contact." *FBI Law Enforcement Bulletin*, July 1997.

Dyer, Joel. "On the Run." *Mother Jones*, June 25, 1997.

Farley, Christopher John. "Remember the Texas Embassy?" *Time*, May 12, 1997.

Fitzwater, Marlin. *Call the Briefing! Bush and Reagan, Sam and Helen: A Decade With Presidents and the Press*. New York: Random House, 1995.

Gamino, Denise. "Wife's phone call brought peaceful end to tense siege." *Austin American-Statesman*, May 5, 1997.

Hardin, Stephen L. *Texian Iliad: A Military History of the Texas Revolution*. Austin: University of Texas Press, 1994.

Harmon, Jim. *The Great Radio Heroes*. Garden City, N.Y., 1967.

Hernandez, Debra Gersh. "Covering Disasters: Report defines role of the media." *Editor & Publisher*, October 8, 1994.

Higginbotham, Jeffrey. "Legal Issues in Crisis Management." *FBI Law Enforcement Bulletin*, June 1994.

Huntress, Brooke. "One JP's experience: The day that everything changed in Waco." *County*, September/October 1994.

Jacobson, Lucy Miller and Mildred Bloys Nored. *Jeff Davis County, Texas*. Fort Davis: Fort Davis Historical Society, 1993.

Karpf, Jason and Elinor Karpf. *Anatomy of a Massacre*. Waco: WRS Publishing, 1994.

Kay, Michele. "Smaller militia groups are seen as big threat." *Austin American-Statesman*, July 19, 1997.

Kurtz, Howard. "Murder rate falls, but coverage of the crimes soar." *Austin American-Statesman*, August 13, 1997.

Lawler, Jack. "DPS SWAT Team Does Front-Line Duty At Fort Davis Stand-Off Crisis;" "The Fort Davis Crisis As Seen By Two Troopers." *Texas State Trooper*, May 1997.

Lucasville Media Task Force Report. Dayton, Ohio, March 1994.

McDonald, Archie P. *Texas: All Hail the Mighty State*. Austin: Eakin Pess, 1983.

Madigan, Tim. *See No Evil: Blind Devotion and Bloodshed in David Koresh's Holy War*. Fort Worth: The Summit Group, 1993.

Malone, Jess. Interview with author, November 10, 1997.

Merk, Frederick. *Slavery and the Annexation of Texas*. New York: Alfred A. Knopf, 1972.

"The Militia Threat." *New York Times*, June 14, 1997.

Moore, Evan. "McLaren had many missions, all unfulfilled." *Houston Chronicle*, May 4, 1997.

Noesner, Gary W. and Mike Webster. "Crisis Intervention." *FBI Law Enforcement Bulletin*, August 1997.

Patoski, Joe Nick. "Out There: What I saw at the Republic of Texas stand-off." *Texas Monthly*, June 1997.

Potok, Mark. "Officials fear extremist acts on infamous day." *USA Today*, April 18, 1997.

Reavis, Dick J. *The Ashes of Waco: An Investigation*. New York: Simon & Schuster, 1995.

Report of The Department of the Treasury on the Bureau of Alcohol, Tobacco, And Firearms Investigation of Vernon Wayne Howell also known as David Koresh. Washington, D.C., 1993.

Richards, Don R. "Disaster reporting poses problem for media." *Freedom of Information Foundation of Texas Forum*. Fall 1994.

Richardson, Rod. "Covering The Separatist Siege." *Editor & Publisher*, June 14, 1997.

Rye, Dale A. "Understanding the Republic of Texas and other Extremist Groups." *CLU Criminal Law Update*, Vol. 5, No. 1, Summer 1996.

Scobee, Barry. *Nick Mersfelder: A Remarkable Man*. Fort Davis: Fort Davis Historical Society, 1969.

Texas Almanac 1996-1997. Dallas: *Dallas Morning News*.

Thomas, Jo. "7 Arrests Are Linked to Militia Plot to Attack Military Bases." *New York Times*, July 23, 1997.

Thompson, Frank. *Alamo Movies*. East Berlin, PA: Old Mill Books, 1991.

Thompson, Mark. "A Political Suicide." *Time*, May 13, 1996.

Vance, Doug. Interview with author, August 14, 1997.

Verhovek, Sam Howe. "Republic of Texas Stand-off Leaves Rumors of a Fugitive." *New York Times*, July 7, 1997.

Whisenhunt, Donald W. *The 5 States of Texas: An Immodest Proposal*. Austin: Eakin Press, 1987.

Woolley, Bryan. *The Edge of the West and Other Texas Stories*. El Paso: Texas Western Press, 1990.

Wright, Stuart A. *Armageddon in Waco: Critical Perspectives on the Branch Davidian Conflict*. Chicago and London: The University of Chicago Press, 1995.

Index

A

A Perfect World, 157
A Reporter's Life, 222
ABC, 51, 57, 109, 116, 117, 146, 148, 151, 224, 227
Alamo, Battle of, 72-73, 74, 75, 77, 78, 178, 237-238
Alexander, Dan, 130
Allegheny County (Pennsylvania) Fire Marshal's Office, 61
Allen, Johnny, 189
Alpine, Texas, 83, 84, 132, 145, 148, 155, 167
Altom, Judy, 116
"America's Most Wanted," 226
Annenberg Washington Program, 211
Apaches, 85
Aronovsky, Linda, *see* Cox, Linda
Associated Press (AP), 35, 38, 51, 56, 107, 115, 144, 163, 190, 209, 245
AT&T, 12
ATF (Federal Bureau of Alcohol, Tobacco and Firearms), 39-40, 41, 42, 44, 50, 63, 139
ATF Explosive Ordnance Disposal (EOD), 54, 194-195
Atlanta, Georgia, 228-229
Atlanta Journal, 228-229
Attorney General's Office, 105, 106, 109, 112, 116, 163
Austin American-Statesman, 9, 35, 51, 101, 108, 127, 180, 181, 238
Austin, City of, Public Information, 11
Austin Emergency Medical Service, 16
Austin Fire Department, 95
Austin Police Department, 10, 95

Austin Statesman, 10
Austin, Stephen F., 75, 81
Austin, Texas, 232
Aycock, Johnny, 35

B

Baggett, Donnis, 46
Bailey, Sheriff Steve, 110, 125, 126, 127, 129-131, 133, 142, 168, 169, 182, 204, 248, 252, 264, 265, 268
Baker, David, 125, 162, 182, 193
Ball, Rex, 248
Bartholomew, Ed, 86, 91-93
Barton, John "Bubba," 162, 167
Beames, Ron, 171-172, 177
Bean, Judge Roy, 85
Benningfield, Larry, 144, 155
Berry, Jim, 147
    V. E. "Red," 82
BeSaw, Larry, 11-12, 13, 38
Bexar County Medical Examiner's Office, 204
Big Bend Memorial Hospital, 127
Big Bend National Park, 83, 145, 149
Blanchard, Ernie, 231
Blanco County, 112
Board of Private Investigators, 114-115
Border Patrol, 131, 133, 135, 142-143, 200
Bradburn, John, 74
Brady Law, 250
Branch Davidian Compound: bulldozed, 67; burning of, 7-8, 49-50, 51, 54, 60, 118; children in, 38, 40, 46, 51, 63; deaths at, 40, 41, 51, 54, 63-64, 67-68; illegal weapons

at, 38, 57; media coverage of, 40-43, 44, 45-46, 48-49, 50-68, 133, 239; media pool visits to, 55, 56, 60, 63, 64-65
Brannon, John, 116, 165
Brantley, Alan C., 250
Branzburg v. Hayes, 215
Braver, Rita, 67-68
Brazos County Jail, 106
Brenham, Texas, 124
Brewster County, 84, 254
Brisbin, Jake, 126
British television, 62-63
broadcast news, 221, 222, 224-226, 274-277
Brock, Ralph H., 248-249
Brodsky, Lew, 15-16
Brown, Randall, 130-131
Buchanan, Sid, 248
Buffalo Bayou, 237
Bulverde, Texas, 100
Bunton, Lucius III, 104-105, 106, 107, 142
Burnet, David G., 80
Bush, George W., 98, 99, 100, 101, 109, 132, 141, 144, 178, 190, 254, 268
   President George, 19, 141, 178
Byrnes, David, 60

C

Caesar, 21
Camel Experiment, 206
Cardona, Sylvia, 197
Carlson, Richard, 175
Carney, Carolyn, 178
Carrasco, Fred Gomez, 9-10, 180
Carswell Air Base, 20
Carter, Bill, 10-11
Casteel, Bruce, 123, 125, 126, 127-128, 131, 132, 133, 135, 165, 247, 255
Caver, Barry, 116, 118, 125, 126-127, 128, 131, 132, 133, 135, 136-137, 141, 144, 155, 165, 167-168, 170, 173, 177, 180, 181, 183, 186, 187, 189, 193, 194-195, 196, 199, 202, 205, 252
CBS, 16, 42, 51, 67-68, 224, 227, 237

"CBS Evening News," 222
Cedar Park, 208-209
Centennial Olympic Park, 228-229
Challenger, 48
Channel 4 (Dallas), 116
Chernow, Laureen, 24-25, 39, 44-45, 50, 52, 55-56, 57-58, 59, 60, 61-62, 65, 66-67, 68, 96-98, 101, 116, 118, 122, 132, 142, 143, 147-148, 149-150, 156, 157, 159, 161, 162, 169, 174, 176, 181-182, 185, 186, 193, 194, 195, 197, 201, 205, 207, 209-210, 243, 244, 245
Cherokees, 76-77
Chinati Mountains, 148
Christopher, Warren C., 99
Clinton administration, 212
Clinton, Bill, 51
Clouse, Ken, 128
CNN, 40, 43, 48, 50, 54, 59, 66, 113, 116, 120, 121, 152, 157, 190, 191, 227, 229, 241, 267
Coffey, Richard, 251
Coggins, Paul, 201
College Station, Texas, 106
Colorado Bend State Park, 251
Colorado City, 200
Colorado County, 30
"Come and Take It" incident, 77
Connally, John B., 10
Constitutional Convention, 94-95
Continental Express, 30
Cook, Maurice, 52-54, 58
Cooper, Bill, 32-34, 35, 36
   D. B., 253
   Gregory, 250
Cootes, Glenn, 11-12, 13
Cos, Martin Perfecto de, 77-78
cover-ups, 229
Cox, Alicia, 23, 24, 52, 55, 56, 62
   Betty Wilke, 256
   Bill G., 256
   Hallie Dorin, 5, 16, 37, 69, 114, 117, 184, 192, 207, 208, 256
   Linda, 5, 16, 29-30, 35, 37, 38, 40, 41, 52, 57, 62, 69, 184, 185, 192, 207, 208, 210, 256
"coyotes," 82

crime rate, 226
"Crime Stoppers," 157
crises, media coverage of, 211-219,
238-246, 276-277
Critical Incident Response Group, 143
Crockett County, 87
Crockett, Davy, 71-72, 73, 78, 87,
158
Cronkite, Walter, 222, 237
Crow, Dr. Rodney, 60
Cummings, Fred, 34
Cunanan, Andrew P., 233

D
Dallas Book and Paper Show, 113
Dallas Morning News, 40, 42, 46, 118,
172, 224
Davidson, Dan, 232
Davis, Jefferson, 85, 206
    Paul, 105
    Tommy, 122, 126, 132, 182, 194
Davis Mountain Land Commission, 90,
99
Davis Mountains, 145, 151
Davis Mountains Resort, 1, 4, 89-90,
92, 107, 110, 118-119, 125,
127, 131, 136, 158-159, 167,
171-172, 182, 196, 252
Davis Mountains Resort Volunteer Fire
Department, 135
"Davy Crockett at the Alamo," 71-72
de Zavala, Lorenzo, 74
Dean, Marshal Jack, 107, 127-128,
201
Dearen, Patrick, 36
DeGeneres, Ellen, 7
DeGuerin, Dick, 46, 59, 139-140, 173
DeHart, Kenneth, 141, 252, 254, 255
disasters, 211, 213-219, 234
Disney, Walt, 71-72, 74
Dorsett, Michael Leonard, 251
DPS: at Killeen shooting, 24, 27, 29,
31-36; at ROT public rallies, 98-
99, 101; at ROT stand-off, 115,
116, 131, 133-137, 153, 155,
161, 163, 165-166, 167, 172,
175-206, 247-255; at Waco siege,
38, 39-40, 41, 42, 43-44, 50-
58; communications center, 58;
counseling, 68; crime laboratory,

31, 34, 54-55; Dive Recovery
Team, 166, 191; Division of
Emergency Management, 24-25,
43, 160; Headquarters, 24, 25;
Motor Vehicle Theft Service, 27,
32, 36; Personnel and Staff
Services, 25; Public Information,
10-11, 16-18, 20-21, 23, 39, 44-
45, 49, 50-68, 116-117, 133-
137, 146-147, 157-160, 161-
162, 175-176, 181, 184-185,
190-191, 209-211, 213, 271-
273, 274-277; Safety Education
Service, 116, 161, 167; Special
Crimes Service, 144, 163, 252-
253; SWAT team, 39, 40, 62,
123, 132, 135, 142, 181, 182-
183, 189, 191; Traffic Law
Enforcement Division, 153, 161
Driscoll, Mike, 140
driver license photographs, 36
Duderstadt, Kenneth, 25-26, 27, 34
Duffy, James E., 250
Duncan, Dave, 116, 132-133
Dusek, Ron, 106, 116

E
Eagle Lake, Texas, 30
Earp, Wyatt, 86
Eastland County, 113
Eastwood, Clint, 157
Ector County Sheriff's Office, 195
Edwards, Benjamin, 76-77
    Haden, 75-77, 104
    Tom, 163
Effective Communication School, 55
El Paso, Texas, 84
El Paso Times, 175
Elite Café, 121
Ely, Glen, 36
England, Mark, 38
ethics, in media, 227-230, 278-279
Evans, Joe, 104
    Tracee, 118

F
"48 Hours," 227
"Face the Nation," 59
Fairfield, Texas, 112
FBI, 9, 41, 42, 46, 47, 48-49, 50, 55,

57, 102, 111, 112, 113, 126, 127, 129, 131, 133, 135, 142-143, 144, 152, 155-156, 185, 187, 188, 228, 249, 250, 251, 253, 254, 269
Federal Aviation Administration, 193, 216
First Amendment, 215
First Kansas Mechanized Militia, 251
Fitzwater, Marlin, 19
Flying J Truck Stop, 154
Fore, Jody W., 32, 33, 35, 36
Fort Davis Chamber of Commerce, 83
Fort Davis Drug Store, 92
Fort Davis High School, 136
Fort Davis, Texas, 83-91, 169, 181-182, 197
Fort Hood, 26, 251
Fort Stockton, 199
Fort Worth Star-Telegram, 108, 164
Foster, Steve, 155
Foundation for the Advancement of Space Laws and Sciences, 151
Fox network, 224
Fox, Michael J., 21
Franks, Darrel Dean, 107
Fredonia Rebellion, 75-77
Fredonia Republic, 104
Freedom of Information (FOI) Act, 227
Freemen, 102, 105, 249
Friend, "Skinny," 92

G
Gamino, Denise, 181
General Land Office, 81
Gibson, Charlie, 59
Glasscock, Andy, 254
Glover, Bradley Playford, 251
Gomez, Arnulfo, 155
Gonzales, Texas, 77
"Good Morning America," 57, 59, 227
government communicators, 18, *also see* spokespersons
Graham, Charles, 153
Grand Kempinski Hotel, 103
Gray, Paul, 60
Green, Sherri Deatherage, 116, 118, 122, 143, 153, 167, 176, 190, 208, 209-210, 243-244
"Gridiron Show," 157

Griffith, David M., 32, 36
Gulf War, 19
Guthrie, Marvin, 32, 36

H
Halbison, Boyce Eugene, 179
Harris County, 99, 104
Harris County Jail, 253
Harris, William, 102
Hart, Judge Joe, 105, 107, 112
Hartnett, Will, 109
Haut, Walter, 19-20
Hays, John Coffee, 81
Headliner's Club Award, 13
Hendrix, Ray, 168-169
Hennard, George, 27, 31, 33-34, 35
Henson, Kenneth, 32, 36
Hobby, Bill, 95
Holt, Robert, 141-142, 156, 157, 159, 190
Hopkins, Julie, 173, 180-181
Horton, Billy, 197
Hostage Response Team (HRT), 41, 143
House, Boyce, 17
Houston Chronicle, 38, 56, 121, 248
Houston Fire Department, 60
Houston, Sam, 75, 77, 78, 79-80, 97
Huberty, James Oliver, 26
Hunter, Lisa, 98
Huntsville prison, siege of, 9, 42, 180
Hye, Texas, 112

I
Independence Day, 19
Institute for Crisis Management, 211-212
Institute of Texan Cultures, 248
Internal Revenue Service (IRS), 101, 112
International Court of Justice, 98
International News Service, 10
Internet, 223, 225, 255
Internet law, 164
Isbell, Bill, 123, 132
Iwo Jima, 192

J
Jackson, Wayne, 180
Jagger, Todd, 163
Jahn, LeRoy, 53

Ray, 53
jargon, 235
Jarrell, Texas, 208-211
Jeff Davis County, 83, 84, 90-91, 99, 115, 128, 129, 130, 158, 169, 206
Jeff Davis County Courthouse, 1, 151, 168-169, 252
Jepson, James, 163
Jewell, Richard, 228-229
Johnson, David, 110
Jones, Anson, 80
Jordan, Montana, 102, 105
Justice Department, 67, 111

K

Kansas Bureau of Investigation, 253
Kaus, John M., 61
Kennedy, Peter D., 164
Kerrville, Texas, 88
Key, Gene, 202
Keyes, Richard Franklin, 3, 4, 118-119, 120-121, 126, 127, 136, 178, 190, 191, 195, 196, 198, 201, 205, 252-253, 255
"kill the messenger" syndrome, 245
Killeen Police Department, 31, 32, 33, 35, 227
Killeen, Texas, 24-36, 212, 227
Kind, Richard, 21
King, George, 98
Klanwatch, 249
Klause, Ruth E., 100
KLBJ Radio, 238
Korean War, 239
Koresh, David, 7-8, 38, 40, 41, 44, 46, 50, 57, 62, 67-68, 70, 118, 160, 238
Kriewald, Melvin Louis, 179, 266
KRLD Radio, 40, 41, 67
KTBC Radio, 238
KTRH Radio, 116
Ku Klux Klan, 95, 96
KVLF Radio, 84
KVUE 24, 276-277
KWTX-TV, 40, 41
KXAN-TV, 55
KXAS-TV, 65

L

Lamar, Mirabeau B., 80
Langtry, Texas, 85
"Larry King Live," 59
Last Command, The, 175
Law Enforcement Bulletin, 250
Leno, Jay, 6-7
Limbaugh, Rush, 267
Limestone County, 61
Limpia Canyon, 85
Limpia Hotel Restaurant, 197-198
Linda's Happy Time Tavern, 46
Livingston, Rachel, 59
    Rebecca, 59
    Sara, 59
London Times, 45-46
Lone Ranger, 220
Los Angeles Times, 51
Lowe, Archie, 103, 106, 109, 106, 178
Lubbock, Texas, 100
Luby's massacre, 24-36, 227, 238
Luckie, Laura, 209
Lumpkin, John, 56

M

Magnolia Oil Company, 73
Malone, Jess, 156, 168, 170, 171, 185, 186, 187, 188
Marfa Lights, 148-151
Marfa, Texas, 2, 84, 90-91, 126, 131, 148
Matson, Mike, 164-165, 178, 190, 191, 195, 196, 198, 201, 204-205, 238, 241
    Ralph, 164-165, 204
May, Janice, 249
McCormick, Darlene, 38
McDonald, Archie P., 77
    Chuck, 52, 56-57, 66-67
McDonald Observatory, 151, 243
McDonald's, 26
McEathron, David, 208
McLaren, Evelyn, 128, 173, 174, 178, 179-180, 181, 186-188, 201
    Richard Lance, 75, 77, 82, 83, 86, 89-93, 97, 99, 101, 102-103, 104-110, 112, 118, 119, 121, 125, 127-128, 130-131, 136-138, 140-145, 147, 151, 155,

158, 159, 160, 163-164, 165,
166, 167, 169, 170-174, 176-
206, 241, 242, 248, 252, 254,
255
McLennan County, 42
McLennan County Jail, 56
McVeigh, Timothy, 111, 249
media in crisis situations, 211-219,
238-246, 276-277
media relations, 64-65, 66, 211-219,
220-236, 238-246, 271-275,
280
Media Studies Center, 226
Medical Assistance Surgical Team, 203
Menger Hotel, 73
Mersfelder, Nick, 85, 86, 206
Mexican Army, 73, 77-79
Micheletti, Missey, 29
Midland County, 189
Midland Police Department, 195, 254
Midland Reporter-Telegram, 224
Midland-Odessa, Texas, 84
"Mile High Town," 83
Militia Task Force, 249
militias, 249-252, 267-268, 269-270
Missouri State Highway Patrol, 251
Mobil Oil, 73
Monahans, Texas, 105
Montana Human Rights Network, 111
Moore, Edwin, 79
Morales, Dan, 102, 103, 104, 105,
107, 109, 178, 254
Morris, Al, 32
Morse, Samuel, 81
Mother Jones, 253
Mount Carmel, 44, 47, 50, 59, 60,
160, *also see* Branch Davidian
Compound
Mount Locke, 151
"Mount Media," 144, 153, 174, 180,
191
mountain lions, 144-145
Murphysville, Texas, 83

N
Nacogdoches County, 104
Nacogdoches, Texas, 75, 76
National Association of Government
Communicators, 15, 278-279

National Crime Information Center
(NCIC), 161
National Guard, 146
National Public Radio, 116
National Weather Service, 207, 208
NBC, 59, 108, 116, 224, 227, 229
Nesbitt, David, 200, 204
New Braunfels, Texas, 36
New London, Texas, 51
New York Herald-Tribune, 14
New York Times, 18, 108, 146, 223,
249, 253
news leaks, 228
newspapers, *see* print media
Newsweek, 224, 231
"Nightline," 109-110
Nixon, Richard, 234
"no comment," 232
Noesner, Gary, 143, 156, 179
Norris, Chuck, 53
North American Aerospace Defense
Command, 112

O
"off-the-record," 230
Oklahoma City bombing, 111, 113,
114, 249
Old Stone Fort, 76
Onyx, 60-61
Ortega, Cosme, 154
Oswald, Lee Harvey, 48
Otto, Robert "White Eagle," 108, 118,
121, 132, 136, 144, 163, 171,
178, 189, 196, 252, 254, 255
Overland Network, 163
Overland Trail Museum, 206
Overton, David, 42
Ozona, Texas, 87
O'Rourke, Terrence, 137-138, 139-
140, 141, 167-170, 173-174,
175-176, 177, 178, 180, 186,
187, 242-243

P
Paradise Mountain Ranch, 125
Pareya, David, 67-68
Parker, Fess, 71, 72
Parrack, Roy, 32, 36
patriot support groups, 249
"Patriots' Day," 111

Patterson, Gary, 24
Paulson, Gregg, 3, 119-121, 136, 137, 163, 178, 189, 195, 196, 252, 255
    Karen, 3, 120-121, 136, 178, 189, 196, 252, 255
Pechacek, Joe E., 202-203
Pecos River, 36
Pecos, Texas, 153-154
Peerwani, Dr. Nizam, 60
Permian Basin Drug Task Force, 169
Peterson, Daniel E., 102
Phillips, Jim, 35, 36
Point of Rocks, 133
Pool, Brady, 95
Poteet, Texas, 20
Potok, Mark, 64-65
Powell, Gene, 255
Presidio County, 3, 84, 90-91, 129, 130-131, 161, 169
Presidio County Jail, 205
Presley, Elvis, 121
Press Agentry, 14
print media, 221-224, 225, 274
Pruitt, Bill, 51, 52
public record, 36
Public Safety Commission, 141
Public Utility Commission, 12
pull-out quotes, 231-232
Purcell, Laverne, 10, 23

R
Rabel, Ed, 42
radio, *see* broadcast news
Ramey, Roger, 20
Rather, Dan, 51, 227
Ray, Richard Lee, Jr., 106
Reasoner, Harry, 16
Reconstruction, 82
Red Cross, 136, 169
"redbacks," 80
Reeves County, 129, 154
Reid, Daniel, 220
Reno, Janet, 51, 67
Republic of Texas (1836-1846), 77, 79-82
Republic of Texas Defense Forces, 118, 119, 142, 154
Republic of Texas group (1990s): activities of, 99-100; arguments of, 75, 82, 97-98, 99, 103, 119, 248-249; bogus liens/documents issued by, 99, 102, 103-107, 109, 112, 125, 128, 201, 260-263; charges/warrants against members, 127-128, 136, 137, 141, 158, 170-171, 175, 201; continues, 248-249, 255; deemed nonexistent, 105, 106; electricity cut, 170, 172-173; "embassy" of, 107, 108, 130, 159, 164, 165-166, 167, 177, 183, 193, 195; flag of, 108; "General Council" of, 100, 101, 107, 179; holds rally, 96-98, 100, 101; investigates Waco siege, 103; media coverage of, 102, 108, 110, 117, 118-119, 120, 121, 127, 133-135, 137, 144, 146-147, 151, 152, 157-160, 163, 167, 170, 172, 175-176, 180-181, 190-191, 197, 215, 227-228, 238, 241-244; membership in, 103; "orders"/ "proclamations" of, 100, 101, 103, 106, 108-109; "rebirth" of, 100; stand-off of, 115-121, 125-185; surrender of, 186-206, 241; sympathizers of, 142, 153-155, 158, 160-161, 164, 167, 171-172, 183, 249; takes hostages, 1-5, 115, 118-121, 125-131; threatens war, 109, 110, 112, 151; weapons of, 106, 130, 154, 161, 189, 254; website of, 142, 144, 163-164, 223-224, 255, 264-268
Republic of Texas Navy, 79
Rhea, Reggie, 202-203
Richards, Ann, 52
Richards, Ed, 210-211
Ricks, Bob, 50
Riordan, Joe, 12-13
Robertson, Peggy, 181
Roswell Army Air Field, 19-20
Roswell Daily Record, 20
Roswell Incident, 19-20
Rowe, Joe, 1-5, 90, 118-119, 125-131, 139, 142, 146, 164, 192, 253-254, 255, 265, 268

Margaret Ann, 1, 118-119, 120-121, 125-131, 146, 164, 255
RoweVista, 1-5, 121, 127, 131, 132-134
Rubin, James, 18-19
Ruby, Jack, 48
Runaway Scrape, 79
Rutledge, Lisa, 173, 180

S

"60 Minutes," 16
Salvation Army, 43, 162, 215
Sam Houston National Forest, 253
Sam Houston State University, 58
San Angelo Standard-Times, 11, 27, 88, 116, 140, 224
San Angelo, Texas, 27
San Antonio de Bexar, 77-78
San Antonio de Valero, *see* Alamo
San Antonio Express-News, 108, 163
San Isidro, California, 26
San Jacinto, Battle of, 75, 77, 79, 103
Sanders, Joe, 172, 177, 182
Santa Anna, Antonio Lopez de, 77-79, 237
Santa Fe Expedition, 80
"Satellite City," 42-43, 46, 56
Scheidt, Robert Jonathan, 118, 126-127, 130-131, 132, 135, 136, 146, 176-178, 252
Schlacter, Barry, 108
Schweitzer, LeRoy, 102
Scobee, Barry, 85-86, 88-89
Seguin, Juan, 74
separatist movements, 75-77, 82, 90-91, 96, 102, 140
Shackelford, Dr. John, 74
Shannon Hospital, 27
Shawnee County, Kansas, 120
Sheraton Hotel (Killeen), 32
Sheriff's Association of Texas, 247
Sherwood, Texas, 252
Sims, Malissa, 57
Sinatra, Nancy, 46
Smith, Clayton, 32, 62-63
Smith County, 143, 189
Smith, Coy, 189, 202
    Danny, 43
    J. B., 143
    Lee, 182

Smithsonian Institution, 61
Snyder, Texas, 103
Society of Professional Journalists, 157
Soldier of Fortune Magazine, 168, 176
Southern Poverty Law Center, 249
Southwest Texas State University, 54
Southwestern Bell, 12, 13, 42
speculation, 233-234
"spin control," 17, 21
"spin doctor," 17
"Spin City," 21
spokespersons: defined, 16-19, 38; tips for, 11, 13-22, 64-65, 131, 211-219, 220-236, 271-275, 280
St. Marys, Kansas, 120
Standifer, John, 192
State Aircraft Pooling Board, 122-123
State Department, 18-19
State Preservation Board, 96, 109
Stephen F. Austin State University, 77
Stewart, Larry, 90, 91
    Robert, 254
Stewart Title Company, 104
Strawberry Festival, 20
stress management training, 68-69
Striker, Fran, 220
Sunset Commission, 23

T

Tarrant County, 101
Tarrant County Medical Examiner's Office, 54, 60, 67
Telegraph and Texas Register, 237
television, *see* broadcast news
Texas, annexation to U.S., 79, 81-82, 90, 97, 99, 248-249, 258-259
Texas Army Guard, 142, 155, 192
Texas Bill of Rights, 95
Texas Book Festival, 256
Texas City disaster, 51
Texas Congress, 79, 80
Texas Constitution, 80
Texas Department of Criminal Justice, 109, 155, 199-203
Texas Department of Protective and Regulatory Services, 38
Texas Department of Public Safety, *see* DPS

Texas Department of Transportation, 205, 215
Texas Forest Service, 160, 196
Texas Governor's Office, 25, 52, 56-57, 66
Texas Highway Patrol, 40, 65, 115, 135, 162, 197, 200
Texas History Diagnostic Quiz, 77
"Texas History Movies," 73-74
Texas Legislature, 90, 91
Texas Nature Conservancy, 91
Texas Parks and Wildlife Department, 183
Texas Rangers, 9, 17, 20, 29, 31, 34-35, 40, 44, 50, 51, 52-54, 55, 56, 58, 62, 81, 85, 115, 118, 126, 132, 135, 154, 163, 165-166, 167, 169, 170, 176, 178, 181, 182-183, 187, 191, 199-203, 227, 253, 267
Texas Revolution, 74-79
Texas Senate, 94
Texas State Capitol, 94, 95-96, 101, 108-109, 111
Texas State Historical Association, 74
Texas State News Network, 115, 153
Texas State Technical College, 44
Texas, subdivision of, 82
Texas Supreme Court, 99
Texas Tech University, 248
Thomas, Dudley, 23-24, 35, 39, 40, 68, 93, 122, 181, 182, 184-185, 191, 194, 208
Time, 224
"Today Show, The," 55, 227
Todd, Larry, 16
"Tonight Show, The," 6-7
Tonto, 220
Toole, Ken, 111
tornado: Jarrell, 208-211; Waco, 51
Torres, Lucila, 116, 169
Tourtelott, James E., 106
Travis County, 209
Travis, William Barret, 178
Treece, Richard, 167
Turner, Jo Ann Canady, 118, 112, 264
TWA crash, 219

U
UFOs, 19-20, 151

U.S. Attorney's Office, 50, 53, 56, 61, 62, 131
U.S. Coast Guard, 231
U.S. Marshal's Service, 133
U.S. News and World Report, 224
U.S. Postal Service, 26, 107-108
U.S. Space Command, 112
U.S. Supreme Court, 215
United Nations, 18
United Press, 10
United Press International, 10
University of Houston, 248
University of Texas, 249
University of Texas Tower, 147, 238
USA Today, 18, 64-65, 108, 111, 223

V
Valadez, Albert, 128, 140-141, 172-173, 252
Valentine, Texas, 84
Van Kirk, John C., 97, 98, 100-101
Vance, Doug, 123, 127, 132, 189
Vandiver, Don, 238
Vaughn, Steven, 43
Verhovek, Sam Howe, 146
Vickers, George, 203-204
Vietnam War, 95
Violent Crime Control and Law Enforcement Act, 250

W
Waco Police Department, 57
Waco siege, *see* Branch Davidian compound
Waco, Texas, 45-46, *also see* DPS at Waco siege; Branch Davidian compound
Waco Tribune-Herald, 38, 40
Walker, Stanley, 14
"Walker, Texas Ranger," 53, 110
Wall Street Journal, 223
Waller, Frankie, 25, 208
Walls Unit, 9
Ward County Jail, 105
Wardlaw, Frank, 134
Warren, Mark, 55, 148
Washburn, Charles, 13
Watergate, 234
WBAP Radio, 116
Weathers, Carl, 154

Western Outlaw and Lawman History
   Association (WOLA), 91
WFAA-TV, 34, 151
Wheeler, Sharon, 41
White, Mark, 96
Whitman, Charles, 238
Wilke, Adolph, 94
   L. A., 73-74, 86-88, 94, 256
Williams, Mike, 168
Williamson County, 208, 210
Wilson, Bill, 16
   James, 35, 36, 51, 52, 53, 56, 65,
      103, 123, 245
wine industry, 89
WOAI Radio, 116, 118, 163
Wofford, John, 125, 204, 252, 266

   Mary Lynn (Rusty), 125, 162
Wofford Ranch, 126, 131, 133, 135,
      142, 144, 145, 161, 265, 266
Woodhull, Nancy, 226
Woodie's Hill, 44
World Court, 98
World Wide Web, 223
Wright, Larry, 148
WXYZ Radio, 220

Y
"You Are There," 237

Z
Zewe, Charles, 152
Ziegler, Ron, 234